Writing Feature Articles

Writing Feature Articles presents clear and engaging advice for students and young professionals on working as a freelance feature writer. This fifth edition not only covers producing content for print, but also for digital platforms and online.

Mary Hogarth offers comprehensive guidance on every aspect of feature writing, from having the initial idea and conducting market and subject research, to choosing the right target audience and publishing platform and successfully pitching the article. In addition, the book instructs students on developing their own journalistic style and effectively structuring their feature. Each chapter then concludes with an action plan to help students put what they have read into practice.

Topics include:

- Life as a freelance
- Building a professional profile
- Telling a story with images
- Developing a specialism
- Interviewing skills
- Profile and interview articles
- Working in publicity and advertising
- A career in magazines and newspapers
- Getting published overseas
- Understanding issues in media law and regulation

The book also provides an extensive range of interviews with successful media professionals, including a newspaper editor, a money, health and lifestyle journalist, a copywriter and an award-winning columnist, where they share their own experiences of working in the industry and offer invaluable tips on best practice.

Mary Hogarth is an experienced educator, media specialist and writer, who was previously Head of Features Journalism at Southampton Solent University before joining Bournemouth University. Mary also runs a consultancy practice, The Magazine Expert Ltd (www.themagazineexpert.com), specialising in advising on new title launches, audience engagement, editorial development and developing sustainable magazine business strategies.

Writing Feature Articles
Print, Digital and Online

**Fifth edition
Mary Hogarth**

LONDON AND NEW YORK

Fifth edition published 2019
by Routledge
2 Park Square, Milton Park, Abingdon, Oxon, OX14 4RN

and by Routledge
52 Vanderbilt Avenue, New York, NY 10017

Routledge is an imprint of the Taylor & Francis Group, an informa business

© 2019 Mary Hogarth
Law and ethics: a rough guide © David Mascord
A career in magazines and newspapers © Miriam Phillips

The right of Mary Hogarth, David Mascord and Miriam Phillips to be identified as authors of this work has been asserted by them in accordance with sections 77 and 78 of the Copyright, Designs and Patents Act 1988.

All rights reserved. No part of this book may be reprinted or reproduced or utilised in any form or by any electronic, mechanical, or other means, now known or hereafter invented, including photocopying and recording, or in any information storage or retrieval system, without permission in writing from the publishers.

Trademark notice: Product or corporate names may be trademarks or registered trademarks, and are used only for identification and explanation without intent to infringe.

First edition published by Heinemann 1989
Fourth edition published by Focal Press 2006

British Library Cataloguing-in-Publication Data
A catalogue record for this book is available from the British Library

Library of Congress Cataloging-in-Publication Data
Names: Hogarth, Mary, 1968– author.
Title: Writing feature articles : print, digital and online / Mary Hogarth.
Description: Fifth edition. | London ; New York : Routledge, 2019. |
Includes index. Identifiers: LCCN 2018054430 |
ISBN 9781138238152 (hardback : alk. paper) |
ISBN 9781138238169 (paperback : alk. paper) | ISBN 9781315298016 (ebook)
Subjects: LCSH: Feature writing. | Journalism–Authorship.
Classification: LCC PN4784.F37 H64 2019 | DDC 808.06/607–dc23
LC record available at https://lccn.loc.gov/2018054430

ISBN: 978-1-138-23815-2 (hbk)
ISBN: 978-1-138-23816-9 (pbk)
ISBN: 978-1-315-29801-6 (ebk)

Typeset in Goudy
by Newgen Publishing UK

Contents

List of figures vii
List of tables viii
List of contributors ix
Foreword xi
Acknowledgements xiii

1 Introduction 1
2 Life as a freelance 9
3 Ideas are everywhere 20
4 Market research 39
5 How to pitch successfully 55
6 Turn ideas into articles 72
7 Research and interview techniques 91
8 A cohesive structure 114
9 How to develop a strong style 136
10 Images tell a story 151
11 Copywriting and PR 167
12 Specialist features, columns and reviews 181
13 Interviews vs profiles 212
14 Worldwide markets 233
15 A career in magazines and newspapers 243
    MIRIAM PHILLIPS

16 Law and ethics: a rough guide 252
DAVID MASCORD

17 Last word: an editor's perspective, with Jonathan Telfer 261

Appendix 1: Example of a freelance workflow income spreadsheet 267
Appendix 2: NUJ Code of Conduct 268
Appendix 3: IPSO – Editors' Code of Practice 269
Appendix 4: The Society of Authors' Guide to Copyright and Permissions 275
Appendix 5: Syndicates, news and press cuttings agencies 284
References 286
Bibliography 291
Index 295

Figures

3.1	Cover of *Men's Running*	21
3.2	Six-step feature model	25
3.3	Mapping your ideas	26
4.1	Magazine facts	42
4.2	*Food and Travel* cover	44
5.1	Magazine hierarchy model	57
5.2	An article's perceived value	60
5.3	Cover of *Food and Travel*	63
7.1	Five essential interview steps	97
8.1	An example of mapping sources to note headings	118
8.2	Three-stage map of a first draft	125
8.3	An interpretation of the inverted feature pyramid model	126
8.4	*Writer's Digest* cover July/August 2018	133
9.1	*Vegan Living* spread	146
10.1	Mapping a publication's feature imagery	153
10.2	Five essential interview steps	161
10.3	*National Geographic Traveller* cover	164
10.4	*National Geographic Traveller* Namibia spread	165
11.1	Processing the five Ws	171
12.1	Words, sentences and structure grid	186
12.2	The reviewer's map	200
13.1	Contact methods	215
17.1	Cover of *Writing Magazine*	262

Tables

2.1	Example record of pitches sent	14
4.1	Categories of national newspapers	50
5.1	Targeting multiple publications using one theme	64
5.2	Example of a workflow chart	66
7.1	Feature summary of key research	102
8.1	A feature plan for membership model article	116
8.2	Turning a theme into a feature package	131
9.1	Analysis of writing styles	143
12.1	Four key themes of a column	195
12.2	The core components of a review	203
13.1	Summarising quotes	225
16.1	Main defences in the 2013 Defamation Act	254

Contributors

Ann Luce

Ann Luce is a Principal Academic in Journalism and Communication at Bournemouth University where she teaches Features and Digital Journalism. A journalist-turned-academic, she now writes extensively on the ethical and responsible reporting of suicide using digital storytelling techniques.

David Mascord

David Mascord has more than 25 years' experience in journalism, teaching, training and development. During his career, he has been a staff and freelance journalist writing about everything from beer to business and weddings to widgets. He is a training consultant specialising in media law, journalism and business writing, and also lectures in Media Law and Journalism at Bournemouth University and at Solent University, Southampton.

Miriam Phillips

Miriam Phillips is an editor, publisher and journalism lecturer. Miriam trained as a newspaper reporter for Newsquest working across daily papers in Dorset. She specialised in crime, court and investigative reporting. She has had a variety of roles for *Trinity Mirror*, Northcliffe in London, writing for newspapers and setting up and running hyperlocal news websites before returning to Newsquest as a Chief Reporter.

In 2015, she set up Bright Daisy Publishing and launched a hyperlocal high-quality lifestyle magazine in Poundbury,

Dorset. She now also lectures on the BA (Hons) Multimedia Journalism course at Bournemouth University, specialising in teaching news and online, court reporting, NCTJ units and social media. Miriam has won industry awards for journalism and has been shortlisted for women's business awards. She lives in Dorset with her husband and two boys.

Jonathan Telfer

Jonathan Telfer is an editor and journalist who, in 20 years in the industry, has had over one million of his own words published and been responsible for many millions more. Having joined as Editorial Assistant in 2001, in 2009 he became the youngest-ever editor of the UK's biggest and bestselling magazine for writers, *Writing Magazine*.

Foreword

Ann Luce

In 1996, Bill Gates, founder of Microsoft Corporation, wrote an essay titled, "Content is King". It became the mantra for publishing houses the world over. Quality content, targeted at a specific audience was all that was needed to make money. And while, in theory, that is still true today, the fact of the matter is, our audiences have moved on and want and demand so much more.

When I began my journalism career in the late 1990s, the path to feature writing was different. All I needed was a strong idea, my rolodex, a notebook, tape recorder (optional), pen or pencil, a good pair of shoes and a curious mind.

Today's journalists are conducting their craft in a multimodal environment. No longer is the rolodex the go-to for sources. Instead, the first port of call is Twitter, Instagram or Facebook. Glossy photographs may once have looked good on a double-page spread but now they need to be interactive. Infographics that once made complex topics accessible, should now drive audiences to your website where they can interact with the data themselves.

A strong feature idea may get you started, but it's the overarching *vision* and depth of a story that matters most now.

When *The New York Times* released its Pulitzer award-winning multimedia feature, *Snow Fall: The Avalanche at Tunnel Creek*, in December 2012, it was declared by many (myself included!) that THIS was "the future of journalism". How wrong we were!

Snow Fall may have started us on the journey towards highly immersive digital feature experiences, but by no means was it the pinnacle of the journey; in fact, it was only the beginning.

Your *vision* for a story is more important now than ever. There is an infinite amount of information available to us on our mobile devices, but our time is finite. What will make YOUR story stand out amongst the masses?

When I first started teaching features journalism, writing, editing and design of print pages were the foundational skills I focused on. As time moved on, it was about teaching my students how to design for a digital world, thinking about the user-experience and interactivity.

While strong reporting, writing and editing skills are a must for any features journalist, I now spend just as much time prattling on about imagination, innovation and vision, three core characteristics any good features journalist must have, in my opinion.

I spout frequently that features journalists need traditional reporting and writing skills, coupled with the production techniques of TV or film producers. You're no longer a print journalist, or a multimedia journalist; you are a digital storyteller.

Your story vision needs to not only incorporate video, audio, graphics and commentary from social media, but it needs to be forward-thinking and immersive. Audiences don't want to just read a story, they want to be a part of the story. Augmented reality, 360° video and virtual reality allow your audience to see the story from all angles, to hear the story from all angles, to be IN the story.

In 1996, Bill Gates stated, "Content is King".

Here in 2018, "User experience is King".

What's your *vision* for 2040?

Acknowledgements

Writing this book has perhaps been one of my biggest challenges to date so my first acknowledgement goes to Brendan Hennessy, the original author of *Writing Feature Articles*, for giving me the opportunity to update his work. It's been a privilege and a pleasure.

My grateful thanks to everyone who generously gave up their time to be interviewed for this book – sharing their knowledge and experiences. A big "thank you" also goes to my two contributors Miriam Phillips and David Mascord for Chapters 15 and 16 respectively, and to Dr Ann Luce, for her insightful Foreword.

Throughout my career I have been fortunate enough to be mentored by some great journalists and writers. They too deserve a mention here – John Jenkins (publisher of Writers International Ltd), Max Hodnett, former editor of *The West Briton* and former Deputy Editor of *The Express*, Ted Dickinson.

Lastly, thanks to my partner Tony, friends, family and colleagues at Bournemouth University for their support.

1 Introduction

Journalism is a vocation – 9 to 5 it isn't. You need a curious mind, initiative and must be prepared to ask questions that nobody else will. Good writing skills are learned along the way. To some, writing comes easily, but for others it is a struggle. Experience is a great teacher, yes you will make mistakes – everyone does. But those mistakes can be the making of you … as long as you learn from each and every one.

Still interested? Great, now for a reality check. Whether you are reporter, blogger or feature writer be prepared to always tell the truth and don't follow the crowd. Even if that makes you unpopular at times. The important thing is that you've become unpopular for the right reasons.

Despite the cons, writing is a fantastic job for anyone and technology has made it even more flexible. It is a wonderful way to earn a living. You can start writing at any time of life. Within limits, you can write even when ill. Some writing talent must be assumed, but there is much scope for development. But you also need that doggedness, plenty of curiosity and a strong desire to communicate.

Doggedness means the determination to improve your skills by constant practice, and in particular the perseverance to write and rewrite (time allowing) until the article comes right. In journalism "coming right" is essentially editing. It means satisfying not only yourself but also your editor and the target audience.

Curiosity means being interested in the human condition and the world in general. You feed it by continually learning – that means reading, meeting a wide variety of people and making sense of the world around you. Maintain a lively interest in many subjects, however specialised the field you write about. Developing strong analytical skills is an essential requirement.

The desire to communicate is the fuel for the engine. You may be driven by a "mission to explain" (but don't preach), or by a fire in the belly that makes you want to correct wrongs and demand retribution. You may be interested in getting readers' attention by entertaining them, perhaps making things from a humorous perspective. But keep it factual because journalism demands that imparting accurate information is the essential task that underpins those laudable aims.

Elementary skills and resources

The essential journalistic skill is reporting. To do this well you need a foolproof way of recording facts and quotes. A good recording app on your phone together with a shorthand system of some kind – be it Teeline or one that you've made up yourself – are basic tools of the trade. Being computer literate is not just about having good keyboard skills: you need an encyclopaedic knowledge of Internet resources, social media expertise and the ability to post tasters of stories, which will signpost readers to your main article. These points are covered later in the book.

Learning your trade

Most newcomers to journalism are now armed with degrees. Some have directly related degrees in journalism – multimedia, broadcast or magazine journalism – while others have more general degrees such as media studies that include elements of journalism practice. Graduates may also have in addition – or alternatively – National Council for the Training of Journalists' (NCTJ) qualifications, or a diploma from a College of Further Education or private college. Appendix 6 gives guidance on courses, some of which organise work placements as part of the curriculum. With most internships, you don't get paid but with luck you might get valuable experience in reporting, sub-editing and feature writing, as well as in making the tea and the odd errand. If you're even luckier the work placement might lead to a staff job or at the very least some freelance work to help you build a portfolio.

If your objective is freelance feature writing, a staff job for a while will enable you to build a network of contacts while pursuing your goal at the same time. Remember an article comes as a package, so when planning a feature consider how you will market it before researching the content.

However, once you have determined the right audience and market consider the content for the following elements of your feature package:

- **The magazine's website:** the content should be an extension of your original article, not a repetition. For example, this might be a case study written in the first person from one of your interviewee's perspective.
- **Digital edition:** this is where added value comes into play by including audio and/or video content.
- **Social media:** plan for taster excerpts. This is to signpost readers to all your article's content – in print, online and the digital edition.

This strategy is likely to double your chance of getting a commission – provided of course, that your idea is relevant, original and right for the target publication.

Set up a workspace

If you haven't already done so, make provision for working at home. All that is needed is a small space with a suitable desk, laptop and an all-in-one printer. Whether you're a staff writer doing freelance work for non-competitive publications or a freelance (or prospective freelancer) you will be working at home – or have the option to sometimes. See Chapter 2.

Gathering experience and networking

Whatever your qualifications, training and work experience, it may still be difficult to find the post you want or get established as a freelancer. The digital age is a challenging time for the media. Publications are downsizing, making both staff and freelance work harder to find. Those made redundant are likely to join their former magazine's growing freelance pool. The main lesson to be learned, especially as a freelance, is that you have to promote yourself rigorously and suffer rejections without losing your self-confidence.

If you've had some work experience, use it to develop a relationship with the editor and editorial team. Send in pitches and offer to help out or do some casual subbing. Remember it is usually best to work in a salaried post for a while before making the plunge into freelancing.

Promote yourself in person, online with a good blog and website and use social media as a journalist's tool. Take any opportunity to network. Go to parties and other social press events where there will be journalists who may be useful contacts – they might give you work or introduce you to someone who can. Try getting personal recommendations from friends, relations, and former fellow-students, colleagues who have connections with the business. Never pitch too strongly and desperately to an editor at a social event. Your later pitch will benefit from even the briefest of introductions.

Trial and error is the best means of building work relationships. Make the most of any opportunity offered to meet an editor to discuss ideas. A young journalist, having got printed in a woman's magazine, was invited to meet the editor with ideas. She put her ideas forward with passion. But her ideas weren't what he was looking for. "What I have in mind," he said, "for example, is a feature on '20 things every woman wants in a man'."

She said, "That sounds a bit banal to me." The meeting was not a success and he published no more of her work. The lesson is that at an early stage give editors what they ask for when they won't take what's better (and riskier) from you. Later, when you've proved your worth, you'll get more of your own ideas accepted.

Editors are looking for feature writers who have some kind of profile, which demonstrates that they can write. Get published – in print or online – so that you have something to show and being persistent will help you to get into editors' sights. At first you may have a thin portfolio containing PDFs/screen shots of one or two pieces in a blog, student or small local magazine. Select the best three pieces and send them to your target editors to back up your approaches when pitching. As time goes by you'll be able to broaden your range and you will have gathered a more impressive portfolio to back up your pitches.

Getting published

Editors are looking for writers with some specialist knowledge within their publications' areas of interest and who know how to communicate it to their readers. As a new writer, you will find it easier to get that first break if you can demonstrate this. Therefore, it's a good idea to select one or two publications that you enjoy reading and know well. Everyone has their own specialist knowledge; for example, you may have:

- worked in a restaurant, hospitality or retail to fund university fees;
- gained knowledge of a particular craft or skill;
- expertise in a sport or hobby;
- experience of living on a student budget.

Whatever your specialist area is, that should be your starting point. Select one or two of your interests to specialise in, then undertake an in-depth analysis of those likely publications to find feature ideas and a fresh angle (see Chapter 4). Once you have an idea, prepare to pitch it. Choose your angles carefully, ensuring that none have been covered by staff writers or established columnists.

Unless advised otherwise, send a pitch via email rather than a piece "on spec" (speculatively). Today, more than ever, commissioning editors are time-poor, hence they value short pitches. Always back up pitches with attached examples of your work (in PDF format), together a brief "about me" paragraph at the end of your pitch along with a link to your website containing some published articles/blog posts plus your Twitter feed. The latter will demonstrate your writing skills and engagement with social media.

One way to get knowledgeable about both the selected subject areas and the latest controversies about them is to engage in debate and commentary on the magazine's social media or letters page. This will help you get to know the readership as well as to become noticed by the editor.

Engage editorial teams

Notice the ways in which a publication's features, and especially controversial columns, are followed up or argued about in the letters page. As a freelance you should regularly email, tweet or post engaging, thoughtful comments about the content on the publication's Facebook page. This strategy will help you to get to know the editorial team.

Widen your range of topics and readerships, to see what works best for you. Such topics might include:

- social problems;
- human rights;
- class conflicts;
- failures in the education system or the National Health Service;
- your views on TV programmes, especially the topical themes in soap operas or high-profile, emotive drama series such as Broadchurch.

Today, most readers email, Tweet or post their comments on Facebook, but one way to get noticed is to write a letter, because few people still do. Of course, there are eccentric letter writers, some of whom notoriously write in green ink and who are printed to create controversy or amusement. So, choose your publications carefully, then work out the best method of approach.

It is also worth aiming not only to get your comments published, but to be credited with the best letter/tweet/post etc. It's a good way to get noticed by the editor, paving the way for you to pitch and ask for work experience.

Work placement opportunities

You may prefer to remain a staff writer where your features may be spinoffs from, or an essential part of, your job. Alternatively, you may prefer to go freelance with little or no staff experience or opt for something in between.

Whichever route you want to take it is essential that you first gain some work experience, preferably at a variety of media outlets. This has a twofold benefit:

- The first being that you will make some good contacts.
- Second, you will gain a valuable insight into how each outlet works – be it a magazine, newspaper, online site or broadcast organisation.

Both are crucial for freelance, contract work or starting your career with that first staff job. However, to get your first placement it helps to be enrolled on a journalism or media degree/postgraduate course. Building a relationship as a freelance with an editor can also help secure an internship. Make a list of potential target publications/outlets, but compile it with care. Think about those titles that you would like to work on. Consider why that particular magazine or newspaper and how the placement will be likely to benefit you in the long term. Next, call each outlet to find out who deals with work experience, then speak to them before applying – that way you have established an important initial contact.

Follow up any initial contact with an email application. This should include an attached CV demonstrating your skills and qualifications, PDF cuttings of any work published, plus a couple of article ideas to show you have done your homework.

Preparation is key to any successful internship or placement. Consider which aspect of the business you would like to focus on (features, production or online) and what outcome you would like – this could be a portfolio of published work or broadcasts and some freelance commissions. Study several issues of the publication or if it's a broadcast organisation list/watch numerous shows so that their style, tone and format become familiar. This will enable you to turn up with a basic understanding in order to generate content ideas that have a strong potential.

During the placement, it is important to be enthusiastic about every task you undertake, even if that's making tea or fetching coffees. When an editorial team sees that you can be trusted with small tasks they are more likely to trust you with editorial work such as an article, online post, video or audio piece.

Case study: from graduate to BBC journalist

James Davies is a journalist at the BBC who has previously worked as a producer and reporter for both LBC and the Sunday Mirror. *During the course of his career he has interviewed some high-profile names such as Sir Sean Connery and David Beckham – see more at http://jamesdaviesmedia.blogspot.co.uk. After graduating with a degree in Journalism from Southampton Solent University in 2009, James went on to do a postgraduate diploma at Cardiff University before embarking on a career spanning online, print and broadcast media.*

But how did he get published? By adopting journalistic attitudes from the start – tenacity, not taking no for an answer and using his initiative.

"Having been fairly lucky with many of my ambitious interview requests for sit downs with various stars of stage, screen and sport, I approached a number of publications I thought might be interested in using the transcripts. Fortunately, the high-profile nature of the interviewees helped stir interest and a handful of publications asked me to write up a feature. After a successful first article, one of the publications asked me to write more of my interviews up, publishing many of my pieces. This opportunity eventually led to my first job in national newspapers."

Despite not having any NCTJ qualifications James was able to secure a staff job on the *Sunday People* and *Sunday Mirror* simply through his freelance endeavours, having sold interviews and stories to both publications, during his postgraduate studies.

His first real break came when James rang the news desk of one national title explaining he had interviewed a film star. "I was asked to send my copy, as well as the tape, across and the rest as they say, is history. As well as this, I worked as a freelance broadcast journalist for *Good Morning Britain*, *This Morning* and LBC radio. This opportunity was made much easier having worked as a reporter for *Trinity Mirror* for four years. By this point I had made several contacts and was able to arrange a coffee with various news editors – taking along my scrap book of cuttings."

Being proactive helped James secure a good income from his work and eventually led to a route into a staff job in broadcasting.

"Freelancing was fairly lucrative for a period and enabled me to pick and choose what I wanted to do, gaining experience in many different areas. This helped me secure my current role as a producer and investigations reporter at LBC Radio – where a number of skills are required to do well and survive. Nick Ferrari, who hosts the LBC Breakfast show, is without doubt the best journalist I have worked with and someone who has extremely high standards. As a result I was required to work closely with Nick in a freelance capacity before I was offered a staff job on his team. Freelancing helped me to prove myself. The skills and experience acquired from my time working with Nick Ferrari and then Clive Bull at LBC led to me moving to the BBC's award-winning South East Today in September of this year."

For James, freelancing gave him the freedom to choose those jobs he wanted to take, which suited his life and career goals. But of course, there are pros and cons: "Freelancing enables you to move work environment at a drop of a hat – taking up any opportunities that arise and making new contacts. However, as a freelancer it is often difficult to let work pass you by because you don't know if it'll dry up. This means you are often working more unsociable hours and during public holidays."

The one thing James wished he had known about writing articles/features when starting out was not to be afraid to ask for payment. "Getting your first article published is rewarding – and payment is the last thing on your mind – but journalists need to be paid, otherwise journalism becomes extinct."

Action plan

Evaluate your potential

Journalists, as well as other kinds of writers, and physicians, need to know themselves. Knowing yourself helps you to avoid inflicting your prejudices on others and to focus on what your readers need to know. This assignment will help you to know yourself and to select the areas of interest you'll find it rewarding to write about. Total about 800 words.

- Try to see yourself as others see you. Write a short account of yourself in the third person. Include your appearance, family background and education, character (strengths and weaknesses), main interests, likes and dislikes, beliefs and political views.
- What attracts you to journalism as a career? What are your ambitions?

- List the publications and blogs you regularly read in one column, together with their key editorial themes, now add your own interests and activities in an opposite column. Match up those publications you most enjoy reading with your main interests. Select one match where you detect a possibility, study the publication closely as advised, and when you are ready start pitching.
- List the journalistic skills (research, writing, interviewing, editing) you possess and those that you need to develop further.
- Record some of the books, both fiction and non-fiction, that you have read recently. Consider their usefulness for your career as a journalist, and whether your reading should be widened/deepened.

Engage with editorial

Study the current issues of *The Times* and your local paper. Reply to one reader letter to the editor in each (300 and 200 words respectively). Agree or disagree with the opinions expressed. But do add to the content if you agree.

Research work placement opportunities

List key media outlets that you would like to get involved with, include local, independent titles as well as the nationals. Then prepare the following for your application:

- First research each title's content, editorial themes and the audience, making notes on these points.
- Call all those on your list, find how who deals with work placements and speak to them before applying.
- Create or update your CV, listing your journalistic skills, any articles published, relevant experience, etc. Don't forget to include your website and social media profile IDs at the top.
- Put together a selection of your best three PDF file cuttings to send with your CV. These should include a blog post, news story and a short freelance article.
- The covering email needs to be short, no more than three paragraphs and it should demonstrate your knowledge of the publication/readership as well as why you want to undertake work experience there. Don't forget to provide a couple of feature ideas too.

2 Life as a freelance

If you're a staff writer you are likely to have more resources and equipment to hand. But today, editorial teams are lean operations with many having shrunk by as much as 75 per cent. This has had a twofold effect: first, using a team of multi-skilled journalists; second, cutting hours and encouraging staff writers to work partly from home. As a result, many journalists now combine a part-time staff job with freelance assignments to boost their income.

While freelance writers have often worked as staff writers (and/or as editors/sub-editors) before making the plunge, following the digital disruption era more young journalists are starting out as freelances, before securing that first staff job. So how do you get started as freelance?

The first step is making room for a dedicated workspace in your home. This could be as little as clearing space on the kitchen table to taking a bold step and creating a home office. Being well organised at home is a must. If your budget will stretch to a rented or shared office space, then this might help you establish clearer work/life boundaries. Flexibility in the digital age is key but a little planning will also go a long way. Once you have established a workspace and decided on a working pattern, begin your freelance journey by first defining your immediate and longer-term objectives. It is crucial to ensure that these objectives are then reflected in the way you organise your time, equipment and all the business aspects.

Before you start researching an article, it is essential to first develop good pitching skills. Editors generally prefer commissioned articles to those submitted on spec, sent via email. To avoid writing pieces you can't sell almost always pitch your feature ideas first, although occasionally you may want to send out an imaginative piece which is hard to describe in a pitch. The art of pitching will be covered in-depth in Chapter 4.

Books, equipment and resources

Even in this digital age it is a good idea to keep a few essential textbooks to hand. A list of useful texts can be found in the Bibliography at the end of this book. You will add to this list according to how your interests and commissions develop.

When setting up your workspace I would advise investing in a landline particularly if you live in an area where mobile signals are unreliable. Broadband is essential as you may need to upload large files to a cloud-based system such as Dropbox or directly to the publication's server using FTP (File Transfer Protocol), a method used to transfer such files between computers on a network. FTP is especially useful if you are putting together a feature package with video and/or audio content.

A smartphone with email and a recording app is also essential. Opt for a mobile provider that offers Wi-Fi calling: this is where the phone will run a call through the Internet if the signal is weak. Being able to sync all your devices – laptop, mobile and tablet – is a great resource. Apple products are incredibly intuitive and achieve syncing between devices seamlessly. For example, you can run your iPhone through your laptop to make and receive calls. This function means you can record phone interviews using a desktop app such as Simple Recorder Plus, which also has file-saving facilities in MPEG format. Apps such as these also allow you to edit recorded interviews should you wish to make a podcast as part of a feature package. But always ask the interviewee's permission first.

If working while on the move, consider using a tablet with a keyboard as it will give you the freedom to write anywhere. Tablets are incredibly versatile for working on the go, enabling you to create short video clips, record interviews (with a separate app), access your emails, surf the Internet, as well as post updates or tasters on social media.

A productive home office

Ideally your home office space should have a desk large enough to spread papers out and come with sufficient drawers for stationery such as business cards, paper and other essentials. Make sure your workstation is sufficient to accommodate the following items:

- a desktop computer, or if using a laptop install a monitor on brackets which can be used as a dual screen;
- an all-in-one printer;
- sufficient shelving or drawers;
- landline phone and mobile charging dock;
- a good desk lamp.

No matter how large or small the space is, it needs to be inspiring. Therefore – while functionality is a must – it is also important to make this space as cheerful as possible. Put up pictures or quotes that inspire you and avoid clutter.

Be organised. A good filing system both for hard copies and computer files is a must so that you can retrieve content quickly. Editors will often want to check points in your article so be ready. It's a good idea to have a large shelving area or cupboard for files with space for reference books.

Equip your laptop or desktop computer properly. Don't skimp on this, as setting up with the right software should be seen as an investment. Carefully assess your working needs. For example, if writing is going to be your focus then Microsoft Office should suffice. However, if freelance assignments are likely to include sub-editing or magazine production then you are going to need the additional software. Some publications may insist on you using professional software, usually InDesign and/or Photoshop.

Tools for organising data

Losing important work on your computer (through a power cut, for example) can be a disaster. While working on a document, continually save and keep copies on a USB stick and/or a cloud-based storage system such as Apple's iCloud, Dropbox or Google Docs where they can be accessed from another device if necessary. Back up all the documents on your computer regularly – at least once a week to a portable, external hard drive so should the worst happen your work would be easily retrievable.

Much of your admin work, such as keeping lists of clients, developing contacts, negotiating with editors and so on, can be done digitally using CRM (Customer Relationship Management) tools, or a good address-book app. Basic versions are usually free, but choose an app that allows you to make notes on individual editors so that you remember their preferences. Keep a record of features pitched, those commissioned with deadline dates, and articles currently awaiting payment. Whenever you get a commission always confirm the brief and fee by email. An Excel spreadsheet or Word document should suffice.

Do use a diary, either a desk one or an app on your computer, phone or tablet. It's a good idea to have one for personal use and another for work. iCal on Apple enables you to set up different calendars and colour-code these. This is an excellent idea because you can see events at a glance. For example, I have three colour-coded calendars to keep track of the different elements of my life: the academic calendar is pink, the consultancy practice is purple and my personal/home calendar is green.

Writing is a business

As a freelance you have a product to sell. Your articles won't sell themselves. Unless you have been a staff writer and are starting off as a freelance with a regular contract or two you need to keep up a steady supply of features ideas that are better than those of your competitors.

The best way to cultivate clients is to store up goodwill from editors by keeping to deadlines, working to the briefs, writing well and being accurate. But neglect the business basics – keeping proper records, marketing and making new contacts – and you can watch lesser talents who work hard at these become far more successful. If you can invest in some basic business training – either an evening class or online tutorials – this will stand you in good stead. Get organised and structure your day because in the long run this will save precious time.

When earning a living from freelancing you need to have:

- good time-management skills;
- an understanding of the art of pitching;
- the ability to keep a basic workflow record;
- some understanding of finance such as being able to cost jobs by the hour or day plus being able to record debits and credits to your freelance account;
- provision to ensure that you are operating legally and professionally.

What follows are some basic techniques that will help you achieve these goals.

Organising your time

Schedule writing into that part of the day when you are freshest, then slot in the other activities around it. Award-winning journalist, Chip Scanlan whose credits include *The New York Times* and *The Washington Post Magazine*, is an advocate of time management. In an article he wrote for Poynter.org titled, *Making Friends With A Clock: Time Management For Writers*, he cites organising time as one of the most important self-improvement techniques for writers and advocates writing daily:

> This is the key to productivity, says psychologist Robert Boice, who found that productive writers don't chain themselves to their keyboards all day long. Instead, they follow the pattern of Pulitzer Prize-winning novelist Michael Chabon: "Keep a regular schedule, and write at the same time every day for the same amount of time." Regularity, not overwork, is the key to productivity.
>
> (Scanlan, 2002)

Other activities in terms of freelancing will include market analysis, reading up on your subjects, researching your features, interviewing, correspondence, phone calls, managing the business. When arranging deadlines, calculate the time likely to be required for the various tasks. For a complex feature the actual writing may take up about a fifth or less of the total time whereas some features may be written off the top of your head in an hour or two. Does the fee proposed reflect the work involved?

Keeping fit is crucial. Ensure you have a comfortable chair that keeps your back straight, don't spend too long at your desk in one session. Take regular breaks from your desk and find time for fresh air and exercise. Some gentle stretching while sitting in your chair will also help.

As a freelance you must keep a record of time spent on producing each feature, which must also include research time. The more efficient you become at writing features the higher your hourly rate will be. Having started out as a typist (many years ago) being able to touch type has stood me in good stead as I can record phone interviews by typing as I am talking – thus saving me hours of transcribing. That said, if you can touch type I also recommend you record every phone or Skype interview to check for accuracy. However, while mastering the art of touch-typing will increase your speed, be careful to avoid back and neck strain, or even Repetitive Strain Injury (RSI). There's good advice online from Patient UK (www.patient.co.uk) and RSI/UK (www.demon.co.uk/rsi).

Getting commissions

Develop ideas and pitch them to publications you've studied, as described in Chapters 3 to 5. Before you've established an effective network of clients and contacts (see Chapter 1) you may find it useful to promote yourself in more general ways including having your own website to showcase your work. Social media is also a good place to start building your profile. I advise students to set up a professional profile on those key social media platforms with which their target markets and readers are most likely to engage. These include:

- **Twitter:** helps to build up a network of editorial contacts and demonstrates a writer's interactive skills. It can also be used as a research tool.
- **Facebook:** enables writers to signpost their work. It is also a good research tool as it can also be used to find potential interviewees or case studies.
- **Instagram:** is great for those writers with iconic, specialist interests such as food, craft or fashion.
- **LinkedIn:** enables writers to build contacts, demonstrate experience and showcase work.

Freelancers must use social media as a network and marketing tool – follow writers, editors and publications you would like to work for and engage them. LinkedIn not only provides the opportunity to connect with a professional network of potential work contacts, it is also great for building testimonials (recommendations) and gaining acknowledgement for your skills.

Press Gazette (www.pressgazette.co.uk) and Journalism.co.uk are among various sites that advertise freelance jobs. There are also directories such as Response Source (www.responsesource.com) where freelance journalists can register and upload their profile. Keep in touch with contacts from any related work experience or media jobs. Spec emails can also work well too, although the success rate is low. That said, I have gained quite a few assignments this way.

When pitching, do emphasise any specialist knowledge and signpost perspective clients to websites where samples of your work can be accessed. Create your own website with a CV emphasising your journalistic/writing experience with links to articles published as well as to your profiles in freelance directories.

A key skill of any freelance is their ability to generate work. Ideally you should allocate a day or two each week to getting new assignments. Aim to get regular commissions from at least one or two clients. When one source of work dries up immediately find another to replace it. Diversify to keep up with current trends, and always follow up a successful sale with new ideas.

Workflow and business records

As a freelance you must keep a record of workflow – and the time spent on producing features. This will enable you to chart your success rate as well as your earning power. I keep a record of all my pitches to ascertain my success rate.

An example of this can be seen in Table 2.1. It is a simple table created in Word listing article pitched, target publication, date sent, editor's response and whether it was commissioned.

Cross-reference these with your publication contacts list. These will include commissioning editors' names, phone numbers and email addresses along with brief notes on each editor's likes/dislikes, etc – and update regularly. Always review the history of your dealings with an editor before making your next pitch.

For organising your contacts there are various apps/programmes. Opt for one that is flexible and allows you space to distinguish between different groups, i.e. editors, research contacts and interviewees. Having all Apple products, I use the brand's own Contacts app, which enables me to customise each entry and create contact groups. For example, when writing this book (using the prefix of Book 3) I have created the following contact groups:

- Book 3 – Contributors
- Book 3 – Publishing contacts
- Book 3 – Production
- Book 3 – Publicity

Table 2.1 Example record of pitches sent

Article pitch	Target publication	Date sent	Editor's response	Commissioned
Your guide to the top 5 eco-friendly spas	*Vegetarian Living*	28/10/2016	Positive, but would like eco spas with vegetarian/vegan menus	Not yet, re-pitch with amended angle
How to write a biography: Geoffrey Wansell reveals the secrets of his trade	*Writing Magazine*	04/11/2016	Liked the idea but has asked for more interviewees as opposed to focusing on one writer.	Yes
Interview with Terri White, Editor-in-Chief of *Empire* magazine	*InPublishing*	11/11/2016	Positive response	Yes
Five minutes with Freya North	Lovereading.co.uk	18/11/2016	Interested	Yes

The plus side of using an Apple app is that I can sync my contacts between all my devices: laptop, iPad and iPhone automatically, enabling me to find contact details for anyone in my virtual address book. However, there are many equally good contact book apps out there, do some research to find the one that suits you best.

Before accepting any work, always agree the fee and any allowable expenses first, in writing. Sometimes an editor may allow you expenses in addition to your fee. Do keep a full record of these expenses, including the receipts. This may include travel, hotel and restaurant bills. Such records can be kept either on a spreadsheet or in a notebook.

A good system is to create a table with the following columns running along the top:

- article title;
- where published;
- deadline;
- time spent on article;
- agreed fee plus any permitted expenses;
- date paid.

In the UK, the tax year runs from 6th April and ends on the 5th of April the following year. Therefore, it is a good idea to update your spreadsheet of expenses regularly so at the beginning of April you can either opt to submit your tax return via Self Assessment or prepare your record of expenses and income for an accountant. More can be found on Self Assessment tax returns at www.gov.uk/self-assessment-tax-returns. Do keep an eye on the time spent on each article then cost it out by dividing your fee by the number of hours worked. To organise a record of assignments and expected fees I use a freelance workflow and income spreadsheet. For an example of this type of spreadsheet see Appendix 1.

Set the rate and rights

Negotiate the fee before writing the feature. Although you may be willing to accept low rates early in your career when eager for the opportunities, demand a fair price for work accepted once you have a good portfolio to show. The proper price means at least the minimum rate that the publication should be paying for features. If you accept lower fees, you will be doing other freelances out of work. Also, always agree any expenses at the time of accepting the commission.

The *NUJ Freelance Guide* (www.nuj.org.uk/work/freelance/) lists varying minimum rates for feature articles, news reporting, casual subbing, book royalties, and radio and TV scripts. These are the rates agreed with various book publishers, newspapers, magazines, the BBC, the Association of Independent Radio Contractors (commercial radio) and Independent TV Contractors Association (commercial TV). Most freelance work is negotiated directly with editors, and once you are established, you should be obtaining rates higher than the minimum ones.

When negotiating rates do discuss serial rights. Ideally you should negotiate for First British Serial Rights (now more commonly referred to as single use licence). If you sell all rights (English language) to a magazine or website, the fee should be higher. When commissioned, the writer is entitled to a "kill fee" – this is usually around 50 per cent of an agreed fee for when the commission is cancelled before it has begun. Delivered work, which was commissioned, should be paid for in full, whether it is used or not. Always get commissioned in writing. Be aware that a phone conversation with the commissioning editor who says: "we'll have a look at it" is not a commission. And don't complain if you haven't fulfilled what was promised. Read more about this in Chapter 4.

If there is no definite publication date for ordered work, try to negotiate a date of payment – perhaps within a month of submission of the work. I always send an invoice with my copy and follow up within a week if it hasn't been acknowledged. If you manage to negotiate a contract for regular articles or a column, try to get an agreement for a severance payment included – usually one month's expected earnings for every year of contributing – and for some paid holiday time.

The magazine business is volatile. Outlining the importance of making a living in *The Magazines Handbook*, McKay (2013) states: "It follows that a freelance should ideally build up a number of regular commissioning contacts so that if one editor leaves, the writer is not left without work." (McKay, 2013, p44)

McKay also warns about the difficulty freelances can have getting paid for their work, including delays of up to three months (from submission to publication) as traditionally many titles only pay in the month following publication. If payment is not forthcoming ring the commissioning editor before trying to talk to the accounts department. From such conversations you should be able to deduce from the reaction whether delay is common. If you haven't been paid for a couple of months (following publication of your article) and still have outstanding commissions think very carefully before doing more work as the magazine/newspaper might not be in a position to pay you.

Many years ago, I was a regular contributor to a small, quarterly magazine. The first year was fine, but then my invoices stopped getting paid and various excuses followed. Sadly, the magazine went bust and eventually its publisher filed for bankruptcy. In the meantime, I had let the situation build up by producing more content without getting paid, hence I advise caution. Let no more than two invoices go unpaid before you cease to contribute. When trying to recover money owed, if all else fails consider taking out a summons through the small claims court.

Membership of a professional organisation will be a source of valuable support. The National Union of Journalists (NUJ) promotes and defends the incomes and conditions of employment of journalists, and provides various benefits and legal assistance. It is the largest member of the International Federation of Journalists, which links journalists throughout the world.

Apart from the Fees Guide the NUJ publishes *The Journalist*, with its articles about trends and strikes, management problems and future prospects for the industry. www.journalism.co.uk is also a great resource for freelancers with articles on getting started, plus it also has a directory where, for a modest fee, you can advertise your services. Freelancersintheuk.co.uk also offers a directory where freelances can register for just £10 per year. Other useful contacts, including online resources, are listed in Appendix 5.

Lastly, some important advice – keep your professional and personal life separate online and on the social media platforms you use. Editors will be evaluating how effective you are on such platforms and they may be put off by that fabulous party photo your friend took.

Case study: understanding copyright

David Mascord is a training consultant specialising in editorial training, media law and business writing skills. He lectures in Media Law on BA (Hons) Multimedia Journalism and Masters programmes at Bournemouth University and is an examiner for the National Council for the Training of Journalists' Essential Media Law and Regulation examinations, and Court Reporting examinations.

Below he defines copyright, explaining the rights that writers are likely to have to sign over when selling their work and offers advice on negotiating copyright.

So, what does the copyright law actually mean in today's terms? Mascord defines it as protecting "the product of people's *time, energy, labour and skill*".

According to Mascord, the creator of a piece of writing in print or online owns their work until they pass ownership to someone else by signing a contract. "Employed journalists assign copyright to their employer when they sign an employment contract. However, any articles, blogposts or features a freelancer produces are theirs until they sign the copyright over when they are commissioned."

"The law gives individuals the right to protect their work. For example, if you feel your copyright is being breached and you've exhausted all the 'friendly' approaches, the first formal legal step may be to pay a solicitor to write and send a 'cease and desist' letter requesting someone to stop publishing your work without permission. If you want to go further, you can sue in the civil courts."

What rights are writers likely to be offered? "In my experience as a freelance journalist, a media law trainer and lecturer, and as someone who has worked in a range of media companies, publishers are asking for total copyright assignment, i.e. they want to know they own the copyright in work outright. This makes it more straightforward for them if they wish to re-purpose material. Obviously, there are a number of opportunities for them to re-use, update and re-package copy in a digital age."

Are First British Serial Rights (FSBR) still offered to staff or freelance writers? Mascord says not, adding that he hasn't seen the term First British Serial Rights on a staff or freelance journalism contract for some time.

"Staff journalists give all copyright in work produced to the company they work for when they agree the terms of employment. I have encountered a few smaller publishers who do not ask you to assign copyright when they commission you. But in general media publishers usually buy total copyright assignment in freelancers' work when they agree the commission."

"It is possible that occasionally publishers may agree to licence work. Some journalists may wish to consider asking for an exclusive single use licence – which is much the same as what used to be known as FSBR. This is a contract that states the work will be published once in a given format and rights to the work will be held by the publisher for an agreed period – after that the copyright ownership reverts to the journalist."

"Alternatively, some form of joint ownership may be agreed. Writers with more experience and popularity, e.g. major columnists, may be agreeing these."

Mascord agrees that writers should always try to negotiate for a single use licence, but must be realistic. "Most freelance journalists will find that they have little choice but to sign a contract granting total copyright assignment. In a few cases they may want to try to negotiate an exclusive use or single use licence. But a great deal depends on the individual journalist's negotiating power, i.e. how important and successful your work and your by-line or 'personal brand' is as far as that publisher is concerned."

"My view is that in the digital age it's very hard for most freelance journalists to agree to anything other than total copyright assignment in relation to day-to-day journalism they produce. However, I feel writers should aim to regain some degree of copyright ownership – and work harder to negotiate payment terms – in more substantial work they may be commissioned to produce, such as books or any other long-form, potentially long-lasting, material online or in print."

"Journalists who are members of the National Union of Journalists or the Institute of Journalists can get advice from their respective unions. There's also plenty of information online from reputable organisations."

Details of such organisations can be found in Appendix 5.

Action plan

1. Create an effective workspace which will inspire you to write and get organised. This can be either at home or a rented office.
2. Create a professional online profile.

- Buy a domain name (in your own name) and set up a basic website containing your professional profile together with examples of your work.
- Create relevant social media platforms including a Twitter account, and start connecting with potential contacts and industry experts.
- Build a profile on LinkedIn and other networking professional sites/directories.

3 Start building your network, get to know commissioning editors of those magazine you wish to target.

3 Ideas are everywhere

Feature ideas and opportunities are everywhere but perhaps the hardest lesson for many journalism students to grasp is that editors want ideas, not subjects. Many don't appear to know the difference. For example, *Racism* and *Racism in London* are both subjects – if you were to propose either of these to an editor you will be asked: *what is your angle?*

Therefore, it is crucial to understand that article ideas evolve from a subject. *The Ignorance that is Racism* is an idea. However, while the angle or viewpoint is clear it is more akin to the title of a book than that of an article and might make an essay type of column for an intellectual weekly, but needs a narrower focus for most publications. I always advise students to try to think of angles in terms of potential headlines.

Narrowing an angle down geographically if it is for a local magazine or newspaper can also help. For example, to narrow and further develop the racism theme a student might use the angle: *The Ignorance that is Racism in Bradford's Schools*. This would then suit a local paper in the Bradford area if it hadn't already been covered. If you narrow it down thematically to *Pre-School Infants Are Not Racist* you may have an acceptable idea for the education section of a national paper or for a Sunday supplement.

By bringing a subject into focus, the angle will become clear. Writers must always be able to differentiate between a statement or title and an angle. Statements such as *The Danger of Noise* can become *Discos Can Make You Deaf*, while *The Police in Britain* turns into *When Should the Police be Armed?*

This chapter will examine ideas in-depth from a staff writer, exploring potential sources for ideas as well as from a freelance perspective. It also contains practical advice on development tips using a mind map.

Ideas as a staff writer

The staff writer has the advantage of living in a familiar world of ideas that has built up around the publication. In some publishing houses, editorial meetings are held on a regular basis, during which feature writers pitch ideas either individually or collaboratively. Press releases and other material, either emailed or posted via social media, can be the source of topics for articles, as can news items that are trending online. As they are embedded in the magazine's identity, staff writers can judge immediately which ideas fit the publication they work for. Furthermore, they are backed up by extensive resources.

Ideas come to staff and freelance writers in different ways, but they can learn from each other. If an idea is resource heavy in terms of man hours and expenses, then it will probably be given to a staff writer. This will tend to happen if there's a risk inherent in the idea – that it might not come off, for instance – or if it will need careful day-by-day developing in the office.

However, David Castle, Editorial Director of *Men's Running* magazine (Figure 3.1) published by Wild Bunch Media warns that the number of staff

Figure 3.1 Cover of *Men's Running*. Credit: *Men's Running*

writers is shrinking, particularly on smaller titles. "It's an ever-diminishing number. At Wild Bunch Media each magazine now has one full-time editor, with support from the multimedia editor and social media editor, plus a freelance budget."

As it's a small team on *Men's Running*, David admits content planning is mostly left to the editor with themes and ideas agreed in advance with the commercial team. This is then filtered down to the monthly website content plan. As a result, the traditional editorial conferences are "unfortunately" a thing of the past.

"The focus on print has lessened in favour of more commercially-led 'native advertising' pieces. These are discussed at length. The front cover still gets attention from the senior management team, but we trust our editors to make the right decisions with regards to content."

Yet no matter how small a team, inspiration is still crucial. When asked where inspiration for feature ideas comes from for his title, David cites events, nutrition, footwear and health as the main sources. "I'd like to think that *Men's Running* is simply not just a cyclical running title repeating the same content year in, year out. We aim to be at the cutting edge of developments in running, training and tech."

Because of the low ratio of staff, freelance contributions equate to around 70 per cent of the magazine's editorial content. This means that the *Men's Running* freelance budget is disproportionally high with freelancers having the lion's share of the content provision. "It's the editor's role to police content coming in, sub copy and give final page approval."

So, where are good feature ideas most likely to come from on *Men's Running*? Again, the secret lies in that old adage about knowing your audience and being relevant.

"Good ideas come from brand-relevant originality – something that enables the reader to be either enthused or inspired, or both", says David, adding that once an article is commissioned his social media editor then repurposes the content, extracting snippets for the magazine's various platforms.

Meanwhile, for those fortunate enough to secure an editorial role on a magazine or newspaper here are some key sources a staff writer might use.

News stories

Reporters on local papers begin to turn into feature writers when they develop straightforward news reports into news features. For example, a reporter is covering a landslide into the sea. Cracks have appeared in houses near a cliff edge. The district council says the houses will now have settled and that it is planned to shore up the bank with some boulders to prevent further erosion. End of news story. But the editor tells the reporter that ten years ago the same reassurances were given to people living in an isolated house near a cliff edge some miles further down the coast. Their house collapsed in the middle of the night, and they were lucky to escape with their lives. A sea wall was eventually built.

"Investigate it," the editor says. "It may be that the sea wall needs to be extended. Get as much as possible from the cuttings, then go back to the surveyors on the council."

The reporter might discover from cuttings sources that might be contactable, not only to update on the topic but to extend it and develop a more ambitious background. Gaining perspectives from expert sources will turn an idea into an investigative article.

In term of the landslide story, experts to interview might include:

- the Department of the Environment;
- the Landslide Response team at the British Geological Survey;
- a Professor of Geology at the nearest university;
- the local secretary of the Farmers' Union if the clifftop includes farm land;
- a local resident who lost their home in a previous landslide.

With such a rich list of potential sources the editor will most likely be persuaded to allow more time and the story begins to shape up into a strong, long-life feature as there is also an opportunity for potential follow-up pieces.

Looking at news from a wider perspective, one big story can set the tone for an emerging theme which then trends to produce a mass of related news stories and features. One prominent example of this – which has sparked a worldwide conversation – is the numerous new stories and features emerging on sexual harassment. At the time of writing this chapter the Harvey Weinstein story had not long broken.

In a short space of time the Weinstein topic became headline news. In *Folio*, Greg Dool reports how the media went into a frenzy over Weinstein's alleged abuse. The story making the covers and prominent editorial pages of publications such as *Page Six* and *Time* magazine. In his article, *National Magazines Take On the Harvey Weinstein Scandal*, Dool reports:

> Among magazines that frequently found themselves in Weinstein's orbit over the years, *Vanity Fair*, *People*, *Entertainment Weekly*, *Us Weekly*, and *Variety* have each published dozens of online stories on the fallout from the scandal, although *Vanity Fair*'s November 2017 issue went to press too soon to weigh in.

Out of this one story a strong theme has evolved resulting in numerous news headlines worldwide and subsequent features with writers developing their own angles to suit the target audience.

The lesson? Always keep up with news stories for potential leads.

Press releases

These may yield material best suited to a feature rather than a news story. Suppose a local paper receives a press release about a novelty act called The Three Charlies, based locally, which involves clowns combining playing instruments, juggling and contortions. It mentions that the trio has achieved some national success and has TV and film engagements lined up. With a few changes the release makes a news item.

Then the item is passed to the features desk to expand on the story. While undertaking initial research, the journalist discovers that the show is based on a famous music hall act at the turn of the century. There are articles on the original troupe performing at the now defunct theatre in the area. A local antiques shop has posters that can be reproduced. The paper's cuttings library and database are searched, publicity agents are contacted and the performers interviewed. Thus, the story then becomes a feature for the newspaper or its supplement.

However, a feature such as this also has the potential for further development from a freelance perspective. It could then be pitched at a specialist magazine such as *The Stage* and perhaps also targeted at English-speaking markets around the world.

Social media and the letters' page

No longer restricted to the mail, the letters' page now includes letters, emails, Facebook posts and Tweets. In response to the digital disruption, magazines are also changing the name to be more digitally inclusive and encourage wider reader engagement. For example, the letters page in *Good Housekeeping* is now titled *Worth Sharing*.

These pages and a magazine's social media feeds are a fantastic resource for ideas both from a staff writer or freelance perspective. Audience engagement in this way not only encourages feedback from readers, but often provides follow-up ideas from existing articles, as well sparking a debate, which can – with skilful subbing – be continued for several issues.

However, in this digital age it is crucial to understand that today's reader wants an interactive relationship with the publication's writers. In editorial offices worldwide, the focus is now very much on interactive engagement, with writers encouraging their audience to share, comment and feedback usually via social media platforms. This is particularly apparent when analysing the letters' page.

It demonstrates how the process has moved on from Lazarsfeld, Berelson and Gaudet's original *Two-Step Flow of Commmunication* (Lazarsfeld et al., 1944), which has been used for decades to illustrate the dissemination of news and stories to the masses.

Now, instead of a two-step flow, the process has evolved into a full cycle, starting with the article developing into a conversation between the writer and audience, with readers actively engaging in the process as illustrated in my six-step feature model in Figure 3.2.

My model demonstrates how the interaction between the magazine, writer and the readership has now become a continuous cycle, with each step leading to the next. Step 5, however, also has the potential to develop a follow-on story. Therefore, feature writers should always read the letters' page of their target publications to spot conversation trends. These are a rich source of leads, with the potential to be developed into a new angle even if it is a familiar theme.

Figure 3.2 Six-step feature model

How to get ideas as a freelance

The distinction between staff and freelance ideas is blurred to some extent. Both have access to a wealth of resources. However, it could be argued that the freelance may have a more creative working environment as he or she is likely to have more freedom. While some freelances have launched themselves following a stint as a staff writer thus having gained inside knowledge, others might have started as students during a journalism degree or postgraduate course.

Some freelancers will specialise as columnists or reviewers for one or two publications. But the tyro freelance may have to be adept at finding different kinds of ideas and at matching them to different targets. In addition, they will also have to provide their own resources and develop a strong network of contacts.

As a lecturer, I have always encouraged my students to freelance while undertaking their under- or postgraduate degree. During such discussions, a question often asked is: should we have come up with an idea then find a suitable market or vice versa? There is no right answer, just the requirement to have a good understanding of magazines and how to analyse their editorial pillars and target audiences. The general rule is that freelances first come up with an idea, then find a suitable market.

For those just starting out a mind map can be a helpful tool to turn a vague idea or subject matter into a potential article. To further demonstrate this, I have created an example. Figure 3.3 "Mapping your ideas" shows how to come up with an original and relevant idea from a familiar theme by noting down associated links.

So how exactly does the map work? For my map in Figure 3.3 I have used the theme of dementia as it is topical, poignant and relevant as it affects many lives – young and old alike. However, as we know much has already been written on this subject, so how might I come up with a fresh angle?

The answer lies in the map. By mapping out key associations then linking these, ideas and potential angles begin to emerge.

For example, if I were to focus on alternative therapies as the theme, this could be the basis of a great package piece – consisting of the print article, a digital adaption perhaps with audio content and an online piece with featuring a short video clip. To avoid repetition, it is crucial to develop different aspects for each component. Therefore, if I were to develop or pitch a feature package on this theme, I would use the following angles:

Figure 3.3 Mapping your ideas

- **The print article:** *how alternative therapies can support dementia patients* – the article will outline two or three successful therapies such as music and consist of interviews with a medical practitioner and a couple of therapists, plus a patient in the early stages.
- **A digital adaptation:** this would be the same as the print piece, but would also include hyperlinks and interactive questions to spark a conversation with digital readers. A short two-minute audio piece would give added value. This could be a narrated recording of a therapist giving an in-depth account of how a session is constructed.
- **An online component:** titled *My story* – this might be an interview with a relative of a dementia patient looking at how or if the therapies have helped the patient from their perspective. It could be written in first person and include a short video clip of an actual therapy session.
- **Social media content:** snippets from the online and print pieces could be posted. This aspect is crucial to signpost the article, start a conversation and thus widen audience participation.

As a freelance it is now important to always think from a multimedia perspective as most publications tell a story (the feature) across several mediums. Again, fresh content and a clear link between each component is crucial as repetition is a big turn-off for readers.

Finding suitable target markets

Professional golfers about to compete on a golf course spend many hours getting to know the course in practice rounds. They get to know the shape of it well, every bump in the ground, the contours, the gradients, the length of the grass in different parts. They can then play it in their minds. Professional feature writers are no different as they must compete for space on a publication. Therefore, all freelancers must undertake a comprehensive market analysis of their potential target publications.

Suppose you want to tackle *Bullying in the Workplace*. First, you might make a list of a few potential target publications. This might include:

- *Daily Mail*;
- *The Guardian*;
- *The Economist*;
- *Management Today*;
- *Woman's Own*;
- *Marie Claire*;
- *Psychologies*;
- your local paper.

After doing some initial research it becomes clear that you haven't got one potential feature but many. However, a word of caution: unless you have an impressive track record, you might find many of the above publications difficult to break into.

But back to the list. Take a close look at your potential targets and decide which are the three most likely prospects for you. Each publication will require a different treatment, which means developing a relevant angle, content, structure and style. You study each publication carefully (several recent issues) and decide on the kind of treatment that will work. Remember when developing content for a target publication you must answer the questions about the subject that its audience would ask, in such a way as to command its attention.

For example, consider which publications will be most interested in the effects of the bullying on the efficiency of the company, which on the psychologies of bullies and victims, and decide what range of workplaces would be covered by each publication. When evaluating your target markets also answer the following questions:

- **Depth of articles:** will the magazines want drama, cool reasoning or in-depth specialist content?
- **Article lengths:** what lengths are their average features in each publication?
- **Tone and style:** which of the target markets use humour or lean towards academic seriousness?

The *Daily Mail* and *The Guardian* are likely to bring politics into it while *The Guardian* (having many teachers among its readers) could relate it to bullying at school. But *The Economist* will be interested in the damaging effects of bullying on the efficiency of businesses and *Woman's Own* in how parents can help victims. How would you develop the idea for each of the other publications?

Having chosen a target, check that the subject hasn't been dealt with recently and that their editorial policy for features hasn't suddenly been changed (for example, by a new editorial appointment).

You may prefer to concentrate on first developing ideas before looking for target markets. Whichever, once established as a regular writer for a publication, the whole process will be more of a collaboration with the editor, who will adapt a briefing policy to what they know you're capable of. More on this in the following chapters. Let's get back to ideas.

Where to look

Freelance writers have the advantage that they can come up with the more unusual ideas. Publications can get in a rut sticking too rigidly to a formula. Editors can then be excited by the passion and commitment of a freelance with fresh ideas and above-average writing ability.

Freelances are sometimes paid for just submitting a good idea, especially by newspapers, when a staff writer is considered to be better placed with connections, and better qualified generally, to develop the article. Be wary of giving too much away before getting a commission – ideas can be pinched as well as pitched.

You need to be open to ideas and ready to capture them. The poet Louis MacNeice spent 25 years learning how to write poetry, then suddenly one day realised he had poems flying past his right ear. All he had to do was move his head a bit to the right. According to Kate Connolly in *The Guardian*, the German poet Schiller found ideas came more rapidly if he had rotting apples in a drawer of his desk (Connolly, 2009), while Ernest Hemingway sharpened a lot of pencils before starting to write (Palimpsest), and our former Poet Laureate, Andrew Motion, once admitted to taking a cup of Lemsip to boost his creativity. You will find your own ways of getting into a receptive state of mind. Be as mystical about it as you like if it works. But for the moment let's stay on a practical level.

As journalists, you need to be practical, in terms of size (seriousness, importance) of idea and the kind of markets targeted. As well as the latest technology always carry a notebook and pen everywhere as many ideas will come when you least expect them. Some will come in the form of a word or a phrase or a sentence, perhaps a title. Others will demand a page or more of your notebook. Transfer likely ideas to a folder where they can be developed by adding notes, cuttings and other materials (see Chapter 2).

But where should you look for ideas? Here are some likely sources.

- **Personal experience:** features can be written about a first- or second-hand experience. Examples might include the domestic upheaval of moving house, a change of career, an unusual travel experience, office politics, dangerous dogs or a conversion to Buddhism. And so on.

    It's probably best to develop such a piece with a target in mind. In which case, make sure that it will appeal to the readership aimed at as it is too easy to assume that what has deeply affected you will interest others. There have been numerous articles published on such topics as those listed above, so consider what have you got to add? Can you think of a fresh treatment or combine your experience with that of others gleaned from your cuttings files? Perhaps you can find interviewees who would add a dimension or two?
- **Conversations noted:** at a party you've been identified as a good listener by a woman of a certain age who is being lengthy about her studies as an Open University student. You are edging away when she says, "I had to do something when I lost my husband and two children in a car crash." You begin to contribute to the conversation. Avoid getting out your notebook right away but do ask if she would mind your taking a few notes for an article you see on the horizon.
- **Events observed and other opportunities:** deepen your particular interests and areas of knowledge by attending associated events. If you want to write features for a local newspaper, find out which organisations and activities are not covered by the paper. Street entertainers, sports such as swimming and running events, surviving rural skills, amateur dramatics, a restaurants guide? Then develop convincing arguments for their inclusion and email it to the editor along with a sample of your writing.

    If you are taken on as a regular contributor (which could lead to the offer of a staff job), not all your reports are going to be used, but you might be able to negotiate a retainer fee. Put yourself on the mailing lists of the organisations. Attend some meetings and make yourself known to the organisers. Having contributed news items to the paper on this basis for a while, you may find it easier to get space on the feature pages.

Many years ago, I found an idea for a feature while browsing in my local library. Sitting on the table of new publications was *Behind With The Mortgage And Living Off Plastic*, by life-coach Lynette Allen. Its amazing title gave me an idea for an article on how to organise your life. The article included an interview with Lynette and was published in *City Life*, a south coast publication.

- **Broadcasts:** radio phone-in programmes, like the letters pages of newspapers and magazines, are natural homes for the cranky and the quirky and can be a fertile source of ideas. Child abusers should be castrated, you may hear someone say, or sterilised, or the public schools should be abolished and the buildings sold to create social housing. While such remarks may amuse or annoy they probably start you thinking about the subject.

  Radio and TV documentaries on such subjects as drug addiction, the prison system, immigrants, increasing obesity and business frauds may throw up some aspect that grabs you: then you grab your notebook. Such programmes will suggest possible contacts. Note that tonight's TV documentary may have been made a year ago: check and update the material.

- **Newspapers and consumer magazines:** read the popular as well as the quality prints. Collect cuttings that add something new to one of your subjects, that may suggest future features or provide facts for them. Collect articles you consider good models for particular kinds: for a celebrity interview, a political background piece, a film review or whatever. Carefully tear out these articles or photocopy them noting publication and date then file in acetate to preserve them. It is always useful to make comments in the margins so that you don't wonder several months later why you cut them.

A good tip when extracting an idea from one market is to reshape it for another where it will be less familiar. A medical breakthrough analysed in an upmarket weekly may lend itself to a more light-hearted human-interest treatment for a popular paper or magazine. Conversely an interview with a young woman in a local paper who has survived a dysfunctional family and drug addiction and launched a career in TV may suggest how some researching will discover stories that might add up to a feature for a national magazine.

Read industry publications such as the *Press Gazette* (www.pressgazette.co.uk) regularly to keep up to date with the journalism business, and a writers' trade magazine for up-to-date market information and articles on idea forming and writing techniques.

Ideas from B2B magazines and professional journals

Some news stories don't break in newspapers but are run in B2B business-to-business magazines and professional journals. Keep an eye on them. You can corner ideas worth wider dissemination.

You spot in a catering magazine, for example, that a famous hotel company, in its bid to take over another, accuses the latter of various management faults. One fault mentioned is a failure to use technology efficiently in hotels. You note that this aspect has not been covered by newspapers or the business magazines, which have concentrated on the financial aspects of the conflict. Names are mentioned in the catering magazine article that could help you to write a piece on the new technology, or lack of it, in hotels. A national newspaper or a consumer magazine might be interested.

Such ideas frequently revolve around new products or new technology. Information in a business-to-business or technical journal about a new kind of computer for use in schools, or about a court case concerning an accident caused by a department store escalator breaking down, may have wider implication. The news media may not immediately realise the news value of such stories or see how to interpret them to a wider audience.

Ideally placed to do so would be part-time freelances whose main jobs are in hotels, computer technology and store management. In journalistic terms, they are the "experts". But your most valuable trick is in knowing who the experts are and in getting them to talk to you.

Books are a great source of inspiration

Reference books of various kinds are worth digging into. Consider *Chambers Dictionary of Dates*. The following entries for 25th March section include:

- 1843: the 1,300-foot Thames tunnel, from Wapping to Rotherhithe, was opened.
- 1867: Arturo Toscanini born.
- 1975: King Faisal of Saudi Arabia assassinated by his nephew.

Some library research into these subjects will develop ideas about famous tunnels, musicians, assassinations. Staying with anniversaries, reference books of different kinds can tell or remind you of forthcoming, notable events such as National Book Week, World Diabetes Day, Mother's and Father's Day or World Town Planning Day and so on. But avoid the anniversaries all those other freelances pick up.

Looking through the London South East Yellow Pages telephone directory I found the following intriguing entries: chimney sweeps, diamond sawing, fallout shelters, gold blockers, hairpiece manufacturers and importers, naturopaths, noise and vibration consultants, pawnbrokers, portable buildings, robots, ship breakers, toastmasters. Nothing stirs you? Have a go yourself in your local Yellow Pages. And yes, they still exist although they are somewhat thinner than their pre-digital age counterparts.

A word about techniques

Whether you're a staff or freelance writer – or both – you need techniques to make your ideas grow. Ideas are tender plants. Some you've just got to let grow, others need to be fed and watched over but a few are likely to be beyond any surgical intervention. Although in time you will find your own ways. In the meantime, experiment with the suggestions below to discover what sort of activity works best for you.

The growing process, as described earlier, is probably best done using a desktop folder marked IDEAS, which might include scans of cuttings, notes, icons and images. Start a folder by collecting as many cuttings/notes as you can, then add to it when you can. Organisation is key. I find the best method is to organise your cuttings alphabetically in subject order. Go through them regularly to remove the out-of-date ones and decide when you've got a good idea to sell.

At any stage of this development, inspiration and creativity will be your stepping stones to success. Therefore, it's crucial to experiment with different brainstorming methods to see what fits the idea or your way of thinking. Here are a few suggestions.

Get creative

In journalism, the originality of an idea resides in treatment – that's getting the right angle, achieving a magazine's house-style and a strong structure. Ensuring the idea is topical and relevant is crucial too, as is avoiding the obvious content. That means gathering your information from places not too familiar, finding contacts if you can who know more than has been revealed and taking a wider perspective by talking to the *not-so-obvious* sources.

Here are a few examples of how to develop potential ideas from these three sources – one is hypothetical, while the other two are based on my own experience:

1 **A news item:** you read a short news article about a pub which is going to close in a nearby village. This is the third pub in as many years, but to get an original angle and develop the piece you first decide to research pub closure statistics in your area and nationwide. By looking at the issue as a problem-solving opportunity a relevant idea becomes apparent taking the angle *Avoiding closure: how publicans can survive a downturn*. Such a piece would suit a local business magazine and a trade publication such as *The Publican*.
2 **The experience:** being a bike enthusiast I was sad to see that only one bike shop remained in our town. One Saturday afternoon I went to the said shop on a fact-finding mission to look for my next bike. It was unusually quiet with only one assistant holding the fort. He seemed preoccupied with a computer task at the desk and clearly did not want to engage with me. Angry, I left the shop but an idea began to evolve in terms of a question: *what does great customer service mean?* This could provide angles for national, local and trade magazines either in the form of a vox pop piece with shoppers giving their views or as an insight using an interview with a retail specialist.
3 **A conversation:** often I have gotten ideas from overhearing conversations. A few years ago, while at a train station, I overhead two older ladies talking

about their dreadful bra fitting experiences. Being Fashion and Beauty editor on *City Life* at the time it sparked my interest and resulted in my article *How to get the perfect bra fitting*. The feature included interviews with expert fitters and fashion stylists plus a *how-to* guide. It was not only relevant but empowering as it enabled readers to go shopping with a good understanding of the basics.

On a more complex level the power of imagination helps you to yoke together disparate notions in inventive ways. As a feature idea grows and you have notes from various sources you need to use your imagination to experiment with them, juxtapose them in different ways, to liberate yourself from the weight of information and to let illumination in. Sometimes you will find yourself on an unrewarding journey, and you may have to abandon the trail and start again with another brainstorming method.

Using formulas and word associations

An idea can begin with a word or phrase that lodges in the mind for no particular reason. For example, Animal can turn into Animals Anonymous, and that might suggest animals with behaviour problems being organised for some kind of treatment, or more sinisterly, for genetic experiments.

There are formula ideas, hundreds of them, that work well for popular markets:

- *what your ... should tell you about yourself* (hand, handwriting, earlobes);
- *what is the best ...?* (age, diet);
- *the ... of the future* (toys, careers, bodies);
- *behind the scenes at the ...* (opera, TV centre, film studio, football stadium);
- *the world's biggest ...*;
- *the world's smallest ...*;
- *can ... survive?* (personality, conversation).

Some intriguing lists can be turned into articles such as *The great bars of the world* or *Five top eco spas*. But of course, most of them are likely to have been overdone, so turn the ideas on their heads: *The world's worst bar* or *Five cheapest eco spas*.

Looking at a subject's contrary can make a possible idea. Phrases such as *Fortunate Accidents, Unhappy Millionaires, Ingenious Mishaps, Tragic Trifles* at least start you thinking.

As some of these formula examples show, a good idea can come to you in the shape of a good title. But a good title is sometimes hard to find, and the ones that immediately suggest themselves may be well worn. Work at finding a good title (aka a headline or sell) because that will help you develop the idea and keep you on track. Experiment by listing possible titles on a piece of paper or on your screen. Try to make them reflect your angle and suit the publication aimed at.

You might have a problem interesting an editor in a piece on *The danger of noise* but a title such as *The top five causes of hearing loss* may have a better chance. Such alliteration helps to make them memorable, as do rhythm and puns and other verbal tricks. On the other hand, you have to avoid using these factors in predictable ways.

Many headlines are changed by the sub-editors. Your title needs to harmonise with the other titles in the issue, and if you aren't a sub-editor you can't always anticipate them, nor the design of the page where your article will appear and therefore the size wanted. A publication's sub-editors are closer to the readers and therefore have inside knowledge. Nevertheless, work at creating a good headline, or at least a good provisional title, because it will help you to sell the idea or the article, and to keep you on track.

Linear-logical thinking

Developing a feature outline from a subject in a linear-logical way can unleash a few ideas. You see the possibilities and can select an aspect that strikes you as fruitful. Suppose the subject is surgery and your angle the question: *is it skilful enough?* You might discover such a pattern as:

- medical training for surgeons;
- where technology is up to date;
- where lacking;
- cutbacks in the Health Service;
- priorities in budgeting;
- criteria?
- too many errors?
- law;
- ethics;
- compensation;
- insurance.

If you're knowledgeable about a subject – and know more or less where you are going – then this way of thinking is productive. If you need to be open to different possibilities, if you want to discover how you see a subject, to stimulate your thinking about it, the linear-logical approach can be restrictive and a brainstorming technique is recommended.

Develop a specialism

Subjects are in and out of fashion, magazines come and go, so feature writers are wise in the early stages of their career to develop ideas out of a variety of interests and cultivate specialist knowledge in a subject that interests you. Interests will vary as you get older but a lively curiosity about the world in general and in people of different age groups is needed if you are to communicate with wide readerships effectively.

Write about what you know, especially perhaps when starting out, but keep in mind that it is what your readers need or want to know that you can find out. An idea is a paltry thing unless it can be supported by facts and put across persuasively.

At the same time, it is good to have a specialism or two because specialist magazines are numerous. Newspaper editors will begin to remember your name. They will begin looking for you when your subjects are in the news, and you will welcome the time you can subtract from selling and add to writing. Making a mark in specialist writing can also lead to work in broadcasting.

Of course, once you are well established with a specialism or two, you may need to concentrate on them. But don't let specialisms take you over completely. Theatre and music critics, for example, can impress with their analytical powers yet disappoint if they show few signs of knowing much else.

An essential checklist

You can waste a lot of time not only writing pieces that are rejected, but outlining ideas that are rejected. After doing some initial market research put your idea through a test but before proposing an idea to an editor.

Here is a checklist to help you decide whether an idea has potential or not:

- Is the idea too broad, or too narrow?
- Is it fresh, or has it been overdone recently?
- Can you update the published information you have seen recently on the subject?
- Is fresh information readily available? Where from?
- Will the idea appeal to the target readers?
- Are the facts likely to be of the kind that the readers will need or want?
- Is there a clear theme/angle/point of view?
- Is the idea significant, important, relevant, timely?
- If not timely, does it have enough timelessness about it?
- Is it a good time for you to handle it. Why?
- Are there any dangers of libel, or other legal or ethical considerations?
- Do you really want to write the feature or do you think of it as a chore?
- How much will the feature cost you in money and time?
- If it doesn't work for your target editor, might it appeal to others?

Lastly, having run through this list then identified a target publication it is also a good idea to also test your idea using what I define as the three "whys?". Because having answers to these three will not only ensure your article is relevant, it will also help pitch the concept convincingly to an editor by summarising why he or she should buy the copy.

1 **Why this?:** clearly identify what it is about your idea that is unique, topical and relevant to a specific readership.
2 **Why now?:** it is crucial to be able to pinpoint the timing of your idea, for example, is this subject trending or have there been related new stories, etc?
3 **Why me?:** demonstrate why you are the best person to write the feature.

Case study: an editor's perspective

Below, former editor of Woman's Weekly, *Diane Kenwood, gives her perspective on what makes a great feature idea, how to research the market and pitching, while also sharing the wisdom of her experience.*

The most important thing is that you have a story to tell because what makes a strong feature is a good story. There are no new stories anywhere in the world anymore but there are new angles and what makes a good article is something that really engages with the audience. It should either speak to their passion, interests, emotions and intellect – any or ideally all of those depending on the publication.

However, it's crucial to understand the differentials – an idea that makes a good feature for *The Economist* won't make a good piece for *Woman's Weekly* and vice versa. When targeting a magazine like *Woman's Weekly*, remember the focus is on women in their homes – articles must be on subjects that are useful, informative, entertaining and inspiring to those readers.

When researching a target market, new writers have lots of opportunities, the tools at their disposal are more varied than when I started out. If you are thinking about writing for a particular market then study publications aimed at that audience – really look at them properly and thoroughly. Give yourself a broad overview by also looking at all the platforms – viewing content from vloggers, bloggers and Instagram.

This is just the same if you're focusing on an older market. Many people are under the ridiculous misconception that the over-40s don't use social media, which is nonsense because they do. However, they do use it in a different way and it is very instructive to analyse that. Another tip is when looking at readers of a specific market, such as the *Daily Mail* for example, always dig a little deeper. Whether it's an online article or a blog, read the comments, they're very instructive too.

If you're targeting a specific title, make sure you analyse the magazine in-depth and that means reading more than one issue. Don't imagine by reading just one issue that you will know everything about that title because writers need to see at least three issues before they really get a sense of what a magazine is about and get a better grasp of its DNA. Go to a library or similar resource where you can view previous issues, or, if you have to, buy consecutive editions. This will give you a much broader picture, because looking at one issue is like seeing the magazine in 2D, but analysing a few issues gives a 3D perspective.

Pitching tends to be where many new writers fall down. The art is to sell your idea and yourself, so firstly you have to make it absolutely clear that you have actually read the magazine. Show the recipient that you're not sending a round robin email and address it to the editor in person. I used to get so many emails where the sender had clearly sent the same pitch to numerous editors and just changed the name. My name was always clearly printed in the Editor's letter at the front of every issue yet still I received numerous pitches starting with Dear Editor. Really? That's not the best start!

And if you are unsure, or can't find the name in the publication, then phone the magazine or newspaper and ask who the commissioning editor is. But whatever you do when pitching don't, under any circumstances, tell the whole story or send the finished feature, just don't do it.

So, what is the best way to pitch? Always be concise. Try imagining what you'd say if you were standing in front of that person with only one minute to convince them. Be pithy but clear. Make it sound exciting, interesting, emotional, inspiring, whatever is relevant, but keep it tight.

Also, make it clear you have access. If it's a real-life story confirm you can get the person to talk to you and that they are willing to have their photograph taken. This is very important as pictures are crucial. Or, if it's the kind of story that is sensitive and therefore the subject/s might not be willing to be shown, demonstrate you have ideas for how it can be presented visually. That shows that you have thought it through.

Do try to build relationships with commissioning editors. I appreciate this is tricky because obviously so many people are trying to get themselves noticed or known. Talking to an editor on the phone always helps, say that you are just starting out and "want to know the best way to approach you with ideas as I would love to write for you". It's nerve-wracking but remember that everyone working in the industry started somewhere, so they should have enough professional empathy to give somebody a couple of minutes of their time.

Phoning is always preferable to email as the trouble with emailing is that everyone now just gets so many. But if you do send an email try to personalise it, give it some character, do something that demonstrates your personality and engages the editor in some way. Above all avoid the bog standard "Dear Sir/Madam, I would really like to write for your magazine and I have some really good ideas that I would like to send you …".

It is tough and there is no point in pretending it isn't. But my best advice to new writers – aside from all of the above! – is start writing for yourself. Young journalists in the current market have a huge advantage compared to when I came into the industry, as there are so many platforms for their words. There are opportunities now that didn't exist even a decade ago. And yes, of course, we'd all love to write for a national publication, but everyone has to start somewhere. Put your stuff out there, just write. Start a blog, it can be your calling card. Approach an editor saying "I've been writing this blog …".

Posting regular blog pieces gives you a chance to get your work seen, but more importantly it enables you to start developing your own style, ideas and ways of conversing. If I received an email pitch or a request for work experience and the writer had put a link to a blog or website then I would always look. It's very instructive because you can tell a lot about someone's writing, it doesn't matter what they are writing about.

Having writer's block is a common issue that every writer comes up against. What I always say is: when you are stuck or find yourself writing in an awkward way imagine you are telling your best friend whatever it is you are trying to say, and write it like you would if you were literally saying it to him/her. It sounds weird, but it releases you from the bounds of writing in a strange formal style. I still do that now.

Most of all though, writers need to find their voice and that only comes by working hard and writing as much as they can, as often as they can.

Action plan

1. Produce a mind map using one of the following subjects: noise, dyslexia, fox hunting or earthquakes.
2. Use the mind map you've created to develop an angle for a feature of 800 words.
3. Now identify three potential markets which might be interested.

4 Market research

Market research is an essential part of feature writing, more so in today's climate where editors expect a succinct pitch as opposed to an article on spec. Often, new writers often find editors a tad reluctant to commission a piece on the basis of a pitch, unless it is accompanied by a portfolio of published work. That said, if the idea is a good one and it's clear the writer has done their research, then the editor may respond with "we'll have a look at it but no promises".

For those who think they have a brilliant idea based on their own experience, it's advisable to tread carefully in the first instance. It is unlikely that an editor will respond enthusiastically to a piece about getting lost in the Brazilian jungle, meeting a long-forgotten tribe or about your life-after-death experience. However, if you truly believe you could do something brilliant with one of these stories then write it. But instead of sending in the full article, pitch it making sure you include a headline, stand-first and intro to demonstrate the relevance of your idea – as well as your ability to write in the style of that publication.

While there is still a small market for "specs" – this tends to be only with smaller magazines. It's worth seeking these out as writing the occasional piece on spec is beneficial as this can get you out of a rut, liberate your creativity, open your mind to more possibilities while increasing your potential.

In terms of feature writing, most of your time should be spent on researching potential markets, building contacts, pitching, before preparing and writing commissioned features. The most common reason for rejection is not defects in the content, structure or writing, but unsuitability for the market. Learn from rejection, to rewrite if asked to or to submit to another market. Sometimes rejection can be about timing so it's prudent to file some of those rejected ideas (or spec articles) then revive them at a later date.

This chapter aims to give you a grounding in market research for magazines, websites/blogs and newspapers. It will look at how to gain an understanding of publications, news values, audiences and editorial pillars – all of which will give you a head start when pitching your idea.

Researching magazine markets

Once you have a good idea, think about which sector it will suit then choose three potential markets. But first, the most important lesson is to understand the different sectors. These are as follows:

- **Consumer:** the lifestyle sector is massive, covering news and mainstream magazines such as *Good Housekeeping*, *Marie Claire*, *Women's Health*, *Shortlist*, *Stylist*, *GQ* and *Esquire*.
- **Specialist:** this sector covers a range of titles from politics and culture, to sport and hobbies. Note, there is often some crossover between specialist and consumer market. For example, magazines such as *Women's Health* and *The New Statesman* fall between these two sectors.
- **Customer publishing:** these are magazines published by businesses for their customers. It is a growing market with numerous brands names commissioning publishing houses to launch their magazines including all the main supermarkets, Marks & Spencer, Boots, Virgin Media and of course the airline industry's inflight titles.
- **B2B (business-to-business):** A lucrative sector which pays well for articles, there is a publication for every aspect of businesses from banking and retail, to plumbing and agriculture. Business owners, graduates and professionals will pay for specialist industry knowledge.
- **Localised:** local, independent magazines are thriving and they are certainly worth considering as a viable target market. Their editorial covers a specific area focusing on lifestyle, leisure and business.

Think about which sector your idea suits best. Once you have chosen the sector, then decided on the target magazine.

Analyse adverts

While newspaper audiences are more clear-cut as they are defined by categories – quality, middlebrow and popular as explored earlier in the chapter – magazine readers require a more forensic approach.

Most digital and print editions are heavily dependent on income from advertising which also includes promotional content. As much as two-thirds of the space in a consumer magazine may be devoted to it. With the growth in promotional content articles (features which are in fact advertising products/services in a subtle way) adverts can be as much part of the reader appeal as the editorial content. Therefore, these too should be included in your analysis.

What media kits will tell you

Target markets in publishing are big business, so editors and advertising directors invest heavily in monitoring their readership using surveys to collect a great deal of information about their readers, the results of which are then put into a media kit, aka the rate card. This is a key selling tool for the magazine's advertising sales executives and can often be found online by looking at publishers' websites.

For feature writers, media kits contain a wealth of information about the audience demographic, the readership – their hopes, dreams and fears, etc. – plus the magazine's key editorial pillars.

There are various formulations of a media kit/rate card. *Food and Travel* magazine published by Green Pea Publishing, for example, has a media information page entitled *Magazine Facts* in addition to its rate card (see Figure 4.1). This includes a wealth of information on *Food and Travel* as well as key data on its audience. Therefore, by going through the media kit any writer wishing to pitch a feature idea can find out a wealth of information including:

- The magazine's background, launch and publication frequency details.
- Circulation and readership figures.
- A comprehensive profile of the magazine's readership including age range, male/female ratio, household incomes as well as lifestyle habits and interests.
- Details on related brand extensions.

While this data provides a good start, further analysis, which should focus on the key editorial pillars, is crucial. Go through at least two issues noting the key editorial pillars or themes, while at the same time looking for potential follow-on article ideas or the opportunity to create a short series for the magazine.

Content analysis

In-depth analysis of the magazine's content is crucial to gain a good understanding of the content, as well as the style, length and tone of articles. Go through a few back issues as well as the current one, noting the following essential style points:

- **Headlines:** length and style.
- **Stand-firsts:** how many words, tone/style and is the writer's by-line written into the text?
- **Article length:** what is the average length of each article? This is important as it's no good pitching a 1,500-word feature if the publication's standard length is 1,000 words.
- **Writing style:** is the writing style formal or informal and how many quotes does each feature contain?
- **Interviews:** note how many sources each article uses. Also, are these interviewees high-profile? If so your sources need to reflect this standard.
- **Type of articles:** examine what type are preferred. For example, are there a few *how-to* pieces or is the focus on investigative journalism? With regards to profile/interview articles, what is the preferred format – Q&A, statement and answer or a standard profile piece.

An intelligent study of the content across all publication's platforms is the best guide for any writer as this should reveal continuity as well as potential opportunities for follow-on pieces.

MAGAZINE FACTS

Food and Travel is an award-winning consumer print magazine published ten times a year in the UK. Our readers are passionate about food, wine and travel, and have come to trust and rely on recommendations and insider tips found in every edition. *Food and Travel* is packed with inspiring and beautifully photographed food, drink and travel stories, which appear alongside seasonal recipes, news, reviews, exclusive offers and competitions.

After 20 years of successful publishing, in the UK and around the world, the magazine's readers are well worth targeting – advertisers can benefit from the trust and loyalty they show the title and its contents. Please find more information below:

UK circulation	31,000
UK readership	103,000
UK frequency	Monthly (10 per year), full colour, glossy publication
Launched	UK edition: December 1997
	German edition: June 2010 (bi-monthly)
	Mexican edition: June 2011 (monthly, 10 per year)
	Turkish edition: October 2013 (monthly, 10 per year)
	Arabian edition: April 2014 (monthly, 10 per year)
	Italian edition: November 2015 (8 x year)
Reader profile	Affluent lovers of food, wine and travel
	Predominantly professional individuals, AB adults
Age range	66% of readers aged 26-54
	26% aged 26-44
	40% aged 44-54
	34% aged 55+
Sex	55:45 female to male
Household income	95% earn more than £50k a year
	33% earn £50k to £75k a year
	38% earn £76k to £100k a year
	27% earn more than £100k a year
Attitude	*Food and Travel* readers are innovative, trendsetting opinion-formers

Figure 4.1 Magazine facts

Remember that most titles are launched to meet an observed demand, therefore a magazine must adhere to its editorial pillars which have been carefully developed by the editor or publisher. A subtle shift in direction might be made to increase or hold a circulation, stave off competition or recognise new trends, but only as much as will not disturb the existing body of loyal readers. Feature writers, especially freelance, should become familiar with the volatility and keep abreast of the trends.

Gregor Rankin, publisher of *Food and Travel* (Figure 4.2), advises freelances to read at least three issues when researching a magazine as this will give an idea of seasonality as well as a general style. "When developing feature ideas, the best way to research a target publication is to read it cover to cover", says Gregor. "Speak with friends and family members who you think fit the target demographic to see if your idea has 'legs'."

He also suggests checking out the target title's media pack to see who they say they are targeting, although caution is advised as this may be different from those who *actually* read it.

When asked what freelancers/journalism students should have found out about *Food and Travel* before pitching, Gregor reiterates the importance of knowing who the target reader is, and considering why would the editor want to run this piece. "Also, consider the possibility that the title has already run a similar feature. If so try and put a different spin on it."

Online opportunities

Following the digital revolution which began at the start of the twenty-first century, there are now more opportunities than ever to write for online markets – and get paid for it. Whether it be blogging, writing short articles for websites or developing social media posts there are some great opportunities for new writers to hone their skills and get paid for doing so.

A couple of years ago I started writing for Lovereading.co.uk as I enjoy profiling authors and was keen to expand into new markets. The opportunity came about while searching for potential online platforms which focused on creative writing/books and didn't have additional editorial content. My initial analysis of the site showed that Lovereading fitted the bill.

The next stage was to undertake a thorough audit of the platform, which involved an analysis of:

- **Type of site:** specialist website focusing on writing.
- **Key editorial pillars:** these included news on fiction/non-fiction releases and reviews, awards, plus writing competitions.
- **Blog posts:** these were mainly in-depth reviews by staff writers.
- **Potential audience:** although no demographics were available a study of the style and tone revealed the average user was likely to be in the ABC1 audience demographic category, aged between 30 and 50, probably a writer or book club member with a good disposable income.

44 Market research

Figure 4.2 Food and Travel cover. Credit: *Food and Travel* magazine

- **Style and tone of posts:** in-depth reviews of a range of books across fiction and non-fiction genres, all written in a relatively informal style.

My research also revealed that there weren't any author profiles, hence I had spotted a gap in their content, which had the potential to add value to their platform. After sending an initial pitch within a short time I had a regular commission for profiles on high-profile and debut authors.

Here I have built up excellent contacts so I'm now able to access high-profile authors, but those starting out can still use the core lessons of this research analysis. Just as with any print market, research and getting to know the publication (or in this instance platform) is key.

Target new start-ups

Getting in early is a great way to build a relationship with an editor, so look for new online launches, particularly independent platforms as those often have low budgets and are looking for good writers. It is from opportunities such as these that roles can grow. Many years ago, a student of mine started writing for a new start-up to gain experience and fund her studies.

Being passionate about a green lifestyle, Alexia was keen to pitch to this market and came across a new magazine that had recently launched. A brave approach netted her first published piece, which wasn't paid but the second article was and soon she was earning more from writing than she would stacking shelves a few hours a week. Not only did her writing skills and confidence soar, by the time she graduated the following year a job offer as features editor was waiting. The key to her success was her initial eagerness and determination. Hard work always pays off in the end.

How can you find a new start-up? The first step is a search on Google for online magazines in your chosen subject – be it on lifestyle, fashion, beauty, sport, food or eco living. This search might just yield a new launch, but if not the next option is to search the publishing industry's news sites of which there are numerous sources including:

- **PPA (Professional Publishers Association)** (www.ppa.co.uk/): has a news section with the latest stories on all aspects of digital, print and online magazine publishing.
- **InPublishing Magazine** (www.inpublishing.co.uk): a quick search under news revealed *Livingetc launches website* (InPublishing, 2018) a story about Time Inc launching a new platform for the Livingetc brand.
- **What's news in publishing** (http://whatsnewinpublishing.co.uk/): is also a good source for new launch stories.
- **Press Gazette** (www.pressgazette.co.uk): carries a range of industry news including launches across all sectors print and online.

Newspaper markets

While magazines remain a popular target for ideas, newspapers also have opportunities for getting published. Although, due to current economic constraints, freelance fees are likely to be much lower. However, for those seeking their first by-line, writing articles for local papers is good training, those features are also more likely to get published.

For convenience, newspaper editorial is labelled "news" or "features" although the lines of demarcation can be blurred. With the increased need for background to the news already broadcast, posted or printed, there are hybrids such as "news features". Background or "current situation" articles deal with politics, the economy and social questions, while for local papers the focus is on issues relating to that specific area and its residents.

Research features at some length and depth may be called investigative. They have in the past covered such themes as dangerous drugs put on the market with insufficient testing and aeroplane accidents due to negligence at trial stage (notably in *The Sunday Times*). Such features are often linked with campaigns to obtain better compensation for victims. They may be running stories produced by a team of reporters, feature writers and researchers.

Human interest stories ("people journalism") are rated highly in most newspapers. For this editorial theme, editors are looking for ideas that focus on:

- TOTs – triumph over tragedy stories;
- people being victimised;
- domestic violence;
- sexual abuse/harassment;
- fraud, particularly incidents that have occurred online.

Other ideas might include struggles against illness or misfortune rather than with the statistics of social problems because that's the way to get readers' interest. The expert on social problems draws on such material, of course, for case studies.

Similarly, it's usually more interesting to read about people being successful than organisations being successful. Notice how business section features hunt out the human angles. Notably "human interest" now forms a key part of a publication's editorial strategy. Why? Because readers are essentially voyeurs and editors need to sell their papers.

Colour pieces are descriptions of such events as the Oxford–Cambridge boat race or an interview with a writer-in-residence perhaps based at a prison. Their effect depends on an imaginative use of language to create atmosphere and on qualities such as humour and pathos.

An emphasis on features

There's a constant interbreeding process between the print and the broadcasting media. Since there is 24-hour online broadcasting of news, newspapers – unable to compete in topicality and fighting ever-declining sales – have to add something to what's already known. Hence editors have shifted their emphasis from news to features.

The distinction between the two (especially in the UK) is often blurred. Newspapers do, mainly with features, what it's more difficult for the other media to do by including background stories to the news – involving analysis, various investigations, social problems, extra angles, thoughtfulness, human interest. They compete with the political weeklies and magazines in some of these areas. Despite the digital age, print remains the best medium for in-depth investigations and sustained argument pieces, because the general consensus is that these are easier to read on the printed page than online.

Specialists in demand

Freelances have a much better chance of getting work for newspapers if they're pitching as a specialist. They may need more than one specialism and must be versatile, adapting to different audiences. Specialist features include:

- parliamentary sketches;
- arts reviews;
- special interests such as photography, archaeology, music and amateur dramatics;
- expert commentaries on law, medicine, science and technology, education, fashion, and so on;
- sports from tennis and bowling to swimming, running and triathlon events.

Then there are the regular service columns, giving advice on shopping, holidays, DIY and so on, most of these are done by staffers or those on work experience.

Specialists know exactly when it's time to analyse a trend, propose an article and start researching it. The likeliest opportunities are in areas where it's difficult for a staff writer to keep up. Success is only assured if a freelance can develop the popularising, jargon-free writing skills required, as described in Chapter 8.

The obvious candidates for such openings are scientists, doctors and professionals in general who can make a useful second income by writing. However, there is still room for freelance writers to specialise in one or two areas so that their knowledge and experience can quickly be called upon when required.

Local papers

According to BRAD (British Rates and Data directory), there are currently 1,467 regional newspapers in the UK including independents and those owned by newspaper groups. If you can get hold of a copy, the analysis of local papers done by Ian Jackson in *The Provincial Press and the Community* (Manchester University Press) in 1986 offers some useful insight. He identifies four functions of local paper features:

1 reflector;
2 booster;

48 *Market research*

3 watchdog;
4 pump-primer.

The reflector function is carried out, says Jackson, by articles on local history that "deepen the sense of community identity". Despite the digital disruption news agendas remain the same. Therefore, Jackson's theory is just as relevant. Booster features are stories of local heroes, champions of local causes, sports champions.

Watchdog campaigns are frequently started off or sustained by public annoyance or concern. Attempts to stop a planned motorway spoiling a particular area is an example of a watchdog campaign that has been waged all over the country for years. In rural areas, the risk of genetically modified crops contaminating the fields of organic food growers sounds many an alarm. Pump-priming includes those general environmental concerns over urban developments, local transport problems, lack of recreational facilities for children.

Examples of local stories

Here are a few examples of stories taken from three UK local papers, *Worcester News*, *Western Gazette* and *The Dorset Echo*. All three have the potential to become news features.

- ***Tribute to cyclist killed in van crash***, *Worcester News* (Barnett, 2018): this topical front-page lead has strong potential for further investigation as encouraging cycling is part of a nationwide campaign thus it is newsworthy and relevant. A starting point would be to look at the number of bike accidents in this area and investigate the council's funding for cycle lanes/paths.
  Potential outputs: news feature for *Worcester News* and an article on the benefits of cycling for the paper's magazine, *Living and Worcestershire Life*. Also, there is an opportunity to turn this into a national piece using an angle such as *Britain's cycling blackspots*.
- ***Successful online gift business to quit town***, *Western Gazette* (Mumby, 2018b): although this is an online business, a news feature angle could examine how to save our high street.
  Potential outputs: *Western Gazette*, *Dorset Life* and for a national target market the angle could be *The top 6 thriving high streets in the UK*.
- ***School children go to the polls to elect MYPs to serve county***, *Dorset ECHO* (Stretton, 2018): as well as taking the angle what MYP means for Dorset's youth, there is also an opportunity here to profile the county's new MYP once elected.
  Potential outputs: *Western Gazette*, *Daily ECHO* and a national angle could be *The impact of MYP*, *Five most influential millennial MYPs* or *Why young people benefit from service roles such as MYP*.

Freesheets (free local newspapers) can offer a promising market for the local freelance particularly those starting out who need to build a portfolio of published work. In fact, I had my very first feature published as a student in *The Andover Advertiser* – a profile piece on a local woods craftsman and hurdle maker. It was my first published article, although I didn't actually get paid for the feature; this kick-started my freelance career as a student and landed me my first reporter job on a freesheet soon after graduating.

Usually, freesheets focus on localised business and community stories. Also included are new product/services pieces and other news items are often connected to advertisers' businesses.

Reporting experience

If you are aiming at contributing features to a local paper, experience of straight reporting will be invaluable as it was for me when I started out. Build your contacts, make a note of groups, societies, associations, clubs and committees in your area. Consult your friends/acquaintances as well as the social media sites of libraries, town halls, community groups and the like. Don't, however, approach the paper's regular sources – the police station, local council, town hall, fire brigade and so on – without checking with staff reporters first.

Plug the gaps. Find out which local organisations and activities are not covered by the paper, then find stories which will justify their inclusion then email a pitch to the editor with some samples of your work. If successful, put yourself on the mailing lists of the organisations. Attend some meetings and make yourself known to the chairs or secretaries of these organisations, who can provide dates or outcomes of any future meetings. The contacts should soon provide a few feature possibilities.

National papers

A politician in the TV sitcom *Yes Minister*, a great success in the 1980s, said:

> The *Times* is read by the people who run the country.
> The *Guardian* is read by the people who think they ought to run the country.
> The *Daily Mail* is read by the wives of the people who run the country.
> The *Financial Times* is read by the people who own the country.
> The *Daily Express* is read by the people who think the country ought to be run as it used to be run.
> The *Daily Telegraph* is read by the people who still think it is.
> The *Sun* readers do not care who runs the country provided she's got big tits.

Despite the digital age, there remains some truth in these labels and they do give an idea of the vast differences in the national papers of Britain. It is enough

Table 4.1 Categories of national newspapers

Quality papers	The middlebrows	Popular papers
The Times	Daily Mail	Daily Mirror
The Guardian	Daily Express	The Sun
The Independent (online)	Mail on Sunday	Daily Star
The Financial Times	Sunday Express	Sunday Mirror
The Sunday Times		The Sun on Sunday
The Sunday Telegraph		Daily Star Sunday
The Observer		Sunday People
The Independent on Sunday (online)		

to compare the circulation figures of the qualities and the populars (*pressgazette.com* regularly gives the circulation and readership figures) to appreciate how different the contents are going to be, in length, depth, complexity and language.

Table 4.1 illustrates how the nationals can be categorised into the following three key segments:

1 quality papers;
2 the middlebrows;
3 popular papers.

Remember each category of paper will have a different set of news values and agenda, as well as their individual ones. Also, let us not forget the special interest papers such as *The Jewish Chronicle*, the *Catholic Herald*, the *Socialist Worker*.

Features with topical pegs

Articles for national newspapers (particularly) must have topicality. A feature tends to be pegged to a news event. Readers want to know the background, or the ramifications, or the possible consequences.

A writer scrutinising a news item about a company collapse may notice a hole in it. Something is being held back, covered up. The writer digs further, finds more figures, finds the real story, perhaps, that the reporter, being busy, missed. There may have been misappropriation of funds or some rapid and unreported changes of staff.

For example, consider this scenario: a news story about a rape case was followed up by articles in many nationals. The story was of a 16-year-old youth who was detained for life after attempting to rape a 10-year-old girl and leaving her bleeding and unconscious. His father blamed the sex and violence on films the family watched.

Among the questions raised were:

- Who or what is to blame?
- Was the father right?

- How should the blame be shared?
- What's going wrong with family life?
- What's the law about selling and renting films?
- What kind of censorship is in operation?

Some of the articles stayed close to the story, whereas others took off into other aspects of censorship, pornography, rape, family life, using the story merely as a starter.

National papers call on specialist writers, especially for background-to-the-news features, even though the current tight budgets require staff writers to be used whenever possible.

When local becomes national

Look for stories in your local papers that might, or must, have national implications or be of interest outside the area covered. It might be a certain kind of pollution of river water, faulty building construction, nepotism in the awarding of local council contracts, wildlife dying a mysterious disease.

Such a scenario happened to me when working as a reporter on the *Avon Advertiser*, when animal rights activists cut the perimeter fence at Crow Hill Farm in Ringwood releasing 400 mink into the New Forest area, which caused havoc and threatened the survival of other wildlife and pets. The story achieved headlines in several national newspapers including *The Independent*, which ran the article entitled, Mink meet grisly end (Blamires, 1998).

Why did this become a national story? There were two key reasons:

1 It was part of an organised attack by animal rights activists on fur farms across the country, which also endangered the lives of other animals, therefore it had a national human-interest focus.
2 The story ticked many of the nationals' news agendas as it also highlighted a campaign to close fur farms resulting in the Labour Government at the time promising to close the UK's remaining 15 mink farms.

You wonder how widespread such cases are, why they are not being investigated on a national level, what are the loopholes in the law that make them difficult to prevent?

A celebrity living locally can provide an opportunity for an interview for a national paper if you can find a topical angle. For example, the celebrity might have just written his or her autobiography or become a patron of a well-known charity. This can also be rewritten for a local paper, and if you got a lot of material recorded you may have aspects that can be written up for various other markets including a writing magazine or if it's the latter the charity's own publication/media platforms.

The proliferation of the media has meant a welcome reduction in newspapers of pomposity and dogmatism. On the minus side, some papers have allowed circulation-boosting attitudes to result in a loss of authority. Yet on the plus side, feature writers have more opportunity than ever to redress the balance with well-researched, investigative pieces.

> **Case study: advice from a former newspaper editor**
>
> *Alan Geere, newspaper editor, international editorial consultant and journalism educator shares his experience and advice on what makes great stories.*
>
> Targeting newspapers isn't always a good way to start freelancing as a student. Newspapers can be rather demanding, so I tend to steer students towards websites or online publications that have both the time and space to accommodate young writers. Also, newspapers are now getting so much content for free from bloggers and special interest groups that are just keen to see their name in print that paid-for work is at a premium.
>
> That said, where newspapers do score, though, is by offering "shifts" reporting, subbing and increasingly working online. As ever, start off with work experience, make yourself useful and get on the shift rota.
>
> If you do have a great story it's probably best to avoid approaching a newspaper editor by phone. The editor will not answer and it is unlikely you will get a call back. Email is fine, but you must be distinctive. As an editor, I received around 200 emails a day. I need a reason to open yours, so have a catchy subject line and suggest some story ideas or have an engaging opinion in your message. Otherwise, use social media. A cheeky tweet or post on Facebook/Instagram is likely to get his or her attention.
>
> When it comes to hooking an editor, the angle needs to be new and different, even if it is a follow-up to a current issue. Student journalists are ideally placed to fill a gap in the knowledge.
>
> What makes the best human-interest stories? There is still a market for TOT (Triumph over Tragedy) stories. Look at the lower end of the women's magazine market; crammed with them. But I prefer a "doing something" or "being there" approach. Don't just talk to the people who run the food bank, go home with the people who have picked up a parcel. Trying to clear the town of rough sleepers? Spend the night out there with them. Whatever you come up with will be new and different.
>
> Despite the digital disruption post-2008 news agendas are largely unchanged, but what has changed is the mountain of media there is out there. From armchair experts to niche interest websites there is likely to be someone out there already doing what you are thinking of. Do plenty of research and make sure you are leading not following.
>
> My advice to those who want to freelance? Having freelanced myself I urge caution. I got started by following my own advice, I did shifts, including while holding down a full-time job elsewhere. In addition, I also ran a news

agency for a while, providing stories for the nationals, which is an existence that really concentrates the mind.

There is nothing like going in to work not knowing where the next pay cheque is coming from.

Further resources

When researching potential markets, be it newspapers, digital/online or magazines, there are numerous sources which will help you to develop a deeper understanding of your intended audience. However, the most valuable three in my opinion are as follows:

1 **BRAD Insight** (https://bradinsight.com/about-us/what-brad/): aka the British Rates and Data directory, BRAD is a comprehensive guide to more than 12,000 UK media titles. Resources include the latest circulation data, audience data and an editorial profile – and in some cases the brands' media kits are available to download. To access BRAD you must sign up to a paid subscription, however, undergraduate and postgraduate students can gain free access via their institution's library.
2 *Writers' & Artists' Yearbook* (www.writersandartists.co.uk/): is updated annually and published by Bloomsbury at £16.99. In addition to online resources, this text is a comprehensive guide to both book publishers as well as magazines and newspapers in the UK and overseas. Each entry includes contact details together with a brief synopsis of the publication and freelance opportunities. There are also numerous resources including practical guidance on finance and copyright law.
3 *Writer's Market*: is published yearly by WritersDigest.com – America's largest resource for writers priced US$29.99. It lists thousands of publishing opportunities in consumer and B2B magazines worldwide plus advice on how to develop your author brand, charging guide and funds for writers.

Action plan

1 Identify three target markets to write for; if these are print then buy a couple of issues or for digital magazines download at least two editions to your tablet. If a market is online then subscribe to the site.
2 Build up an in-depth understanding of each of your chosen three markets by evaluating:
  - **Target audience:** produce an audience demographic including age range, male/female ratio and category i.e. ABC1, etc.
  - **Core reader/user:** develop a reader profile of the typical reader identifying the median age, job, lifestyle as well as hopes, fears and aspirations.

- **Editorial pillars:** what are the key themes the content is built around?
- **Editorial style and tone:** note the average feature length, plus the length of article headlines and stand-firsts, formal or informal style of writing, plus are sub-headings used, and how many per article?

3 Now come up with a feature idea for each market.

5 How to pitch successfully

> An editor: a person who knows precisely what he wants – but isn't quite sure.
> (Walter Davenport, quoted by Bennett Cerf in
> *Saturday Review Reader*, No. 2)

What editors overwhelmingly want are good ideas. There's no use being a skilled writer if you have nothing to say. Walter Davenport's editors are quite sure what they want when presented with a fresh idea well expressed that fits the features formula of their publication and yet is different in some way from anything that has already appeared in it.

Good editing is about knowing when to "drag the readers into a story that they would never before consider reading" (Henry Porter, 2000, "Editors and Egomaniacs", an essay contributed to *The Penguin Book of Journalism*). What Henry Porter is emphasising here is that the good editor should have the imagination and leadership to sell the quite unfamiliar, perhaps complex and challenging piece from time to time. Also, that an unfamiliar product is sometimes a speculative ("spec") article, one that any proposal or outline could not have described satisfactorily.

However, as stated in Chapter 4, the majority of articles are sold on the strength of the journalist's pitch and if the commissioning editor is confident in the writer's ability to produce quality content. The previous chapter demonstrated how to identify then research target markets and their audiences, now it is time to explore how to sell your idea (and yourself) to achieve the end goal of getting published.

Key areas covered in this chapter will include:

- understanding the editor's point of view;
- preparing to pitch;
- pitching methods;
- using your network;
- organising the assignment;
- sending specs;
- dealing with editors.

An editor's point of view

Features editors are keenly aware of the market they're in and of their publication's needs. They must be able to respond rapidly to changes in needs and to successful moves by competitors. On newspapers, such responses are most likely to mean commissioning staff writers or those freelances whose work is well known. Thus, a young outsider must develop strategies for breaking in.

From an editor's point of view, commissioning involves choosing the right person for the right job, not as easy as it sounds. Choosing "the safe pair of hands" is the tendency when the pressure is on, but on the downside this can lead to a predictable set of feature pages. The trick is to know when the safe is the best, and when you need an unusual combination to lift a feature out of the ordinary.

Features editors must commission with a clear brief, then give follow-up briefings or there will need to be much rewriting, by themselves, the subs or indeed the author. A news-pegged article on a national paper needs to be as near as possible right first time as there may not be time for much rewriting. Commissioning policy on any publication will be influenced by the special requirements of different subjects, by the traditional ways of dealing with them, and by the relationship that has been developed between the editor and writer, in the course of trying to get on the same wavelength.

Following the digital disruption, freelance writers are today expected to visualise their feature idea when submitting pitches. Therefore, this must include:

- headline;
- stand-first;
- details of images for the feature (pictures or an infographic);
- added value such as a short video clip or audio piece.

Thus, today freelancers – particularly those targeting magazines – should be multi-skilled in storytelling as well as expert interviewers. They need to visualise how their feature could be projected on the page (be it printed or digital), what images would sell the piece and how to choose the best interviewees to make an impact. It's crucial for writers to think about how they hope a typical reader will feel after reading the article, or in what way their attitude to the subject might change.

The turnaround for a newspaper staff writer's feature may be a day or two, or sometimes an afternoon. The space requirement may change, pictures may be found that the writer didn't anticipate, breaking news may require some rewriting at the last moment. Section editors and subs may have to work on it in the middle of the night.

For magazine freelancers and staff writers, deadlines are generally longer as the publication's frequency is usually weekly or monthly. Therefore, if a feature isn't quite what the editor wanted or more information/clarity is needed, then they are more likely to be briefed to make the changes themselves, or at least to be consulted on edits. On the other hand, staff writers are more likely, provided there are none of the above emergencies, to get it right first time. They can instinctively anticipate exactly what their publication wants. To get ahead a freelance must focus on developing a deep understanding of every magazine they write for on a regular basis.

What all commissioned writers must understand is that editors, despite the insight described above, will often not know exactly what they want until they see what they don't want. An editor and a writer must work effectively as a team. A staff writer can strengthen that teamwork by informal chat and by participating in the formal conferences and group meetings. Therefore, a freelance should engage the editor or commissioning editor and develop a relationship. A short call to clarify a brief or develop the pitched idea further will always pay dividends. In the end, an article is a finely judged compromise – having to satisfy the editor, readers, writer, lawyer and, to varying degrees, proprietors.

Preparing to pitch

You have a great idea, have diligently studied your target audience and publication, so what's the best way to secure that commission? First, find out who is responsible for commissioning features/articles. This requires a quick call to the magazine or newspaper's editorial desk and remember to check name spellings and email addresses – nothing annoys an editor more than misspelling their name.

Today, editorial teams – particularly on magazines – are much smaller as reflected in my magazine hierarchy model illustrated in Figure 5.1. The editor is not always the person who commissions features; this responsibility could fall to the deputy editor, features editor or commissioning editor so always double-check.

Also, check to see if the magazine or newspaper publishes any writer's guidelines. If so, there may be a specific email address for pitches. If you're not known to the editor, then you must sell your writing skills as well as your idea. A good pitch must demonstrate why you are the best person to write the article. Give an indication of your relevant experience, a *show not tell approach* is the best

Figure 5.1 Magazine hierarchy model (Hogarth, 2018)

way to do this, so, if you can, include a PDF of a previously published article as well as links to your website and blog.

Make sure you've undertaken all aspects of the market study described in Chapter 4, and have included in this study the website, media kit (if available), editorial pillars and writers' guidelines.

But before you pitch, double-check that your idea is:

- Relevant to the magazine's readership.
- Reflective of your target market's editorial pillars.
- Timely and topical.
- Has an original angle and has not been covered by the publication or its closest rival.

If you're new the editor is unlikely to commission straight away, but if your idea appeals you may be encouraged to "send the piece in and we'll have a look at it". You may also be given valuable suggestions about treatment. Occasionally you may be fortunate enough to get feedback with a rejection stating why your idea isn't right for the publication. When I was deputy editor of *Writer's Forum* I would often send back a few lines of suggestions to help a new writer – providing it was clear that they had researched the market and demonstrated an understanding of the magazine. If rejected always scrutinise the idea and the target again, and consider sending the proposal to another publication.

The pitch

As everyone in business knows there's no point in having a good product if you lack salesmanship. Equally, a good idea can often be buried under an ineffective proposal. Learning to pitch is a skill – one that requires research, diligence and practice.

In today's digital era most pitches are sent via email although sometimes a preliminary quick chat over the phone with the commissioning editor can pay dividends. A word of caution if you plan on making a call: make sure you can present the idea articulately as vagueness will irritate the busy editor you are talking to and – apart from losing you the commission – a poorly thought-out approach as illustrated in Example 1 is sure to leave an unfavourable impression.

Example 1: a travel magazine editor receives a phone call

The caller has had a few articles published in a students' magazine and a local paper and has a pleasant voice and manner. A young writer worth encouraging perhaps? The call goes as follows.

EDITOR: Tell me about it.
CALLER: I'm going on holiday to Vienna for two weeks. I wonder if you'd be interested in a feature when I get back.
EDITOR: We had a feature about Vienna six months ago. Didn't you see it?

CALLER: I'm afraid not ... But I thought I'd do something a bit unusual, like describing the places where Beethoven lived and there's a museum ...
EDITOR: Our feature covered that. Sorry.
CALLER: Actually I'll be visiting Salzburg as well and ...
EDITOR: What have you got in mind for Salzburg? Mozart's haunts? We've done that as well.
CALLER: I wonder if you could suggest something I could look into while I was there?
EDITOR: Not really [the features editor has already been too kind]. If you think you've got something that might interest us, send it in. But study the magazine first.

The features editor had to be vague because the caller was vague. The caller was unwise to call with a vague idea of writing something, no angle and clearly no research of either the publication or its readers.

Example 2: the woman's magazine editor receives a call

This potential freelance is also young, he has had a couple of pieces on sport published and has clearly done some initial research to produce a coherent idea. This conversation – which goes as follows – of course results in a more positive outcome.

EDITOR: What's your idea?
CALLER: [First refers to a summary jotted down in 23 words before responding with] How parents push their children to win at various sports. To damaging effect. The title could be "Champion children – but is the price too high?"
EDITOR: It sounds interesting. What facts have you got?
CALLER: The Sports Council has just published some research on effects on children of different ages. Quite academic stuff. I thought a composite piece, interviews with four or five children and their coaches and parents.
EDITOR: Send me samples of your work plus a brief outline and an intro. I don't promise but I like it so far.

Never pitch an idea without doing thorough research on the publication – and that means reading a few issues, plus analysing the audience, as outlined in Chapter 4. When teaching pitching to undergraduates I tell them that when preparing to pitch it is essential to:

- Know your chosen magazine – make sure you have read at least three issues.
- Understand who your reader is – and what he/she needs from a feature.
- Have a clear angle and succinctly summarise your idea.
- Come up with a strong headline and stand-first – written in the tone and style of your target publication (to use in the pitch).
- Justify to the editor why your idea would engage his/her readers.

Pitch via email

Most pitches today are sent via email. Editors receive numerous emails every day which means you need to keep the message short, around three to four paragraphs should suffice. Do clearly mark your email pitch in the subject box and include a provisional headline. The purpose is to present an appealing writing style so your presentation must be polished. Avoid grammatical and spelling errors at all costs.

Often a good intro technique is to refer to a telephone call being followed up provided you have called ahead and briefly outlined the idea. However, if your email is an initial approach, the first paragraph should be a brief outline and suggested length, followed by proposed headline and stand-first – both written in the style of the magazine to demonstrate your skills. The second paragraph should give some background including potential interviews, opportunities for value-added content, such as audio or video clips for online versions, while the third should be a brief synopsis of your experience. Sign off with "Best wishes" and make sure you include a phone number in your email signature as well as URL links to your website or blog.

When pitching focus on these five essentials:

1 **Who:** make sure you find the right person, this could be the editor, features editor or commissioning editor.
2 **Contact:** always know the commissioning editor's contact details – both email and phone number.
3 **Address:** avoid using "Dear Sir/Madam" at all costs, make sure you have the person's name – and that it is spelled correctly.
4 **Subject box:** keep it simple, stating: Pitch for (name of magazine/newspaper).
5 **The idea:** this must have an original angle even if you are covering a familiar theme.

Remember that as a freelance you must demonstrate why an editor should buy your feature and that means demonstrating its value as illustrated in Figure 5.2.

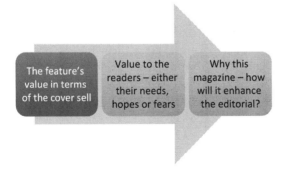

Figure 5.2 An article's perceived value (Hogarth, 2018)

Demonstrating this value is an essential part of selling your idea. After all, if commissioned the editor will be spending their editorial budget to buy your article and that means he or she needs to see a return on their investment in terms of potential value to enhance the magazine's content. Therefore, using what I define as the *three whys* to develop your pitch will also help you perfect your technique.

The *three whys* model has been adapted from my book, *How To Launch A Magazine In This Digital Age* (Hogarth, 2014), where it was used as an example of how to test the sustainability of a new magazine concept. However, while teaching feature writing to undergraduates over the years, I have adapted this model specifically to enable young writers to test their idea – as follows:

1   **Why this article?**: demonstrate why this particular feature would sell the magazine – your idea must use an original angle even if you are using a familiar theme.
2   **Why now?**: this idea must be topical, to some extent newsworthy. Do not start a pitch with last year ... last month ... or yesterday as it implies it's dated.
3   **Why this magazine?**: why would readers of this magazine be interested? Also, think about it from the commissioning editor's perspective – why should they buy this feature?

An example of a pitch

Below is an example of a pitch I previously wrote to an editor of a writing magazine. The magazine, editor's details and the stand-first (aka sell) have been changed – aside from that the content remains the same.

> Dear Jo,
>
> Would you be interested in an interview with Alexander McCall Smith focusing on how to write a series?
>
> **Masterclass: how to write a successful series**
>
> **Alexander McCall Smith marks the 20th anniversary of his No.1 Ladies Detective Agency, which has sold more than 20 million copies worldwide. He talks to Mary Hogarth about the adventures of his favourite characters and reveals how to write a successful series.**
>
> The feature, which could run for 1,000 to 1,200-words depending on your limits, would be an inspirational piece focusing mostly on Alexander's best-selling series *The No1. Ladies Detective Agency* and *Corduroy Mansion*.
>
> It would include the pitfalls of creating characters and how to avoid them as well as how to create a sustainable series with practical suggestions on getting started, plus with tips for readers on getting their book published.

> There is also scope for a short audio clip together with an additional 400-word online version on how Alexander got his first break in fiction.
>
> **About me:** Having worked in magazines for 12 years (former deputy editor of Writers' Forum and managing editor of Weddings Today) I now work on a freelance basis in addition to a career in academia. For examples of my work please visit: *www.maryhogarth.com*
>
> Best wishes,
> Mary Hogarth

Note that in the pitch I have included a suggested headline and stand-first (aka the sell) – all written in the style of the magazine to demonstrate that I:

a) have researched and read the publication;
b) can write in the magazine's style.

The last paragraph is "about me" and includes my website URL where the editor will find examples of my published work. Now, if you are inexperienced your "about me" will not be as in-depth. However, you must demonstrate your professional skills and qualifications such as "student/graduate of BA (Hons) Multimedia Journalism at Bournemouth University (for example) whose published work includes …". If it's a PPA accredited degree, then do state this and don't forget to include your blog or website.

Gregor Rankin, publisher of *Food and Travel* (Figure 5.3), advises those who want to pitch to his magazine to always – without exception – thoroughly research the magazine and its readers first. So, what does he look for in a pitch?

"Insight, originality, accuracy (in terms of what you are pitching) and brevity," says Gregor, adding that they must ensure the pitch contains no spelling mistakes or bad grammar. "It is also essential to have an understanding of the core positioning statements of the title and ensuring these elements are built into your pitch, brevity."

"Consider sending ideas in by mail – editors get lots of pitches every day by email – so think outside the box to attract the editor's attention, and don't send blanket pitches – you'll be instantly consigned to the dump folder. A bullet, not a shotgun approach is far more likely to succeed."

Multiple pitches

Most features have the potential to be reworked. Written in a certain way the same feature can be syndicated all over a country, even worldwide – more on this in Chapter 14. However, ideas can also be pitched multiple times. For example, it is acceptable to send the similar ideas to various non-competing publications, in different cities perhaps, or different countries.

How to pitch successfully 63

Figure 5.3 Cover of *Food and Travel*. Credit: *Food and Travel* magazine

But when pitching, it is essential to indicate clearly what rights you're offering, as explained in Chapter 2. The best way to avoid multiple commissions for the same article is to come up with a theme then develop different angles for each of the publications you intend to target. An example of how to get multiple pitch ideas from the same theme can be seen in Table 5.1.

Table 5.1 Targeting multiple publications using one theme

Theme	Target publications	Possible angles
An interview with crime writer Minette Walters	*Writing Magazine* *Good Housekeeping* *Dorset Magazine*	Masterclass: crime writing with Minette Walters Minette Walters interview: My writing life Crime writer Minette Walters reveals how she finds inspiration in Dorset
Eco-friendly travel	*Vegetarian Living* *The Guardian* *The Green Parent*	The top 5 UK eco-friendly spas Your eco guide to responsible travel 10 green places to stay in the UK
Starting a small business	*Country Living* *Writing Magazine* *Grow Exeter*	Your guide to kitchen table businesses How to earn £££ from your writing Why you should work from home

As Table 5.1 demonstrates it is easy to achieve multiple angles from one theme, all of which can then be developed as pitches for different magazines. In some cases, it will be possible to repurpose your research. The first theme in Table 5.1 – an interview with Minette Walters – is a good example of this whereby the material from the interview has the potential to be turned into three articles as illustrated in the table.

If your pitches are not working, scrutinise them for specific detail. Lack of detail gives a feeling of blandness. Beware, however, of sticking rigidly to any formula given here or in any similar text for any stage in the pitching process.

It's a good idea to have several targets in mind for an idea so that when it's rejected by one you can try it on another. Suppose you get interested in dubious cults being followed in your area (which not many people know about). With a local weekly in mind, while doing some preliminary research including a couple of interviews you discover some multi-purposing could be feasible. For example:

- The local weekly might like *Witchcraft replaces bingo* at 800 words, with some pegging to local history.
- For an occult magazine, you propose *Strange rites in backwoods*. This, at similar length, will incorporate various manifestations of the cult and mention similar cults in the UK.
- A national monthly might consider 1,500 words on *Sects can damage your health*, with a promise to investigate cults that are hostile to the family and that use brainwashing techniques, or that claim association with charities where no connection exists, or where no proper accounts are produced.

There are many reasons why a proposal might be rejected. It may have been covered recently, although this shouldn't happen if you've done an in-depth market study. The idea may be considered boring or potentially libellous, the proposed treatment may be considered inappropriate, or sound too much like a "scissors-and-paste" job. That is where your proposed content is clearly to be collected from other articles and shows no sign that it will be transmuted by some kind of originality.

Develop a network

Your ultimate aim is to have a strong network of connections in high places. Then, when you have a great idea for an article, you phone your contact – the features editor of a national magazine for example – and after a brief chat, you secure a commission. A week later you have another great idea and gain another commission by ringing a contact on a newspaper. And so on. A daunting thought for the tyro.

These relationships take time to build. They can and do go wrong if you occasionally spell a name incorrectly or send a pitch aimed at *Marie Claire* addressed to *Vogue*. This can happen when sending the same pitch to several women's magazines without any attempt to adapt them – it's easy to use the wrong name or email address. Always read every pitch carefully before clicking send.

If you can, take the opportunity to meet editors face-to-face. The advantage is that you can soak in the atmosphere of the publication's offices created by the publication and those who work for it. A deeper understanding will be gained by visiting the magazine. From the editor's point of view, putting a face to your name will help to fix you in the memory. As a result, a relationship may then develop rapidly from which further commissions may be attained.

First make your editor a friend, treat them with care and respect while bearing in mind that they are also a customer. Good customer service should be a core value of any feature writer, as should achieving excellence in terms of content. Trust is crucial in the editor–writer relationship. You've got to work at these relationships, when an editor complains that your feature needs a complete rewrite, try to agree. Always cooperate cheerfully and promptly if asked to "find better evidence for your argument not later than 4pm today". Don't assume you can be a day later than the deadline because the editor is a friend. Nor should you can ring up for a friendly chat in the middle of a busy day, or ask for the highest fee.

Organising commissioned articles

You may be in the middle of several other assignments when another commission comes in so being well organised will ensure you can deliver the correct copy on time. A good method to use is what I would define as a workflow chart to record the article brief, copy deadline and agreed fee as demonstrated in Table 5.2 (note the fees have been changed to protect confidentiality). As writing now forms only a small part of my overall work, I compile my workflow charts on a six-monthly basis and use a table instead of spreadsheet simply because I prefer to work in Word. However, use whatever software you find easiest.

All email commissions should be saved in a new mailbox titled *Freelance work* so that they can be easily retrieved should the need arise. If you received your

Table 5.2 Example of a workflow chart

Publication	Article brief	Deadline	Fee
InPublishing	1,700 words on the launch of *List for Life* – Time Inc. Points to include: why the business model works, how the innovation lab evolved and plans its future development.	21/2/2016	£300
Lovereading.co.uk	Interview with Sophie Hannah – 800 words. Focus on current novel, explore how Sophie created her characters and what were the key challenges she faced.	15/5/2016	£150
The Self Publishing Magazine	1,200 words on how to get an agent. Points to include: how self-published authors can secure an agent, what agents look for in new authors. Interview a literary agent, talent scout and successful author.	11/9/15	£395

assignment verbally, write it down, adding anything that occurs to you while the discussion is fresh in your mind. Then send a follow-up email to the editor confirming the brief and agreed fee so you have a record in writing.

The NUJ advise on minimum fees for articles based on advertising rates – ideally you should not accept less than the minimum, although in these tough economic times you may have to negotiate. However, once you have a good track record you should expect more.

Start a feature file

On being commissioned, immediately open a desktop folder for the article. Include any material you have into the current folder, such as the editor's briefing notes, potential interviewees and their contact details. I often start the article as soon as I get the brief by first drafting a rough outline with a working headline and stand-first. This gives me the basic starting point on which to base my research and interview.

Some writers use bullet point notes or brief paragraphs as an outline, expanding on the brief while leaving gaps to develop with interviews, anecdotes, quotes from experts, pithy quotations or other researched material. This method helps develop a logical structure and ensures all the points in the editor's brief are covered. I always try to arrange interviews as soon as I get the commission.

Getting interviews organised way before your deadline is a must otherwise you could find your interviewees either aren't available or drop out. Then should the worst happen you have time to find some other sources.

Problem features

Every writer produces a dud occasionally, so when this happens to you evaluate and learn from your mistake. Remember failure is one of the best teachers. Writers avoid producing poor articles too frequently by being clear about what you are doing.

A bad feature teaches writers to:

- plan more carefully;
- achieve greater structure/control over research;
- secure interviews early and have a back-up plan just in case interviewees pull out;
- adhere to the brief – or liaise with the editor over any deviation.

If you have any doubt about the editor's requirements or about what you are aiming at, clear this up before you start researching, so that you get your line of enquiry right. Some articles fail despite an apparent agreement between the writer and editor about the assignment. When this happens there has been a failure in communication. The best of editors and writers can end up with the wrong idea of what the other has in mind. So, if you are not clear, ask.

A wise editor judges which writers need a lot of guidance and those who need little – it is a delicate balance. Flexibility in the commissioning policy is necessary. There must be scope for imagination, second and third thoughts may turn out to be best, and some writers do not work well feeling hamstrung or over-briefed. On the other hand, new writers might prefer a more detailed briefing.

When to send specs

Although it is usual to first pitch an idea, there are occasions when it's good to send in an article on spec. Here are three situations when this might apply:

1. **Unusual content:** you had a remarkable experience. You got lost, perhaps, for a week in a Brazilian jungle and barely survived, meanwhile having a *life-after-death* experience. Or you cared for your grandmother who had Alzheimer's disease, or you were converted to Buddhism after hearing voices. Now you want to write a feature about it but find it difficult to describe briefly, nor are you sure how it will turn out until you write it. Write it up then decide who might want to print it and send the copy in on spec.

2. **Unusual treatment:** it may be the treatment rather than the content that will be incalculable. You may want to vaunt your way-out sense of humour in a personal lifestyle column (undaunted by the fact there are already too many such columns). This might be to describe a writer's experience of his or her first book launch, in the first person, or you may want to introduce the surreal, or borrow other fictional techniques, to transmute otherwise ordinary, familiar content. Almost certainly you will do these things on spec.
3. **After a nod and a wink:** a long-established relationship with an editor may result in a commission after a pitch of a few sentences on the phone. Such an editor may also consider sympathetically a piece coming in from you without warning. But don't count on it.

It can be useful to get some feedback on spec features before trying them on editors. If you know a good critic or two whose views you respect, if you are an undergraduate this might be an approachable tutor or lecturer at your university. Avoid members of your family as often they won't be your best critic – unless of course they are journalists or writers.

Dealing with editors

Make sure you submit your feature one time and as agreed when commissioned. However, if when working on an article you find that your original promise or the editor's briefing cannot be fulfilled, get in touch and discuss the problem. Perhaps you have failed to obtain a crucial interview or you realise that you are not sure what the editor wants exactly.

There's nothing worse than producing an article on the deadline which is so far from the brief but it's too late to do anything about it. The piece you've got might be accepted or it might not. If not, you might get a kill fee. The editor may feel that you've communicated your difficulties well and that you've done your best or may accept some of the blame for any misunderstanding.

Dealing with rejection

Always respond positively to rejection – remember it is not personal. If a commissioned feature is rejected with such flaws identified, read it through to decide on future action. Assuming you have not been encouraged to rewrite it, you may be able to identify another publication that might welcome it. At which point you decide whether the new editor would react in the same way and how to improve the piece.

If no comments arrive with a returned spec feature, try to work out why it was rejected. There may not be much wrong with it. Three or four pieces on the same theme as yours may have arrived at the same time. Yours was good, but one of the others was better. Or two pieces on the same theme arrived: yours was better, but the other was commissioned and yours wasn't. Or the editor changed while you were writing your feature and the new one has different criteria.

Some features can be rewritten immediately for another target publication, while others can be filed away to be considered at a later date. A news peg may appear after a month or two that may restore life to the material. Just don't give up because you have had your work rejected. Rejection is the bane of any writer's life – on the positive side it is an opportunity for reflection and improvement.

> ### Case study: from pitch to publication
>
> *Julie McCaffrey has worked as a journalist for over 20 years and freelanced for nine years. Commissions include articles from numerous national publications such as the* Telegraph, *the* Mirror, Cosmopolitan, Glamour *and* Grazia. *Here she shares her experiences – from getting her first job to crafting great pitches that get commissioned and becoming an established freelance.*
>
> Before freelancing I had spent nearly 15 years as a journalist gaining invaluable experience. I got my first by-line while at university, studying English and Psychology. I applied for work experience and achieved a by-line in *The Scotsman* in 1995 – a page three story about the Teletubbies.
>
> After graduating I took an NCTJ course then joined my local paper, the very glamorous *Glenrothes Gazette* as a trainee. A six-month stint in New Zealand followed, before returning to Scotland to work as a news reporter on the Edinburgh Evening News, then feature writer and columnist. In 2003 I joined the real-life exclusives team at the Press Association in London, before joining the *Daily Mirror* as a feature writer.
>
> My freelancing career began in 2009, the year my triplet daughters were born. I remember when my babies were four months old, I was holding one child while breastfeeding with one arm and writing a Britney Spears three-part series with the other. As much as I could, I honed my pitching skills, contacted editors and got commissions.
>
> Learning to pitch is a must-have skill for any freelance – and one that will pay dividends. The key is to keep it simple and concise because editors don't have time to wade through copy to get to the point. Include an impactful headline, some emotive details and anything that could give it a topical hook such as a link to present or future events or some strong stats. But definitely no waffle, emojis, kisses, or "hiya hun".
>
> To get regular work it's crucial to make new contacts by continually approaching editors with ideas. However, this can be often daunting to a novice. The key when making an initial approach to a new editor is to remember that at every level, all journalists need stories. Although it's natural to feel a bit nervous before approaching a new editor, if you have a good story don't be afraid to pitch it.
>
> No editor will write you off as a journalist if you send them ideas that don't fully work, but they will credit you for sending in ideas. Ideas are the

key – even if your approach and writing isn't polished, if you have good ideas you'll stand out. Send loads.

I always make an approach by email because editors are too busy to take calls. Also, I can work on re-shaping an emailed approach rather than blundering into saying something silly in a call. It's important that your genuine enthusiasm for the story shines in your approach. Be sincere – don't tell them you love their publication if you don't because they'll detect it or even test you on it.

I usually send three ideas at a time, preferably tailored to specific parts of their publication. For example, for *Fabulous* magazine: "I thought this story would make a moving read in your 'It happened to me' slot." Or, for *Glamour*: "I hoped this would make a powerful G Reality report." End the email with an invitation to work together in future such as: "I hope the ideas will work well for you, and if not please let me know if there are any story ideas I could work on for you?"

Even if they turn down your ideas, the editors might reply asking you to work on a story their staff haven't got around to doing and there you go – a commission.

But the biggest challenge as a freelance is not finding ideas, hunting for case studies, pitching or writing stories. It's coping with the completely erratic way of being paid. I could work for a long time researching and writing a feature which is sold for four figures, but at the last minute it could be dropped and I'd be paid nothing, or it could be cut to a smaller size and my fee would be halved.

Although most of my work is sold to UK markets, it's also been syndicated to Australia, New Zealand and the US. I'm most proud of seeing one of my features written in Chinese – a *Grazia* syndication.

Getting continual commissions is challenging but achievable, as editors who like my work are more likely to accept my ideas or commission me to produce their ideas. Achieving a healthy cash flow, however, is much harder. I could work tirelessly for a whole month, including weekends and late nights, and end up with zero income if invoices aren't processed on time or an editorial decision out with my control means my features are spiked.

The most important lessons I have learned about freelancing? Try not to turn down work as sometimes an editor will commission someone else, and if they like another writer's work they might continue commissioning them instead of you. It can be tricky to win your way back to the top of an editor's list.

Try not to accept a very low fee, otherwise you forever lower your worth. Be reasonable and not graspy, but don't undersell your work because you won't be able to drive your fees up again.

Lastly, try to have savings to protect yourself against erratic payment. Some publications pay within a fortnight, while others can take three months. This can cause havoc with personal finances so try to have a financial cushion.

My advice to anyone who wants to get published and freelance while studying is firstly don't neglect your studies because that's counter-productive. But try to think of everything else you do in your own time as an opportunity to find potential stories to sell. Could you sell a review of a gig? Would the chatty girl you met at the gym class make a good case study? If you have a part-time job in a shop, maybe you could write an insightful piece about it?

Blogs are a great idea to demonstrate your enthusiasm, dedication and writing skills to an editor whether it's to secure a commission or get an internship. And while I always urge writers never to give their stories away for free, I understand the value of having cuttings in your portfolio.

Most of all, be brave and just do it. I used to worry myself into a tizzy, but now instead of fretting about a pitch I just write it, check it and send it. Be brave, take a deep breath, have ambition and bold ideas – you'll be brilliant. Now send that pitch …

Action plan

Having come up with feature ideas after undertaking Chapter 4's action plan, it is now time to choose a target market – newspaper or magazine – then develop a strong pitch using the knowledge gained in this chapter.

1. First, ascertain who the commissioning editor is then obtain his or her direct email address.
2. Next, sufficiently research your idea to come up with a working headline and stand-first – written in the tone and style of your target publication.
3. Then focus on the three whys (outlined in this chapter), identifying why your idea:
   - Would fit the publication's editorial pillars?
   - Has topicality or is significant at this time?
   - Is relevant to the readers?
4. Now write a rough draft of your pitch including a short paragraph about you. Remember you are selling an idea as well as your ability to write it.
5. Do edit your pitch and ensure there are no mistakes before sending.

I always recommend making a follow-up phone call to the editor the following week. If you pitch hasn't been successful – the call will provide a good opportunity for you to find out why. Do have another idea ready.

6 Turn ideas into articles

You get a sharper insight into publications when you see how differently a particular subject is treated. There follows a list of subjects with mileage, indicating varied treatments, and making some comparisons among publications. Keep in mind that subjects, types, formulas and magazines are constantly changing to meet the demands of the time. Remember, magazines are born to reflect new interests, and die when their remit is out of date. In today's digital age, features are continually evolving – in terms of content, length and those added-value additions such as audio or video clips that can be embedded into digital editions.

Journalism is all about what you can find out rather than what you happen to know, such sources include:

- online news and social media;
- articles published online and in print;
- the legwork of reporting;
- interviews – what's in people's heads.

A more original treatment of a familiar theme might be to take one or two contrasting interviews – an academic expert perhaps, plus one of the streetwise kind. You then need to take time to think out, in the end, how your original attitude to a subject has been changed by your exploration, and to decide where you want to take your readers.

If your research is likely to involve significant travel, try to get such expenses included when you have a pitch accepted. A feature that is going to provide valuable publicity for an organisation may offer a "freebie" – for example, free or discounted hotel accommodation, meals, travel. However, with the current economic uncertainty such perks are mostly restricted to travel features. Having been on a few press trips during my career, these freebies are often incredibly hard work particularly if you are going as part of a group.

For example, when managing editor of *Weddings Today*, I was invited on an all-expenses-paid press trip to Curacao along with journalists from other publications. It was certainly a memorable experience. Yet while the accommodation was luxurious with excellent, authentic food throughout, there was little free time. Mostly we were on the go from 8am to 11pm with just a couple of hours break in the afternoon. This left little time to explore the island's core, to see those less desirable parts and get a real taste of the local culture – all of which can also enrich a travel feature. Free trips are great, but they may have a downside.

Before moving on to writing, first a word about images. If you include photographs with a feature find out the publication's submission requirements. Generally, photos should be 300dpi at print size, but this can vary so always check. If it's a travel piece send in a good selection of around ten pictures as some will be used for the online version as well as in social media posts. Always label picture files and include a caption. A separate list of captions should be included either in the submission email or at the end of your article.

Feature opportunities

In this section, my matching of subjects and treatments although valid at the time of writing may need to be revised based on what you can discover from researching both the subject and target market. With the latter, go through the current issue as well as a couple of back issues. If you're planning a piece on any of the subjects listed in this chapter you may also want to search databases of articles by subject using the public or university library. Alternatively, online searches also will often bring up results on how and where the subject has been covered in the past year or so.

Particularly when writing about a familiar theme digging out the relevant articles should be part of your research. This will ensure that your idea and treatment are fresh, you'll see what needs to be updated and perhaps find a stronger angle to take.

Develop your own preferences and specialisms too. In your capacity as a freelance would you prefer to write for *Cosmopolitan* or *Glamour*, *New Statesman* or *The Spectator*, *The Guardian* or *The Daily Telegraph*, *Active Life* or *The Oldie*, *Woman* or *Woman's Own*? Don't over-stretch your reach – focus on a manageable number of subjects and publications.

Develop a keen sense of the preferences you detect in what different publications demand. Each editor will want a certain kind of subject, treatment, tone and style. Nevertheless, note that one of those preferences is for something original, a piece that is different from the general run of what they publish but still fits.

You will find your own way of studying how different publications cover subjects you've marked as your own. The sections that follows provides, I hope, a useful formula. It contrasts the varied approaches of different publications to a particular subject while pointing to the pitfalls inherent in dealing with the subjects listed. Lastly, it suggests how to vary your own approach when selling a subject/idea to different editors.

Celebrity stories

Journalism has been awash with feature articles within and about the celebrity culture for years. You may deplore the obsession with celebrity and the vacuousness of gossip magazines, and you may believe that the vicariousness encouraged by celebrity culture has replaced the real news values.

Yet, on the other hand, note that the celebrity culture pervades all social levels. Cosmo Landesman in *Prospect* magazine believed that "for most people celebrity culture is escapist fun". He believes that many people tune in to celebrity soap operas of the moment – which at the time of writing are Brad, Ange (and now Jen again), Posh and Becks or the royals – then tune out and get on with life.

Changing times

Between these two viewpoints, there are many complexities to explore. There is cynical pandering to low expectations. Back in 1996, Richard Barber, editor of *OK!* magazine, when interviewed for *The Guardian* by Andrew O'Hagan, summed up his ABC audience demographic C1 and C2 women between ages 25 and 44 as: "a fairly bog-standard female audience in terms of who they are and where they live. Well, their biggest form of entertainment is clearly the TV sitting in the corner of the living room, isn't it?"

This is no longer true into day's digital age – entertainment comes from a variety of electronic, mobile devices. Whether they are from C1 or DE classification readers are becoming more demanding and have higher expectations following the digital disruption. This, together with the emergence of celebrity websites, has impacted heavily on circulations, many weekly gossip magazines are at an all-time low.

For example, according to BRAD, *OK!* magazine had a combined circulation of over 600,000 at its peak – today it's 159,242 taken from ABC July–December 2017 (BRAD, 2017 [2018]). This has resulted in budget cuts, which means fewer commissions for freelancers for print editions.

That said, the market for celeb stories has widened as many editors see these as the key to strong copy sales. Lifestyle magazines, as well as national newspapers, regularly include such stories, interviews or features. In addition, there are also numerous online markets all vying for juicy interviews or stories.

Titles aimed at the 35+ reader such as *Good Housekeeping* also have a celeb focus. GH regularly includes features on the *Great British Bake Off* team. One such example can be found in the January 2018 issue which features Mary Berry on the cover. The five-page interview is headlined *There's Something About Mary* and is pegged on her forthcoming book, *Mary's Household Tips & Tricks*. Then in the next issue (February 2018) Kirstie Allsopp takes centre stage this time – the piece is angled on her weight loss.

Newer celeb magazines do that balancing act perfected by the populars of giving the wicked as well as the wonderful. *heat* makes a point of reflecting the complexity of our fascination. There is prurience and envy mixed up with love and admiration, and the insults and the accounts of celebs' excesses and misfortunes can be funny and occasionally thought-provoking. An example of this can be found in *heat's* cover-lines for the 17–23 March 2018 edition which include:

- Jen: too humiliated to go out;
- Posh's romantic weekend ruined;
- Cheryl's brave face as Liam "goes cold" on her;
- Lauren loses 18lbs to look like Michelle.

The Internet is less regulated. An example is Popbitch (satirical music gossip). It was started by Neil Stevenson (who became editor of *The Face*) because he was frustrated by the way celebrities are overprotected by publicists. A welcome change from vacuity, perhaps, or as media pundit Stephen Glover called it in the *Daily Mail* "an open sewer running with lies".

Pitfalls

Although PR companies, studios, record companies and agents are keen to get coverage for their clients they also want a say in how it is done. Thus, they and their clients often put pressure on editors and the writers to have a say on editorial decisions such as which writer and photographer, plus the length as well as the date of the issue in which the celeb interview will appear.

Editors of newspapers and general consumer magazines have learned to negotiate with some success, but editors of celeb magazines have less bargaining power.

Your approach

Here writers must work closely with editors when making arrangements to interview a celeb, especially when there's a demand by the interviewee or their agent for copy approval. See John Morrish and Paul Bradshaw's *Magazine Editing in Print and Online* on this and other editor–writer collaborations (especially Chapter 5, The Right Words). Morrish and Bradshaw (2012a) determine that a feature must have value citing all editorial as fitting into one of three types:

> financially viable information that saves the reader money or time; emotionally valuable material that the reader finds entertaining, fascinating or stimulating; and socially valuable information that the reader can use to forge new relationships or strengthen existing ones.

The latter two reasons are perhaps most reflective of celebrity features. Often this can lead to conflict where the writer has obtained a juicy piece of information during an interview that the celebrity – or his/her agent/publicity doesn't want printed. Caution is advised if such a situation arises. Always seek your editor's advice.

Also, celebrity status can be short-lived ensuring talents are often overexposed. To fill the gap reality TV – such as *Big Brother*, *Seven Year Switch* and *The Great British Bake Off* – produces a kind of processed celeb out of would-be celebs without any particular talent. Yet some will be an instant big hit with viewers and consequently get into the papers and the magazines as well. Yet another complexity for the writer to come to terms with, to come up with the right attitude for the target chosen.

Competition for celeb stories is fierce. In today's tough market you must have first secured an interview before you send in a pitch. If you have a contact at a magazine or on a news desk of a redtop paper, then phone first, otherwise email. Magazines such as *Hello!* state they are "interested in celebrity-based features with a newsy angle and exclusive interviews from generally unapproachable personalities". Generally, this is true of most publications as competition for the best cover stories is ferocious.

To sum up, if you're going to start writing about the celebrity culture you must have a wide spectrum: where would you fit in, where do your sympathies lie?

Children

Writing about children looks easier than it is. If you're a parent, teacher, social worker or child psychologist: that will be a great help. What is essential is that you have an imaginative insight into children's worlds and an ability to establish a rapport and to interpret what they say.

Different approaches

There are numerous topics for writers to explore in this genre. It may be advisable to become an expert on one specific area. Key topics that are newsworthy (at the time of writing) include:

- child development;
- autism;
- learning difficulties;
- literacy issues;
- behavioural problems;
- drug use and early sexualisation.

There are opportunities for both positive and negative stories. On the positive side, it is said that interaction with computers has raised IQ levels, that listening to them more than was the habit in the past has helped children to grow into more confident and more enterprising adults. It is also said that more imaginative parenting is prevalent today, requiring much more effort than the parenting of the past, that this is commendable and that children's general behaviour speaks of self-expression that should be encouraged rather than bad manners.

It's essential to keep in mind that topics – like fashion – re-emerge, so keep an eye out for familiar themes turning up with new treatments. For example, a while back homework became something of a hot topic again. *The Telegraph* ran a feature on *Homework around the world: how much is too much?* (Goldhill, 2015). Pegged on a story about a primary school in New York ending all homework assignments, the article explored the negative effects of homework in young children before moving on to secondary schools and comparing the number of hours 15-year-olds spend on homework around the world.

Depression in the young is also currently a keen topic, as is dyslexia. In *The Times*, a feature on *Depression risk for pupils who fall behind aged 11* (Bennett, 2018) linked a decline in academic performance in primary school with teenage depression. While the HuffPost took a more personal approach and ran a piece on *What I know now as a teen with dyslexia* (Koppelman, 2017). Here the writer gives a powerful account of her own experiences.

Pitfalls

Those approaching older years must take care to avoid thinking (too often): *when I was a child we were taught how to behave.* If you're just out of college, you may be tempted to discount the views of anyone over 40. My advice is: never assume and don't judge – objectivity should be at the core of everything you write.

Your approach

Watch for familiar topics and consider how you can develop an original angle. Here your core approaches are likely to be interviews with experts together with case studies, first-person style interview/profile pieces and perhaps (like our HuffPost writer) your own experience. Understanding the way children think is crucial so if you don't have any children of your own, talk to those related to you such as young nieces and nephews, or children of friends – and learn from them.

Crime

Crime is a compelling story, drama, conflict, passion, and in its aftermath inspirational messages are to be found such as triumphs over adversity. Media platforms are swamped with crime: in print, online, digital and broadcast media (documentaries, docudramas, series). There are the thrillers, the many feature films and more recently the true crime dramas such as *Murder Detectives* (now *Forensic Files*), *Psychic Investigators* and *48 Hours*. All this means that there's plenty of information and well-informed audiences.

There are pros and cons when covering this genre. The facts must be separated from prejudices, passionate convictions backed up by good evidence. It is a rewarding territory for experts, who include ex-senior policemen, sociologists, psychologists and fiction writers. If you're not an expert, it's a good specialisation as long as you are an articulate researcher and can keep up with changes to procedures and protocols in crime investigation.

Different approaches

In the London *Evening Standard* Paul Barker, Senior Research Fellow at the Institute of Community Studies, under the title, *Send the police out alone on the beat*, wondered why police so often work in pairs. While street crime was rising in every London borough and the London Metropolitan Police pleaded lack of resources, this was a waste of resources he said. If they were on their own, we would be "twice as likely to see one of them in action".

Barker talked to Glen Smyth, chairman of the Metropolitan branch of the Police Federation. The problem was diagnosed as "our public services' paramount (and paranoid) safety culture". Recent changes in safety legislation have "undercut thorough police work … The NHS is riddled with the disease known as defensive medicine, whereby consultants throw every possible test at a patient to cover themselves legally. The police, in their pathetic pairings, are going in for 'defensive policing'."

This is a good model of an op-ed piece carrying a strong point of view on a controversial subject and ending up by proposing a solution. It aroused interest and provoked different points of view, and inspired a continuing debate in the letters pages.

As well as including personal experience, an expert's pronouncement and the evidence of a safety culture, the author backed up his thesis by reference to an American police novel, the *Health and Safety Executive*, the TV police series *Inspector Morse*, and statements made by the Home Secretary and the head of the Metropolitan Police Authority.

Features dealing with the social problems, as well as the human interest aspects of crime, regularly appear in general interest magazines. They draw on the research sources of such organisations as NAPO (the National Association of Probation Officers), the Howard League for Penal Reform, NACRO (the National Association for the Care and Resettlement of Offenders) and Women in Prison. Some of the statistics and brief case studies are put in boxes.

Pitfalls

Be careful with the statistics. For example, the number of people in prison has greatly increased so overcrowding has become a key issue. However, covering this angle requires accurate statistics from credible sources. *The Financial Times* article, *Momentum stalls on UK's private prisons*, which reported a predicted 2,000-inmate rise in the prison population by 2022 is a good example of this (Ford and Plimmer, 2018).

Also with the increase of sophisticated smartphones, CCTV and computers, more crimes are being reported and captured. Therefore, detection is aided by much media coverage but hampered by some.

With crime-related features, facts must be separated from the prejudices and passionate convictions backed up by good evidence.

Your approach

If you're not an expert, it's essential to base your writing on interviews with experts, case studies and legwork, and to check and check again. Topics might include:

- triumph over tragedy;
- cybercrime;
- fraud;
- a rise of knife crimes in schools.

Education

This subject is riddled with controversies and arguments are constantly raging. At the time of writing, there is a drastic shortage of teachers in state schools with many leaving due to high workloads and increasingly hard to manage pupils, plus heated discussions on tuition fees in higher education. Many issues associated with these topics have been unresolved problems since the Education Act of 1944, with each new government trying various ruses, seemingly bereft of a coherent policy.

Different approaches

In *The Independent* Hannah Fearn wrote a poignant piece: *Teachers are leaving the profession in their droves – and little wonder. Who would want to be one in modern Britain?* (2017) which reveals the depth of the crisis, noting that some 10,000 teachers had left the profession between 2010 and 2015. Her feature explored the core issues such as "spiralling workloads" and the growing bureaucracy in terms of "data-gathering and form-filling" that goes with the job. A strong piece – well researched and hard-hitting it demonstrated the writer's expertise.

Since tuition fees rose from £3,000 to £9,000 a year back in 2010 this has been a hot topic – heavily debated on both the for and against argument on scrapping fees altogether. Vicky Spratt, writing for the site *THE DEBRIEF*, questions what difference scrapping fees would make. Following Labour leader Jeremey Corbyn's promise to scrap tuition fees if elected, her article, *Why scrapping tuition fees isn't necessarily the answer to young people's problems*, is somewhat controversial in that it argues repaying student loans is more akin to "paying tax".

Whether the argument is right or wrong is not the point here. Her treatment is articulate with a strong argument backed up by some compelling evidence and key points. Being an online feature this post includes a few well-chosen hyperlinks and Spratt – hoping to engage more users in the conversation – ends with a question: "Could Labour's principled proposal convince them to turn up? After all, isn't voting, above all, about our principles?" Ironically just a few months later *iNews* reported that "tens of thousands of students were expected to take part" in a protest in Central London against tuition fees.

While the debate continues, the point here is about being able to write a conducive argument that presents an alternative point of view.

Pitfalls

Again, as in the subject of children, it's easy to pontificate, to get involved with abstractions. Don't always take the side of a well-worn argument. By being objective, researching the topic then actively seeking out alternative points of view you are more likely to come up with a stronger angle.

Your approach

If you are a teacher or lecturer in Further Education and have offspring being educated at various levels, you might well make education a specialism. If you want to dive in occasionally, get up to date. Essential resources include:

- the education sections of the national broadsheets;
- professional blogs written by experts;
- professional education bodies including HEA (Higher Education Academy) and (NUS) National Union of Students;
- professional supplements and publications such as *Times Educational Supplement* and *The Times Higher Educational Supplement*.

Health and medicine

Specialist features written by medical professionals are discussed in Chapter 13. There are not enough of these experts, however, to cope with the great interest in the subject, so here we are concerned with the non-expert who wants to write about various aspects. There are many non-experts who write well – some particular experience or unusual angle is likely to make acceptance easier.

Different approaches

Science, and more specifically biotechnology, constantly invades the subject so that new ideas are not hard to find. Today, popular women's lifestyle magazines draw largely on personal experiences and case studies. Gareth May reported on male impotence in *Marie Claire* in the April 2018 edition. His feature, *Hard luck: why male impotence is on the rise*, is a mix of personal experience, expert interviews, studies from credible sources and interviews with those who have experienced impotence. It's a strong article which leaves no questions answered, but what makes this stronger is the case study giving the partner's perspective.

In magazines aimed at older readers such as *Saga*, health is a key section and editorial pillar. In addition to a regular Q&A spot with Dr Mark Porter, the July 2017 issue contains a three-page spread written by Lesley Dobson on *The key to surviving prostate cancer*. A comprehensive piece including warning signs, getting a diagnosis and treatment. While this is clearly well researched with lots of facts and figures, a case study would, I feel, have made more impact.

Alternative medicine is getting increasing space, with sections in the newspapers and popular magazines, and the launches of specialised magazines.

While many alternative medicine practices such as hypnotherapy are recognised as valuable by the orthodoxy, readers should be kept aware of the dangers of going for treatment to people who are inadequately qualified. It is reassuring to list within articles one or two dependable organisations which can supply the names of properly qualified practitioners. Indeed, many articles about alternative medicine are written in-house or by qualified therapists who fill a regular slot. Check this out when doing a market analysis as discussed in Chapter 4.

Pitfalls

If you get into questions of diagnosis and treatment a minor inaccuracy could have woeful results for your readers so you must get it right. That means a good medical encyclopedia on your shelves, a good biology textbook, study guides for the aspects that particularly interest you, and the ability to locate the necessary experts.

For such contacts you will need access to the *General Medical Council's Register* and *The Medical Directory*, which gives the background and experience of doctors. Some aspects, such as dieting, though covered widely, must be regarded as specialist areas: careful checking with the experts is essential. Obesity: has there been enough on eat less and exercise more? Please.

Your approach

Where will the ideas come from and where will you sell them? As with most specialist subjects that lend themselves to popularisation, a good principle is to go downmarket for the research and upmarket with the idea (see Chapter 12) or upmarket for the research and downmarket with the idea. That way your audience will not be too familiar with the material on which your article is to be based.

Thus, you will get ideas from the medical specialist *The Lancet* and the *British Medical Journal* that you may be able to shape for general interest magazines and more than one popular magazine – among the men's, the women's, the parents', the teenagers', the elderly's. When, for example, an article in the *British Medical Journal* said that female sexual dysfunction was "the corporate-sponsored creation of a disease" to profit from the drugs manufactured to treat it, there was follow-up far and wide. The over-prescription of drugs in orthodox medicine continues to have mileage.

Old age or retirement

According to the Office for National Statistics data (2016), 18% of the UK's 65.6 million people are aged 65 or over. That is formidable "grey power" – as the advertisers have been quick to recognise – that an increasing number of magazines and feature pages have to cater for. People are "retiring" at 55 (or taking company pensions then and starting another life, some of them a writing life) and living to 85. This is a wide age range to accommodate.

Furthermore, some retirees are comfortably off having paid off their mortgages and securing a decent disposable income, while other retirees suffer from the dwindling value of the inadequate state pension. Today many "oldies" are very active, physically and mentally – incorporating regular gym sessions in their weekly/daily routine – while some are bedridden.

Different approaches

This is a broad genre, therefore articles must be multi-purposing enough to interest such a wide spectrum. To gauge this audience's potential subjects and interests start by evaluating and contrasting the content, tone and style of the following magazines:

- *Saga*;
- *Choice*;
- *Active Life*;
- *The Oldie*.

Pitfalls

You may want to watch for fashions in nostalgia: there are sudden revivals of the tastes of the 1940s or 1950s. But of course, the revivals are short-lived, so the timing must be just right.

A word of caution. You are of course most often addressing the elderly/retired directly. You'd be unwise to have a picture of your 85-year-old parent or grandparent in your sights, however active they might be, when many retirees are aged 55. Today, not only are people healthier in later life and living longer they are also taking up new interests from starting a degree to physical activities such as running, yoga and in some cases weight training. Best advice: don't assume.

Your approach

How-to pieces, interviews with extraordinary octogenarians and significant anniversaries work well, as do comparisons between today and previous decades. A few practical points when making comparisons between then and now. Be specific and accurate. Do the necessary research. Get some names (who was

Prime Minister at the time?). Get dates to pinpoint periods exactly. Make price comparisons only after you have calculated the effects of inflation.

Travel

Travel belongs to a huge market full of opportunities and therefore it gets the lion's share of the space here. But because so many writers want to get into it it's a tough and highly competitive area. To specialise in this genre is hard work, many travel writers I know spend most of their working life travelling – often having to get on a plane at short notice. If you don't want to specialise, you'll probably need to become skilled at multi-purposing.

Readers of travel magazines and the travel sections of newspapers/lifestyle publications not to mention blogs and online magazines have vastly different interests, so that your readership analysis needs to be at its sharpest.

Key considerations are:

- How much have they got to spend?
- What rank of hotels/restaurants should you be talking about?
- How old are they and how active/adventurous?
- Is it two weeks at a beachside resort for a family or a month in the Borneo jungle for a twenty-something between jobs?
- Or if it's a package holiday how much practical advice about insurance, health risks, etc. will be provided by the tour operator or travel agent, or will you need to provide it?

When most of your readers are going to be armchair travellers, you must bring something extra to the article – try to make the piece entertaining in its own right. Aim to recreate the experience instead of merely describe it.

Different approaches

Travel articles can be classified under:

1 *Destination pieces*: the reader's practical guide, as they are probably planning to go there on holiday.
2 *Evocative pieces*: readers including tourists but also armchair travellers.
3 *Exploratory pieces*: which may be written by writers who are trying to understand and describe a country or countries in some depth (and perhaps themselves and the human condition at the same time). Some of these writers also produce books. Most readers will be armchair travellers. Both evocative and exploratory articles may be more concerned with the travelling than the arriving.

The above is, of course, a drastic oversimplification but it does help illustrate this section. The three kinds overlap, and there are numerous sub-sections.

Consider the factors of time and money available to the readers aimed at: age, sex, single or married, with or without children, mode of transport, and so on. Not every reader wants to ride on a yak.

A completely honest account of a trip of the more unusual kind with a mixture of suffering and exhilaration can be refreshingly unpredictable. Not long into my writing career I once wrote an account of our holiday for *World of Retirement* magazine, titled *Greece out of season*. The article focused on how a short break on Zakynthos turned into an epic trip to Delphi – all on a low budget. Although I'm not a travel writer by trade (my specialism being profile pieces and interviews) I have written a few pieces over the years for a variety of magazines, including articles on eco-spas and weekend breaks.

More off-the-beaten-track in both content and style are those travel articles in the male-orientated magazines, such as *Monocle* and *Esquire*. However, don't forget about those traveller publications such as *Wanderlust*, *Traveller* and *Backpacker* that focus on experiences and wilder destinations. Not to mention the numerous online opportunities that now exist.

Pitfalls

Accepting "facilities" from organisations, which means certain expenses paid or discounts on airfares and hotel bills, otherwise known as "freebies", can be restrictive. If you tell the truth about deficiencies in a generous company's services, your relations with that company and even with an editor may be soured. But you are right and they are wrong to expect you to turn into a publicist. That principle holds for all journalism.

If you're writing travel articles for a prestigious, expensive, glossy magazine, they may prefer to pay all expenses so that you won't have to accept free trips and be tempted to bias in what you say.

Avoid brochure-speak, which is a strong temptation if you're doing a destination piece to be written after a short visit with a pressing deadline. Clichés are fewer than they used to be and you won't get away with them. Make a note to avoid those that still slip through the net. What does "authentic cuisine" mean?

Try not to write great stretches of description unless the scene is extraordinary and remote. Bring a scene to life with new facts, action, revealing dialogue, anecdotes that add drama.

Your approach

Build a travel article around a theme: finding a strong working headline (title) is a good start. If you can't find a theme, try to sum up the place or the journey in a pithy sentence. Will that do as a theme? Often a theme can be turned into action – a story with a beginning, middle and end. Whatever angle you choose, be careful to keep the readers' needs uppermost. What will they particularly enjoy in the places described? What will they want to avoid?

Do the necessary research studying guidebooks, online sites and perhaps novels, then put your notes aside when you write. If you're going to a resort take a look on tripadvisor.com to find the truth about building work around the hotel or problems with air conditioning or central heating. However, do look at several reviews and look for reoccurring issues before making a judgement. When you visit anywhere for any length of time, read the local papers if you know the language or get someone to translate relevant news items such as how tourism is polluting the environment or how local people have recently been ripping off or mugging the tourists.

On the other hand, follow E. M. Forster's advice (about the best way to see Alexandria): "wander aimlessly about". Be on the alert for serendipity. Dig out the unexpected, see what other people haven't seen or probably won't see, and you won't end up sounding like your guidebook. Be knowledgeable with a light touch. Don't be a *bon vivant* or come out with foreign phrases to impress. Please allow me that one.

Avoid stretches of description unless you can astonish. Find action, new facts, revealing dialogue. Use fictional techniques.

Use a camera and phone to take pictures and short video clips. If you are artistic take a sketchbook. These mediums will help you to be precise in your descriptions. Don't use photography as a crutch. Note your impressions as they come otherwise your photographs, a day or two later, may not make sense, or freeze your imagination instead of stimulating it and reminding you of precise detail.

If you are a good photographer you will sell many features on the quality of your pictures. A good quality digital camera together with an eye for framing will suffice. You don't have to be an expert to satisfy many markets. But find out whether a publication prefers to use its own picture library or a picture agency or its own photographers. Also, the local tourist board is usually happy to supply some professional quality images in exchange for picture credits, these can accompany your own candid shots.

For longer trips, it's a good idea to make some verbal notes on your phone using one of the free voice-recording apps. I use Voice Record Pro on my iPhone which allows me to save my audio files to my Dropbox account. Such apps are great, for note-taking, interviewing and for recording the sounds of a seedy nightclub in Bangkok or the croaking of frogs outside your hotel window. You may also want to take your tablet or laptop.

Bring back menus, brochures and leaflets that you pick up during your stay. Note striking reactions as you go to capture the edges of fresh reactions but it may be best to leave the writing up until you get back.

Travel is expensive and the fee for an article may fall far short of the cost in time and money. See Chapter 2 on expenses in general. You may be able to make use of freebies if you can avoid the pitfalls mentioned. They are not so easy to obtain these days though. It will help if you have been commissioned.

Freebies come in various forms. You may want to get on a press trip or obtain tourist-office hospitality. On press trips, you will be part of a highly organised group. They are tiring but you can benefit from the opportunities to network with the other writers, some of whom will be travel magazine or section editors. Tourist-office hospitality may involve free hotel accommodation plus meals and sometimes help with air travel as well. But don't accept freebies with conditions that curb your independence in any way.

If you're lacking help with expenses, you may be able to sell the same article to several markets. Make the most of any trip by making notes on various aspects of the place to be written up into various articles. Read any English-speaking publications and the local ones if you know the language. A trip to Milan might find you visiting art galleries, old churches and rundown estates as well as La Scala, talking to drug addicts and illegal immigrants and one or two British expats as well as getting views from business people on what the EU does for them.

Think of the publications you read, and write for. What would their readers want to know about Milan? A woman's magazine might want to know about Italian fashion designers, while a men's magazine such as *Monocle* may be interested in a contrast between London and Milanese art scenes and cultural quarters, and so on.

Here are three multi-purposing treatments:

1 **Destination pieces:** readers looking for holiday ideas trawl the travel pages in newspapers and their magazine supplements or lifestyle titles for holidays they can afford and they want the prices of everything. Use infographics or boxed information where appropriate. Indicate where readers can get further information, about excursions and so on.
2 **Evocative angles:** work out which approach works best for you. Are you the traveller with personality, perhaps some eccentricity, concerned to express your reactions to what you find, whether humorously or painfully? To study this technique, have a look at Redmond O'Hanlon's *Into the Heart of Borneo* and Bill Bryson. Are you, in contrast, the traveller who succeeds in blending into your surroundings, so that the scene comes vividly and purely to life and the reader is transported. (Read the travel books of Norman Lewis.)
3 **Exploratory articles:** the epic dimensions of the quests of the renowned twentieth-century travellers are lacking today, but one can learn some valuable techniques from reading Wilfred Thesiger, Laurens Van Der Post, T. E. Lawrence, Gertrude Bell, Freya Stark and Gavin Maxwell. There may be no more lost worlds or forgotten tribes to be discovered, but there are evils to be unmasked and glories to be unearthed.
4 **Environmental issues:** the disruptive effects of industrialism and tourism on some cultures can make a serious exploratory theme. The attention paid to this issue by *Geographical Magazine* has been mentioned, but it's covered by the more escapist travel articles as well.

Books

Sampling the great travel writers listed in the Bibliography will be worthwhile whatever your market, but essential if you aim to write books. You may want to write as a contributor for books that approach the subject through design, diagrams and striking illustrations rather than through words. See Dorling Kindersley's series and the Insight Guides, for example. Wonderful tasters, but you may be frustrated by the need to hone your piece down to 30 words when you feel it needs a hundred.

Depending on your writing skills, you could write your own travel book. As with many other subjects, if you pull it off you then have more chance of getting commissioned for features – and will of course achieve higher commission fees.

Case study: a travel writer's life

Travel journalist and editor Jill Starley-Grainger has written for some of the world's best-known publications, from The Sunday Times *to* Condé Nast Traveller, *as well as a multitude of editorial and commercial websites. Here Jill – who has also set up her own travel content marketing business, Inscribe Content – shares her inside knowledge and experiences.*

I'm sometimes asked, "how did you get your first break?". An opportunity arose while I was working as a freelance sub-editor. Someone called to ask if I could do shifts on an in-flight magazine. I did shifts for a few weeks, then when a job as deputy editor of the magazine came open, I applied and got it.

Sadly, after a few months the magazine closed but that experience sparked a passion so I returned to freelancing, focusing on travel magazines. At the same time, I started pitching freelance articles to in-flight titles. Subbing shifts on Condé Nast's *Traveller*, *The Sunday Times Travel Magazine* and *British Airways High Life* magazine followed – building my profile and skill sets. Then an opportunity arose to become the launch editor for *High Life's* website. After the site launched, I went back to doing shifts again, but the experience had enhanced my pitching skills as well as my network, so I began to pitch to higher-profile travel publications.

Being in-house doing shifts on the subs desks at various travel magazines made a real difference. It gave me an insight into how these magazines worked, and where it would be easiest to get articles accepted.

I was still doing shifts when someone on a new start-up website called to see if I wanted to be his digital editor. I agreed but within two weeks of starting, I was on the verge of walking out with nowhere to go. Unfortunately, he was a bully who knew nothing about the process and would stand behind my desk watching me work. He seemed to think that it would be easy to write and edit thousands of words of insightful, well-written content each day.

In my third week, as I was contemplating which exit was nearest for my escape, a member of the editorial team on *The Sunday Times Travel Magazine* called offering a maternity cover post for the lowest, worst-paid position on the editorial desk. It was a massive pay cut. Despite this I jumped at the chance, even though I wasn't sure how I'd afford my mortgage on the salary, but figured I could make it work. Over the next two years, I moved up several times, and became Commissioning Editor.

Then I applied for and got the job of Editor of *Which? Travel* magazine. However, much like the job for the start-up, I soon realised the company culture did not align with my work ethos, so after two years, during which time I had redesigned the magazine and was a finalist for two major industry editing awards, I quit.

I returned to freelance travel journalism, and have now also set up my own travel content marketing agency, Inscribe Content, which uses the best newsstand travel journalists in the country to write high-quality blogs, articles and ebooks for brands.

What attributes make a great travel article? Essentially, it is one that provides genuine insights and advice rather than stating the obvious. Everyone can describe a hotel room as luxurious or spacious. But telling people which hotel room is the best one in a set price category – i.e. the corner room that's larger and has better views, but for the same money – is far more interesting.

And avoid clichés like the plague (pun intended). Ask yourself this – if what you're saying could be applied to any similar place on earth, is it useful to include it in your copy? For example, every city is a city of contrasts – they all have rich and poor parts, and most are a mix of cultures. Using tired copy like that isn't helping the readers. Hone in on what makes a place unique.

Articulate engaging copy is a must. Be concise and keep it simple. Don't use a bigger word when a smaller one will do just as well. Try to make your content active – minimise the use of passive verbs, such as is and has – and you'll carry the reader along with you, rather than leaving them bored in the first paragraph.

It pays to widen your focus. Over the years I have written about travel from just about every angle. Advice, travel news, round-ups (i.e. listicles), industry insights, large colour features, interviews. I particularly enjoy writing advice articles. These tend to provide insights that people can apply to most of their travels, such as *How to save money on flights* or *Myths and facts of hotel upgrades*.

Today writers need to be able to work across print, digital and online platforms, but high-quality writing skills function the same across all. The only real differentials are headlines and stand-firsts. For example, with online content, longer and straighter headlines work best, i.e. *17 ways to save money on your next flight* vs *Plane truths*. The former will likely get more hits online, but in print you just don't have the space for those lengthy headlines.

In print you can also be more playful with your headline because it usually sits on top of a gorgeous picture that helps tell the story. Online, however, the headline must stand on its own two feet, with a very straightforward explanation in the stand-first of what people are about to read. Otherwise, they'll click away.

Make no mistake, travel writing – particularly as a freelance – can be hard, particularly with regards to press trips. Everyone gets into travel because they think it funds a high-flying lifestyle, but the reality is that press trips are rarely worth it financially. They take a long time, and freelance journalists don't get paid travel expenses, so I only do them as a loss leader. In other words, if I really want a long-haul holiday, then a commission can help offset some of the costs, but I never earn enough to cover all my costs on those sorts of trips, at least in the short term. I might sell features about the same destination multiple times, but that will often be over years, rather than weeks, so I've written ten times about South Africa now, so over the course of years, that trip has paid off. But if I'd relied on making enough profit from first trip to pay the bills, I'd have been kicked out of my home. Instead, I now do a lot more trips in the UK because the costs are lower, so they're more remunerative.

There are also other downsides. On every group press trip, there's inevitably one obnoxious person, which is why I don't do group trips any more. Every travel journalist has a group trip horror story. My worst one was on a trip to Gstaad in Switzerland. My luggage was lost on the way, yet I needed to look smart for three days of fancy meals. I spent as much time as I could spare, in between press activities, trying to find the cheapest shirt, pants and socks, and it still cost me £125 all in, yet the airline would only cover a max of £50 of expenses for lost luggage, so I was already £75 down – and these were items I didn't even like, but were simply the most affordable in this insanely expensive Swiss town. That was topped off by an older journalist whose only goal on the trip was to drink from dawn until midnight, rack up a huge bar bill and be rude to the lovely PR.

If you're going on a press trip, be nice to the PR, and don't take the mick by drinking every second of every day. If that's all you want to do, don't go on a group press trip. You might have fun, but the rest of us are trying to work, and it ruins the trip for everyone else.

The biggest challenge of the industry today is income. The sad reality is that almost nobody I know makes a living as a full-time travel journalist any more, not even the most successful people in the industry. It has turned into hobby journalism. Unless you are independently wealthy, you will need to subsidise your travel journalism with other work. And you can forget about getting a staff job. They're incredibly rare and badly paid.

Also, you will never sell the same story twice, so banish that idea, too. You can, however, sell different angles for one trip to different publications, so get your first commission, then pitch that destination to multiple publications – each with a unique spin (i.e. maybe as part of a round-up to one publication, and a long feature to another one).

For those wanting to get their first travel piece published, my advice would be to start your own blog, and don't feel like every piece has to be about horse riding naked in Kazakhstan. Most people want to read about destinations they love, so features about Paris or Edinburgh will garner far more interest than off-the-beaten-track destinations. And make sure all the travel features on your blog are edited thoroughly and carefully.

Write your blogpost, then cut it down by half. Doing so will teach you what is important and needs to be in the copy, and what is extraneous and likely to be boring to read. Tight, well-written copy is vital. Once you have published a few pieces on your blog, start pitching to in-flight magazines or websites before you think of targeting newsstands. Once you have a few commissions, you can add published work to your CV and portfolio, which will make it much easier to get something into the bigger titles.

Crucially, do not be precious about your words. Everyone has their copy heavily edited and rewritten – with good reason. Your editor knows their publication's audience much better than you do, so while you might think you've written the most beautiful phrase in the English language, if the editor cuts it or rephrases it, they've done it for a reason. Ask for feedback – but don't expect it – and if they provide it, take on board what has been said, and learn from it.

And finally, the good news: talent is a myth. The most successful writers will tell you that the way they've achieved success isn't by being born with talent. It's by working hard to improve their writing and pitching skills, and being a pleasure to work with.

Action plan

Having come up with ideas and a suitable pitch using the previous action plans in Chapters 4 and 5, now focus on developing those ideas into a more engaging, deeper article as outlined in this chapter. Now it's time put into practice what you have learned about the various treatment options for different subjects.

1. Come up with an idea for an article on one of the genres in this chapter.
2. Find a suitable target market – do aim for the smaller magazines as opposed to the larger mainstream titles are you will be more likely to secure a commission.
3. Now undertake the necessary research then write a working headline plus a stand-first – both written in the style of your target publication.
4. Pitch to your target editors, then once you have secured a commission turn your idea into a 1,000-word feature (or whatever the required length is).
5. Aim for more than one commission. Can you rewrite your feature to fit more than one market?

7 Research and interview techniques

As we have established the basic skill of journalism is reporting – collecting facts to make a story, while ensuring the news value focuses on those facts being of public interest and sometimes in the public interest. To do this, reporters must:

- identify the information that has news value;
- locate reliable sources of information;
- gather accurate (verified) information and communicate it accurately, effectively and quickly.

The last requirement means that reporters fulfil the other objectives as well as they can within the deadline. Those writing features, however, must build on those skills. Although they often have more time and deadlines may at times be extended, there is less excuse for unverified data. Thus, feature writers normally add stronger language skills to the dexterities of reporting to describe, analyse, argue and persuade, but these are the concerns of other chapters.

This chapter concentrates on those core research techniques such as:

- finding reliable sources;
- articulate research skills;
- interview techniques;
- verification skills.

Finding reliable sources

Which are the best sources for your purpose? To identify such sources, it is best to always have a working title (the angle) before at the start, that way you know what you're looking for. Initial background research is essential to find out as much as you can about the topic so that you will be able to ask fruitful questions (and get effective answers). This initial legwork will pay dividends by providing the necessary insight when interviewing sources, and help you make illuminating comparisons.

It's worth reminding yourself of the truism that you may be able to leave out things you know without spoiling your story. But if you leave something out *because* you don't know it, there will be a hole in the story.

When given a complex subject you may be able to get a detailed briefing and recommended sources from a commissioning editor.

Background research

First, see what you've got in your cuttings files – either desktop files or copies of printed articles. If they are lacking, a few searches online and through library databases should turn up sufficient material. Also, try informal exchanges – with friends and colleagues, and social media. Move around with a reporter's notebook look for relevant TV or radio programmes/podcasts, though make sure these contain up-to-date information. Sometimes background information can be acquired from producers or press offices.

Initial background research will lead you to primary sources – experts to interview or those with first-hand experience etc. It will also guide you with regards to what questions to ask interviewees. If you have particular interests and want to specialise in that area, it may be worth subscribing to some publications and online/social media groups which deal with your specific interests.

Other background sources include press cutting agencies who will – for a fee – provide a selection of traditional hard copy press cuttings as well as digital content. You can find a small selection of agencies included in Appendix 5.

Personal experience and legwork

Sometimes having a personal insight can add depth to your article. For example, you are given an assignment for a woman's magazine to describe how the headmaster of your local primary school rescued it from the bottom of the league table. A good starting point might be thinking about your own schooldays, then exploring the current experiences of your offspring or of children you know.

The next step would be background reading, looking at a variety of news stories and articles in print as well as online. Next, follow this up with some legwork – a visit to the school and the area to see what you can observe followed by interviews with the head teacher and perhaps a focus group with some of the pupils. You might fill in by getting information about the area's schools in general from the Local Education Authority by examining press releases, booklets and reports.

From legwork report to feature

Supposedly filed from the war zone in Iraq, reports in *The New York Times* from an American journalist were concocted in the US on his computer. Heed that warning and assume you'll also be found out if you fake legwork or misrepresent any of your sources. The temptation to use computer resources instead of legwork increases, particularly at a time when editorial budgets are so tight. Naturally so, since for some purposes the Internet is vastly superior.

Social media sites such as Facebook and other online sources make it easier to find those case studies which will validate your article. Previously such research might have required time-consuming legwork and phone calls.

It is prudent to avoid being too dependent on online sources (and make sure you know exactly what you're looking for when you go online). That said, the Internet is a great resource for finding credible sources and their contact details. However, there is no substitute for getting out and talking to people. You might have the time and inclination to combine personal experience (literally) with legwork to argue a case.

A lack of legwork can seriously impact on research for some features. For example, bogus begging is a familiar theme and every so often a shocking new story emerges – often providing an opportunity for strong investigative pieces. In 2017 there were several such reports, including one written by Ian Johnson in the *Mirror*. The story titled, *Fake beggars "have homes and pocket more than £2,000 a month in benefits" while pretending to sleep rough*, exposed how the alleged beggars were in fact just topping up their benefits (Johnson, 2017).

However, while Johnson's article uses numerous sources including statistics obtained using the Freedom of Information Act, it was likely – given the limited resources on many national newspapers – that the reporter hadn't left his desk. The lack of legwork resulted in the story including a brief quote from a Labour councillor, but no interviews key sources such as homeless charities, police or any of the "alleged" beggars. While this may be down to a lack of resources on the paper, a bit of legwork could have turned this into a much stronger piece – thus leaving an opportunity for a feature writer to fill in the gaps with a feature investigating the issue.

As well as attributing facts and figures obtained from sources, it is also essential to double-check these when researching a story. Figures can be easily manipulated so don't accept any without first understanding how the original figures have been worked out.

Note taking is also crucial as you will compound any problems of interpretation if during interviews you fail to take notes and record quotes accurately. Ask your interviewee to repeat anything you're not sure of. For example, was that "15" or "50"? Would you spell that name please?

Build up your contacts

Develop good contacts as you go. You may find a Filofax ideal as a hardcopy back-up. But your primary tool should be your phone's contacts book. There are many such contact book apps including Apple's Contacts, which has the facility to organise contacts into groups and record other essential data such as social media addresses and URLs plus notes on each contact. For example, I have quite a few groups of contacts. My freelance group for example is divided into the following sub-groups:

- sources and experts;
- PR contacts;
- commissioning editors.

Remember that one contact leads to another so before you leave an interviewee, ask "Who else could I talk to?"

Indicate the particular expertise of your contacts ("good on progress of parliamentary bills"). Contacts should also include such entries as libraries (and their specialisms), opening hours and the names of friendly librarians. *Press Gazette* produces an electronic database and regularly lists press officers as does *Hollis Find A Client*, a PR database for which – at the time of writing – 12 months' access can be purchased for £229 +VAT. Free access for *Hollis* is also likely to be available in some libraries.

Get on the mailing list of organisations and non-profits you are interested in to receive advance information about developments. Manufacturers will email you press releases and photographs if you write about new products.

Official sources may be generous with time and information, especially if they know your work – and have established a good relationship. But spread your network, do talk to enemies as well as friends, consumers as well as producers.

Do keep in regular contact with people otherwise they might forget you. Also, if getting in touch with someone whom you haven't spoken to for a while remind them of a previous piece you have written featuring their quotes, interview or case study, etc.

Assessment of sources

When researching any feature always evaluate the contribution value of your potential sources. Remember their quotes or input needs to bring value and validation to the article. Here are three essential criteria by which sources should be judged.

Consider whether your source is:

1 **Accessible:** if your feature would benefit greatly from your visiting an institute in New York or Paris, but there may not be time and or budget think of alternative sources.
2 **Authoritive and reliable:** how authoritative are your sources? Some eyewitnesses remember certain things, while others remember different details. Likewise, figures quoted in press accounts can be wrong and the errors repeated. Cross-check one kind of expert against another.
3 **The best informed:** determine who is the best informed, the most credible and up to date.

Assessing sources requires some thought as the traps are endless. There are unreliable sources whose judgement is clouded or memory is impaired, hoaxers who delight in ringing up newspapers to give them false stories as well as convincing gossipers, liars, slanderers, people bearing grudges, seeking revenge at any cost.

When working on a weekly newspaper as a rookie reporter, angry residents and other such local stories were high on my agenda. Based in a small office in Hampshire, people would often drop in to see me with tip-offs or potential stories. One day I had a lady tell me an animated story in which she accused her neighbour of "killing her dog and a few other animals in the neighbourhood". Listening patiently until she had finished I then asked: *So how did the dog die?* "It was poisoned," she replied.

Having asked a few more questions such as who the vets were and had the police been informed I promised to investigate the matter further. A quick call to the vet practice revealed that the poor dog had died of an age-related illness and the lady was sadly not well. It was a valuable lesson. As one of my former editors used to say – never assume, always check the facts to validate any story, no matter how plausible.

However, there's a limit to how much cross-checking you can do, so you must select with care. When you're not sure of the truth of statements you can attribute them in a qualified way: "Certain people believe that …" or "The impression has been gaining ground that …".

For a feature about bullying in the workplace you wouldn't depend on an interview with one victim, but would supplement it with other interviews, with observers, some background research and interviews with experts. Look for the names of experts who are mentioned in professional journal articles, those who have written recent texts or papers on your subject. Universities often have a directory of research specialists listing their prominent academics. Trade magazines (business-to-business) also contain the names of experts in many fields, an online search can also yield potential sources. Experts depend on being recognised as such and will grant interviews readily if you pitch your request for one effectively.

Social media and online resources

Social media also has a part to play here. For example, if you are looking for an expert or case study use Twitter to compose a tweet stating what you are looking for then end with #journorequest.

Facebook is also useful for finding specific groups from specialist interests such as bee keeping or crafts to victims of key events like the recent Florida school shooting, violence or cyber fraud. Used well, Facebook can help you source potential case studies or those who have been part of a major event/disaster/movement, etc. However, a word of caution – you must always identify yourself as a journalist and be clear that interviews will be used in your article.

There are also numerous online expert directories to help you find bona fide sources such as:

- Journalist's Resource https://journalistsresource.org
- Expertise Finder http://expertisefinder.com/
- Elsevier www.elsevier.com/solutions/expert-lookup
- The professional networking site LinkedIn https://uk.linkedin.com/

A word on experts

Bear in mind that sometimes you will find that a disaffected expert will be ready to tell you more than a happy one. Why are there such long delays in, say, hip replacement operations? The happy hip replacement surgeon in your local hospital may give you an interview. But you may find some questions unanswered or avoided and even someone willing to be a whistle-blower to complete the picture.

One such whistle-blower, also a surgeon doing hip replacements, complained that a fellow surgeon was admitting private patients before NHS patients who had waited longer and was getting paid twice. The NHS Trust decided that she needed further training. It was two years later that she was interviewed by a journalist. She had done six months further training, after which no more training had been available and she had been on full pay for two years. She had seen no patient in this period and wanted her job back.

Of course, the truth is never a simple matter. Does the other side have more of a case than you suspected? Find another source to check. You can assess a contact's reliability from the replies to questions to which you know the answer. You know for certain, let's say, that your contact's firm has had to withdraw three products this year after being arraigned under the Trade Descriptions Act. But you ask, "Sometimes in your business firms have trouble keeping in line with the Trade Descriptions Act. Has that ever happened to your firm?" Your readers must make their own judgements about how reliable your contacts are, and your questions and treatment should establish their confidence in your judgement.

Don't be over-cautious in choosing the obvious experts even if they have been overused elsewhere. Remember that the best stories can come from an unusual angle perhaps by matching your topic with one or two out-of-the-way sources.

Interview strategies

Great interviewing skills are a must for the writer's toolkit. To achieve a productive interview, it's crucial to first prepare thoroughly and that means careful research, defining your questions while leaving room for manoeuvre should an interviewee's answer lead on to something interesting, but unexpected. Preparation such as background research – not just on the subject but also your interviewees – particularly those who are experts in their field, will stop you asking basic questions about their experience and background. Your interviewee will

Figure 7.1 Five essential interview steps (Hogarth, 2018)

appreciate that you have bothered to gather some basic knowledge beforehand thus he or she is more likely to go the extra mile.

Figure 7.1 illustrates the key steps to achieving an interview which results in strong quotes that will validate your article, engage the reader and contain additional insight.

Effective approaches

Don't depend on switchboard operators to guide you to a likely source of information. Find the name of your intended contact from initial research.

If you're not known or haven't got a commission from a well-known publication it can be difficult to get past the PAs, assistants, deputies and other such gatekeepers. It helps if you can engineer an introduction, something like: "Brian so-and-so suggested you might be able to tell me about …".

Decide which method of interview would be most appropriate for your subject but be ready to go along with the preference of your contact. Explain the project you're working on and why their contribution would be important. If there is reluctance, remember you article will provide the interviewee with free publicity, thus raising their profile.

You may be able to indicate (tactfully) in what way the published interview will benefit the contact and their work, and that a "no comment" might be harmful. Tell people you want to "talk" to them, not "interview" them. Don't get annoyed if, despite tactful persistence, you fail to gain an interview. It happens to the best of us. Be ready with alternatives.

Some dos and don'ts

Suppose you, fairly new to the game, are asked on Monday to find out why a renowned editor and several other staff had mysteriously resigned from a highly successful magazine, then write a feature about it, detailing its previous success and what has gone wrong. The commissioning editor wants 1,000 words by Thursday.

The editor has provided the name of the most promising contact (let's call him Arnold Baxter), he is a journalist who worked with the publisher for 15 years and left six months ago to become the director of a School of Journalism. Meanwhile, you have arranged an interview on Tuesday with the advertising director of the group, who will tell you something of the publishing group's history and the magazine in question.

What you shouldn't do is fix up a telephone interview with Mr Baxter before you've done some basic research on the magazine and spoken to the advertising director. Because if you fail to do the necessary background study Mr Baxter will be surprised to discover that you know nothing about the magazine, nor its history, nor anything about the resignations. Therefore, the most likely scenario is that he will suggest that you find out about these things, do the Tuesday interview and return to him on Wednesday. But now that he's on the phone you want to make the most of it, so you plough on and ask: *What was it like working with that proprietor and why do you think things have suddenly gone wrong with so many of the staff?*

It is important to reiterate that all interviews should be recorded. This can be done easily using one of the numerous apps mentioned in previous chapters. Mr Baxter is very articulate and talks quite quickly, although you are taking notes having a recording will save you having to ask him to pause frequently or worse still, interrupt him. However, shorthand – also an essential skill for journalists – is another option particularly if your interviewee does not want the conversation recorded.

After the interview Mr Baxter asks, *Can I see the script?*. He is worried that you're going to misquote him. You respond that it's not the policy of the magazine to show interview scripts before publication. *At least, read over to me from your final script what you're quoting me as saying*, he says. *I'll check with my editor*, you say. The interview ends with little rapport and you have lost a good opportunity to obtain illuminating commentary. When you've gone Mr Baxter realises that you have failed to ask key questions that would have produced that illumination such as: *What problems did you have with the proprietor while you were an employee?*

Background research and careful preparation are essential components, you can't expect an interviewee to tell you what questions should be asked. You recognise that you've done a duff interview, but Mr Baxter regrets that he's too busy to give you another chance.

Here are the basic research steps to prepare properly for all the necessary interviews needed for this assignment.

- **A thorough background check on your lead interviewee:** find out as much as you can about Mr Baxter and his career, probably by interviewing briefly one or two others first. Ask the editor why he's the main prospect if you weren't told. Talk to any current or ex-colleague who knows Mr Baxter well.
- **Who else can you talk to?:** decide on two or three main interviewees and the best order to interview them.
- **Get to know the magazine:** buy at least the current issue of the magazine and read some of it so that you know what it's all about, develop an understanding of its audience etc., and look through the titles in the group. Check BRAD and the magazine's media kit if it is available for a history of circulation figures.
- **Find out about the publishing group:** search for any recent articles about the company and the magazine.
- **Record interviews:** even if you have shorthand, do ask for permission to record the interviews be it phone, Skype or face-to-face. I have found that most interviewees welcome it, feeling there's less chance of being misquoted. (Of course, it doesn't always work that way because you'll do a little editing when transcribing and that may result in the interviewee feeling misrepresented.)

Interview notes

Organisation is key in journalism. Poorly organised notes can cause much trouble when it's time to write the piece.

Assuming you will be compiling notes on your laptop or tablet you may want to use a main folder with a few sub-folders such as one for each of your interviewees (for questions and answers, etc), plus another for background research on the magazine, etc. Open a Word document to record general research notes. Whatever device you are using it is worth signing up for a Dropbox account which includes 2GB of storage or, if you are an Apple user, iCloud offers 5GB of free storage to store documents, photos and interviews, etc. For simple Word files and spreadsheets Google Docs, which is free, should suffice. Using cloud-based storage enables you to access and work on documents anywhere. Both Dropbox and iCloud allow users to purchase additional storage if need be. Both applications will sync data across all your devices: desktop, laptop, tablet and smartphone.

Whatever the source of your notes, keep in mind that the published article contains the correct acknowledgements, therefore, you must clearly record the following data:

- name of interviewee;
- date of interview or event;
- authors and titles of books/articles;
- dates of publication;
- page numbers for the references.

This will enable you to verify later that you've quoted or reproduced statements correctly. Back up those points that need authority by acknowledging the source. Well-known facts don't need acknowledgement.

Note sources for figures, especially official figures, to give them authority. Date everything: not only those mentioned above, but also any event mentioned in the course of conversation. If your interviewee says something happened "recently", ascertain the date so that you'll know how you (or a sub-editor) will refer to it on the date your piece is published. Inaccurate notes can bring trouble.

Quoting and paraphrasing

Put quote marks round and highlight significant statements in your notes that will add impact and depth to the feature. You may want to establish the credibility of a statement made by an expert. If you quote and attribute factual statements that might be considered disputable use a caveat such as "according to …". Such care in distinguishing opinion from fact will help to establish trust in your readers. But if there are libel dangers, always seek legal advice on such statements and talk to your editor.

Make sure your notes differentiate between quotes and paraphrasing. Quotes in notes (with "paraph" in brackets) can simply remind you to paraphrase when writing up, thus avoiding the risk of being accused of plagiarism. (It's easy to copy material directly into your notes and forget they are the original words when writing up.) "Style" in brackets after quotes can remind you to use the words in your piece to indicate the writer's or speaker's style.

You may have thoughts about the points you are noting. If so, put them under the notes in square brackets. Note the source at the end of each note, so that you can return to it later if necessary to check: author, title of book or article, publisher or title of publication, date, page number; or name of interviewee with date of interview; or event attended, with date.

Paraphrase facts that are repeated in various sources and introduce them by saying something like: "Most experts/historians/footballers agree that …".

How to organise notes

If you're going to interview several people for a news feature, you should work out a good order to do them in and create a summary of notes so that your understanding and questions are good. After some background research you'll probably – as we've seen in the previous example – start with those most knowledgeable about the current situation. Then you can move on to people who are able to comment on specific detail, before ending the article if necessary with summing up and if appropriate speculation about the future.

However, once your interviews are done, you may think about different ways of ordering the material for interest and effect. To demonstrate let's take a fictitious example of a news feature that requires multiple interviews.

In the county of Jaytonshire, the town of Rowdyborough is about to establish an alcohol control zone in the city centre in a month's time. The scheme will be a trial for six months, and if it works it will be repeated in other towns in the county. Already the city of Peacewick in the neighbouring county of Beldonland, also visited by many tourists, has transformed its centre by creating a dry zone by means of a by-law. You're a feature writer for the *Jaytonshire Gazette* and you've been asked to write a feature of 900 words, with a provisional title of *Will a dry zone work in Rowdyborough?*

The town suffers more from drunks and hooliganism than Peacewick did. You decide on an order of interviews and organise your research so that the story can be clearly seen in summary. Table 7.1 demonstrates how a summary of your key research data for this brief might look.

This demonstrates the right order for your research and subsequent interviews when working on the feature brief. When writing up you could lead in with some colour, set the scene: a typically noisy Rowdyborough centre in the evening (you would go and have a look). Perhaps you could also include an incident that reveals the scale of the problem and the need for action. Or you might want to start with the quote from Mr McManus if it sums up your own viewpoint. And in your lead-in you'd probably introduce as a link an element of doubt that comes with the question of the title, *Will a dry zone work in Rowdyborough?* The laws and the consultation report would have to come early but it's essential to get readers interested in the situation first.

Creative questioning

However well you do your preliminary research, have accurately identified what you need to find out and planned the shape of the final story, creativity will play a key role. Even well prepared, with a strong interest in people, good listening skills and carefully organised notes, you've got to add some creativity. That involves understanding people, adapting your techniques to their personalities and knowing how to phrase a question in different ways to get the facts out of:

- an introvert;
- extrovert;
- workaholic;
- alcoholic;
- people with their own agendas very different from yours;
- those suspicious of your intentions;
- individuals with something to hide, and so on.

Creativity also involves being ready for the unpredictable. You'll discover facts, whole stories sometimes, which are different from what you had expected. Often you will have to adapt or change your prepared questions on the hoof to

Table 7.1 Feature summary of key research

Item	Source	Data
1	**Cuttings, etc:** coverage in the *Rowdyborough Gazette* plus press releases from the council	**Background:** the Criminal Justice and Police Act 2001 and the Local Authorities (Alcohol Consumption in Designated Places) Regulations 2001 give local authorities the power to restrict anti-social drinking in designated places and to provide the police with the power to enforce this legislation.
2	**Report:** Council Report on consultation with local residents and businesses	**Data:** 140 responses, 137 in favour, two don't knows and one in disagreement. Reference also made to noise pollution, street lighting, skateboards, mountain bikes and beggars.
3	**Email:** from R Councillor Joy Luckock, Community Safety Department	**Quote:** "We want to protect R's rich heritage for everyone to enjoy. The alcohol control zone is just one measure we're introducing to make R safer. We're not killjoys. Publicity? Posters, handbills, street signs, warnings from clubs, pubs and shops."
4	**Phone interview:** Deputy Leader of R Council Norman Finch	**Quote:** "We've picked R for this pilot scheme because it's a great attraction for tourists and we can learn from what happened in P. In the evenings people can be intimidated by the drunks."
5	**Phone:** Jaytonshire Police: Inspector Roy Bartlett	**Quote:** "We have talked to our colleagues in Beldonland and Sgt Michael Higgins of Peacewick will be helping us at R for a period."
6	**Phone:** (P) Sgt Higgins	**Quote:** "In the two years our scheme has been operating there have been only three arrests. People drinking in public are asked to move, and they know about the by-law and they move."
7	**Face-to-face:** (R) Margaret Baker, National Association for the Care and Resettlement of Offenders (NACRO)	**Quote:** "The situation in P is not entirely satisfactory. There has been insufficient back-up from agencies like ours for people moved on. Sometimes the police could cooperate more with us. Some of the drinkers in town centres have recently been released from prison, some are alcoholics who badly need help and we lose sight of them. They take their problem somewhere else. You could talk to Shelter."
8	**Face-to-face:** (R) Shelter: David McManus	**Quote:** "There are day and night shelters for the homeless and the scheme will work if people moved on are referred to us."

take account of those unexpected answers. At the same time, keep in mind that an interview for information isn't like a conversation where you're delighted by new vistas opening up that need to be explored. You've already got your vista and must not be deflected by facts, however interesting, that are irrelevant for your purpose.

This kind of creativity will improve by practice, and by studying good research interviews. The following is a list of ten general tactics in sequence.

1 **Prepare simple questions:** use open-ended questions, not requiring yes or no: use your *who*, *what*, *when*, *where*, *why* and *how*.
2 **Formulate a set of good specific questions:** apply your knowledge of the interviewee and of the current situation. Generalities create a fog. You want specifics which make for clarity and readability.
3 **Ask for examples/anecdotes/quotes:** a detective inspector tells you that very personal information about people has been obtained by talking to their neighbours. "Have you got important evidence this way? Can you give me an example – without mentioning any names of course?"
4 **Exploit revelations:** ("I wasn't feeling myself at the time … but we won't go into that.") Avoid being totally occupied with keeping up with the note-taking. Follow up any unguarded remarks that promise a seam worth digging into, but emotions and opinions must be essential to the story if you're going to follow them up.
5 **Collect some colour when relevant:** a little description (colour) usually is. A rowdy evening scene in Rowdyborough (with a description of the participants, unkempt beards perhaps and beer cans), would provide a good intro to that story. If legwork isn't possible, collect the colour and perhaps one or two anecdotes or quotes from those people you interview.
6 **Check some facts as you go:** get names of people and places you're not sure of spelled out. Get anything you don't understand repeated or explained, especially jargon.
7 **Get more information than you need:** this will ensure that you are much less likely to have holes in your story.
8 **Keep the person on track:** be polite, your interviewee may prefer to talk about something else. You've got the list of questions and are making the notes – you're in charge, or you should be.
9 **Loosen the person's reserve:** when you get "I don't like talking about it" or "I've no patience with that kind of activity. Full stop", just asking "Why do you say that?" or "Why do you feel like that?" can open the gate. You may be able to loosen the reserve by showing your genuine interest and concern. Instead of firing another question try reacting emotionally: the lack of a question can have a relaxing effect. For example, "I can understand why you may be reluctant …".
10 **Find time for a review at the end of the interview:** are there gaps in the story you can plug with another question? Is there something that doesn't quite add up?

Questions not to ask

Avoid obvious questions, particularly asking someone how they feel after a momentous event such as winning an award or if a close relative has had a tragic accident, etc. Here are a few examples of what not to ask.

- Were you ready for instant fame?
- Your last play was panned mercilessly by the critics. Don't you think you should try another medium? Or is it too late in your career? Have you ever thought of giving up writing altogether?
- You're the most promising writer of your generation. Are you on a roll, or do such accolades put too much pressure on you?
- Although well known for your large donations to charity, do you try to keep them quiet or is it good for your career/business? (It may be a good question if drastically rephrased.)
- How are the share prices of your company going on the stock market at the moment? (You should already know how and have some idea of why.)
- Have you stopped beating your wife? Don't ask any version of the famous trick question, encouraging an answer, whether yes or no, that implies he used to.

Persuasion techniques

Those more difficult interviewees – especially those with much experience of being interviewed by journalists – present another kind of challenge. Even securing the interview in the first place may require much more obstinacy than is healthy. Secretaries and assistants will tell you he or she is at a meeting, not in the office, will ring you back, will ask if you will ring back next week, and so on. Sometimes these responses will be true, but mostly are often ways of fobbing you off. Keep trying until your target realises that cooperating will be easier than resistance.

Professionals such as information officers and press officers, start from different premises. The quid pro quo nature of the encounter is tacitly accepted. Publicists avoid giving information that may be compromising, the journalist tactfully avoids being used as a vehicle of publicity.

The publicist may give facts that put a product or service in a good light and omit several other facts that do not. Multiple check sources, as has been suggested, may be the answer to this ploy, but the journalist may be hamstrung by the deadline. Try giving the impression that you know those other facts but that you might make them out to be worse than they are.

Spokesmen of business organisations, like politicians, are highly skilled in relaying the information they have decided to give you, while cunningly evading your questions although apparently answering them. Bringing them back on track may require a firm response such as: "You have not answered my question" or "Interesting, but that's not exactly what I asked". When firmness is not enough, get tougher, use questions such as:

- Are you keeping back information that is legally available?
- Do I have to tell my readers that you personally declined to give me this information?
- Won't a "no comment" look bad for your organisation, make the situation look worse than it is? Make it look as if you've got something to hide?
- Do you refuse to let taxpayers (or ratepayers) know what you're doing with their money?

Such veiled threats, however, should be the last resort. Also, note, that they can lose their bite anyway if you can't determine exactly where accountability lies.

Awkward questions

If when asking a difficult question you get an awkward, incomplete answer, wait. Your interviewee will probably feel more uncomfortable than you and may start filling the silence with what you want.

Leave embarrassing questions that must be asked until much later in the interview. Don't start with accusations or damning questions. Get some rapport established and most of the interview done before you go in for killer questions such as "where are those missing funds?" That way if your subject declines to answer or terminates the interview you will at least have a few quotes for your story.

Something to hide?

There are numerous signs that an interviewee has something to hide. For example, you ask for an opinion about athletes taking illegal drugs to enhance their performance. The athlete being interviewed says he has never done so, then explains why he was once suspected of doing so. Guilty conscience?

Or if you have strong evidence that a parent has punched a teacher, don't ask did if he did it, instead ask him why – this might result in an admittance rather than a denial.

When to get legal advice

If an interviewee asks you to keep a statement "off the record", ask if you can use it without attribution. Explain why it's vital to your feature and would not be a problem. If you think publication is in the public interest but that there may be some legal issues have a chat with your editor, who can consult the publication's legal team if necessary.

How to elicit good quotes

Quotes have an important role in any article – they should aim to validate content, engage the reader and add in some cases add a new perspective. At the planning stage – and during the interview – consider these five points:

1. **Authority and expertise:** quotes can indicate that the subject has the knowledge or experience to give a statement authority, to deserve readers' attention. Readers will trust that any facts quoted will be correct, for example. Well-known or easily checked facts, of course (the company's turnover last year was £12 million), don't need quotes.
2. **Interesting quotes:** will come out of who the subjects are, what they do in life, their personalities. Charm, quaintness or oddity rapidly wear thin on the printed page unless there's also some insight into an interesting character. It's up to the writer to awaken the readers' interest in the subject, to ask questions that stimulate interesting answers and to provide the context that will make the quotes not only interesting in themselves but relevant to the piece and illuminating.
3. **Make it engaging:** build up interest in a subject before you start quoting. Looks after his widowed mother with Parkinson's disease? Keeps a dozen snakes as pets? Believes she has psychic powers? You can incorporate an interesting factor within a quote: "I was summoned to the manager's office," said Andre Baines, who had risen through the ranks meteorically in six months. "He told me I was dismissed."
4. **Interviewee's opinions should standout:** you can make it clear that a speaker's words are what the speaker believes and that the view is not necessarily shared by the writer. For example: "The manager had referred to Mr Baines's 'personality defects' and 'lack of commitment to the company'." Leaving out the quote marks would imply that you agreed with the verdict, and you would get into trouble with Mr Baines and could in breach of legal guidelines.
5. **A fair interpretation:** make sure that you represent a speaker faithfully. People say things in anger or with humour or irony that they would express quite differently if they were writing for publication. Those who are not used to being interviewed may have little idea of the impression their words will make when they appear in print. They may need to be warned, "Do you really want me to print that?" On the other hand, when speakers inadvertently reveal the truth, which doesn't show them in a good light, and it's the truth you're after, so when you're asked "You're not going to print that, are you?", there has to be a compelling reason not to say yes.

Choose the best interview method

Should interviews be via Skype, phone, email or face-to-face? To repeat: if you conduct a long interview by phone or face-to-face, record it and take notes. Ask for names, technical terms, and so on, to be spelled out.

There are techniques common to all methods. Your loyalty is to the truth as far as you can ascertain it, not to anybody else's agenda. You must be friendly but firm, professional and persuasive.

You might need more than one method of interviewing for facts. Before making your choice (or after having the choice made for you) consider the advantages and disadvantages of the chosen medium. However reluctant your interviewee, anticipate that you might need to make contact again at the writing-up stage. You may want to clarify a point or two, and even ask one or two more of those vital, specific questions, so ask for the privilege. With good judgement, you should have achieved enough rapport for that to be granted.

When it's not face-to-face, remember that the people you're addressing cannot see the encouragement on your face. For email interviews it is essential to put that encouragement (inspiration?, empathy?, friendliness?) into your words or if on the phone put it into your voice. Where possible when interviewing by email, I always like to have a quick chat with my interviewee first to get the measure of their personality – particularly when writing a profile or interview piece. If this is not possible I search for any video or audio programmes of their previous interviews.

Acknowledge your sources

As described, your notes should alert you to the sources you need to acknowledge. We're now taking acknowledgement a stage further, to where you need to obtain the source's permission to use quoted extracts, as well as to acknowledge.

Appendix 4 gives the Society of Authors' Quick Guide to Copyright. Copyright under the current law expires 70 years after the author's death. Before then, as a general rule you can quote an extract up to a short paragraph without permission as long as you acknowledge it. But the current tendency is to charge for reproducing short extracts and publications vary in their demands.

Establish bonds with contacts

Two professionals have met with different agendas. Therefore, it is necessary to negotiate, mark out the boundaries and perhaps make compromises. It's important to establish a rapport, with the future in mind, but without making too many promises. You may be asked by your interviewee to explain, for example, how the subject covered will be treated, exactly how what was said will be used in the forthcoming feature. Even if you have some idea, it will be wise not to comment, and to say that the editor must be contacted on that question.

Sometimes interviewees ask to see your feature before it goes to press, however brief their contribution. Avoid this. Seeing their words in typescript makes some people regret the frankness and want to substitute platitudes. However, an exception should be made if the material is highly technical, or liable to be misunderstood. In such circumstances, you may want to send a script for verification on condition that changes are made only for reasons of accuracy or to aid understanding. Sometimes reading a script over the phone, resulting in a few minor changes of emphasis, may satisfy both parties.

But, really, it's a matter of trust. If you come across as vague or disorganised, you may find it hard to persuade anyone that sending a script for checking is not usual. If your interviewee comes across as hostile or suspicious however, you will be reluctant to continue the association. A most regrettable situation, which should arise only rarely. Having worked at establishing a rapport this should form the basis of a relationship that will enable you to make contact again should the need arise. For example, something might not be clear, or you may have left out an important question, or your editor comes up with one you hadn't thought of.

Lastly, bear in mind that his or her name is in your contacts book – and therefore this may be a useful contact for future articles.

Verification skills

Although it is essential to find reliable sources so as to avoid the need for too much cross-checking, you must ensure every fact and figure you use in any article is:

- up to date;
- accurate.

Verification is always your responsibility as the writer, therefore you must ensure all aspects of your article are correct.

How many facts make the truth?

A news story can run and run in the papers. New evidence arrives daily. The news writer cannot preface too many statements with "as far as we know". If you're writing a feature based on a running news story you can describe evidence as "circumstantial" to indicate that there are several facts that appear to arrive at a certain conclusion although one of the facts by itself would not be proof. If the conclusion seems less certain you can use the term "anecdotal".

It's natural to make extensive use of media sources. Keep in mind that they in turn often depend heavily on previous reports and articles. Anyone who has spent an hour or two in a newspaper cuttings library will testify to the danger therein. Going back over the life of Elvis Presley, say, or the United Nations' use of force, you are struck by the way an error can be made in an issue of one newspaper and be repeated by that paper and other papers and magazines for months or years. The original may have been a printer's error.

Some of the misuse or misinterpretation of facts perpetrated by the media is careless reporting. For example, the terms used to refer to refugees are often confused. There's a tendency at the time of writing for much of the media, and much of the population, to lump together refugees, economic migrants and asylum seekers with illegal immigrants. Refugees have a genuine fear of persecution in the countries they came from. Economic migrants have been encouraged to come here to fill skill shortages. Asylum seekers are awaiting a Home Office decision to qualify as a refugee. Illegal immigrants are not asylum seekers: they are here without official authorisation.

Verifying figures

Paul Donovan in the *Press Gazette* of 26 July 2002 ("Siege mentality") gave some figures collected by MORI Social Research Institute in a poll for Amnesty International, the United Nations High Commission for Refugees (UNHCR) and other agencies. How many of the world's refugees and asylum seekers ended up in the UK? Most people thought between 10 and 19 per cent. The second most popular guess was between 20 and 29 per cent. The actual figure was 1.98 per cent.

The backing of those agencies makes us feel that we can trust those figures. There are, however, many weaknesses in the way questionnaires are set up and used that can make the results of the polls of little use. How big was the sample, how representative, how many failed to answer, what was the effect of these considerations on the results? These well-known checks are still often ignored.

If you're so bold as to want to use a questionnaire in your research, check the Bibliography for a guide to how to use them. Don't miss Darrell Huff's classic *How To Lie With Statistics*, which reveals the flaws to look for in figure crunching. That "average" we hear so much about: is it a mean average, a median or a mode? Quite different matters, and sometimes the distinction is crucial.

Be wary, similarly, of IQs, the charts and graphs sometimes used by companies to give misleadingly favourable pictures of their progress, and percentages. Percentages of what, exactly?

Evaluating online sources

In this digital age, almost anyone with access to a computer can create a website, therefore it is important to decide how authoritative and reliable an online source is. This is not an easy task and even reputable agencies like the BBC have been caught out. So, when you find that piece of earth-shattering, unbelievable, exciting information on a website, you first need to decide:

- Is it dated, current or timely?
- Is the information cited authentic?
- Does the author have a bias? Is he or she affiliated with a particular organisation or institution?
- Could the page be ironic – a satire or spoof perhaps?

Even if you are satisfied that the information seems authentic, up to date and unbiased, how can you be sure the author is who they say they are. Some clues can be found in the following:

- The URL (website address).
- Is this a "personal web page"? If the page is being hosted on free web-space provided by an ISP, this should be obvious from the web address, which will contain the user's name and often a tilde (~) or per cent sign (%) (aol.com/

members/%joebloggs, geocities.com/users/~joebloggs). This does not mean the information is necessarily unreliable, but it undermines its authority.
- Does the web page claim to be an authorised source? Educational, non-profit, government or other agencies use specific domain suffixes for their sites. Is your web page genuinely the site of a governmental (.gov/.gov.uk), educational (.edu), universities (.ac.uk) or non-profit organisation (.org/.org.uk)?

Decipher who the author is, does the page give contact details where you can verify the writer's bona fides? Have you heard of this person or organisation before? If so, search engines might help to check what has been written by or about them. Is the author qualified to comment on the subject? What background information (education, profession, credentials) is offered – and can you check this against an entry for the person on a professional networking site such as LinkedIn? If there is none, you might want to ask why.

Read the piece carefully. Is there sufficient evidence to support the facts it presents? How does the information compare with other sources you have consulted? Does the author seem to have an axe to grind? If you have doubts about any of these issues, take care to check the source: you can do this by contacting the writer, verifying information using trusted sources or searching using the name of the author or organisation to see.

Lastly, remember if something seems suspicious it probably is so do the appropriate background checks.

Case study: a lesson in investigative journalism

Dr Paul Lashmar is a senior lecturer in journalism at City University and an investigative journalist with 40 year's industry experience. His research interests include mass surveillance, mobile technology and the heritage landscape as well as organised crime. He has broken many exclusive stories during his career and is an advisor to the Centre for Investigative Journalism.

Dogged research is a must in the pursuit of truth, says Paul who shares his experience and those essential lessons he has learned along the way.

During my career, I have had a few great scoops all of which have come as a result of dogged research, hard work and above all talking to people – that's how you find stories. But perhaps the most memorable was the investigative work I did on Hatton Garden, London's famous jewellery quarter, a story that has spanned over decades and revolves around how this peculiar corner of Central London became a hotbed of crime and served as an incubator for financial crime.

By the early 1980s many of London's notorious armed robbers had moved into lucrative VAT gold fraud often walking away will millions of the taxpayers' money. Around the same time banks became more tightly regulated therefore Hatton Garden – an economy that dealt in cash for gold – provided the perfect solution. My work on this took years of painstaking research, developing contacts with a variety of sources including the criminal underworld, Customs and the Met. It was by learning how to smuggle gold and run "legitimate" businesses that these criminals moved into drug dealing bringing in cannabis from Spain and cocaine from Columbia.

But all my research paid off as I've had numerous articles published in the nationals including *The Independent* and *Observer* plus a big feature for *Esquire*. More recently this work has also contributed to my academic papers. I was also well positioned as a journalist when the Hatton Garden Robbery took place as 2015 as I even knew one of the robbers. I was then involved with a TV documentary and a book about this robbery. As a journalist, it's important to look for themes to turn in to longer articles. For example, if you develop a specialism then it's important to consider how to draw substantial pieces out of routine smaller stories to maximise your work. A good reporter learns to be creative and develop a myriad of angles from one story. In today's digital age journalists are essentially storytellers who must use narrative devices such as layering techniques to develop a story. Equally important now is the ability to reformat that story for numerous platforms and audiences.

With long-form journalism, having found a good story the writer should first ask "why should I care about this" and "how is it important to my readers?" It's so much better to read a story on something with which the audiences share empathy. Look for a person who you can tell the story through, as with it comes understanding and an acknowledgment that we can all fall victim to circumstance. The quicker a writer can convey a person and their situation with empathy – particularly if they have suffered unfortunate circumstances – the more impact the story is likely to have. It may even result in a change in society in the longer term.

An example of this can be seen with Dorothy Byrne, Head of News and Current Affairs at Channel 4, who produced a programme early in her career on rape in marriage. As a direct result of her campaign the law changed making rape in marriage a crime. Again, empathy comes into the equation.

While working with female journalists early on I learned to ask a simple question – "how did you feel?" – which helped me to develop emotional intelligence and empathy. Listening to others without interrupting is an essential skill for any interviewer, whether a journalist, broadcaster or researcher. Being a journalist can be transformative in terms of developing a stronger personality because you can't be shy. To do the job properly, you must put any personal feelings aside and be objective and get out there.

For me, a valuable lesson of my journalistic career has been to trust the lawyers – if they are good – when working on a difficult story. When working in a responsible news organisation the lawyers are there to help you to find a way to tell a legally tricky story. I say this because many journalists are wary of media lawyers and that's wrong.

Cooperating with other journalists and pooling resources is also a good idea. Today staff papers have very limited resources, but there is a lot of expertise among reporters and many ways of sharing stories, so you get your scoop and they get theirs. For example, the Panama papers – an unprecedented leak of 11.5m files from the database of the world's fourth-biggest offshore law firm published in 2016 – had journalists from 140 countries around the world working together. It was a powerful story because of a wide collaboration. However, to pool resources on a story the rules of engagement and deadlines agreed at the start. Crowdsourcing is good for investigations. It is also important to record everything. Much of the research undertaken and filed will ultimately provide historical records later therefore they have a recyclable value.

With technology evolving at such a rapid pace, research techniques have changed to some degree particularly with new areas such as data journalism emerging. Having the ability to use data to tell stories is really important if you are doing investigations, as is knowing how and when to use the Freedom of Information Act (FOI) requests. There are now journalists who get all their stories from FOI, it's a formidable tool. In contrast, data journalism provides a range of information such as the impact of obesity, which can result in a powerful story because it is factually based and then you bring in the human element.

On the downside, it is harder to access those in power now. The system has been specifically designed to keep journalists away from key people, thus controlling the flow of information making the country more institutionalised. For example, on BBC Radio 4's *Today* programme, the presenter, who was discussing the appropriate levels of sentencing for criminal offences, had asked to interview a minister from the Department of Justice but no one was said to be available. And this has become a common occurrence as people can be more selective in who they talk to particularly as the power of the press has diminished locally and nationally.

Social media has become a focal point for journalists and editors as it is a distraction as well as a tool. From a negative perspective, it has disrupted what constitutes proper research, real news and the difference between opinion and fact. That said, used in the right context, social media can be a powerful ally if say you want to find a case study of someone who can't get proper cancer treatment.

For anyone thinking of embarking on a career in investigative journalism curiosity, together with an anger about injustice, are fundamental traits. First and foremost, understand that this is not a profession that will make you rich but there is plenty of job satisfaction. Journalists learn their trade by doing the job. It's having that ability to spot what's going wrong before other people do and building up a solid network of contacts, with whom it's important to keep in touch as you never know when someone might come back to you with another nugget that leads to a great story.

If you are serious about honing your investigative skill, then talk to investigative journalists because they like people who care. Get in touch with your BureauLocal – part of The Bureau of Investigative Journalism, which is an independent, non-profit organisation. They are involved with numerous projects around the country, many of which have resulted in a change to society. For example, one successful report on domestic abuse discovered that local council funding cuts to shelters meant that fewer women could seek refuge. The Bureau sent reporters to interview those running refuges about how much funding they had received and how much this had been cut. This may have been a story, but each town has its own, so national becomes local much of the time.

For investigative journalism, you need passion, determination and the nose for a good story. But it's also important to remember that writing is a skill that can be learned, then honed.

Action plan

Practice is an essential part of learning how to interview. Quite simply the more interviews you do, the better you will get. Following on from Chapter 6, start researching your 1,000 article by taking these four key steps.

1 **From your research notes produce a feature summary plan:** this should include secondary sources (background reading, etc), essential points and primary sources (interviewees). I would suggest for a 1,000-word feature you interview three to four people, these might be experts (where applicable), case studies (those who can give an example) and anyone whose point of view/perspective is essential to the story.
2 **Contact your potential sources:** having done some background research first – and set up interviews.
3 **Develop your questions carefully:** think about what you need to find out from each source and in what order. Also, consider the sort of quotes you are seeking, what would validate your content and engage the reader? A mind map can help.
4 **Plan for additional content:** remember you may need to get extra material from your sources for added value content such as the online version of the article and perhaps a two-minute audio clip from your case study or expert.

8 A cohesive structure

As Samuel Taylor Coleridge stated in *The Table Talk*: "Prose = words in their best order" (Milford, 1917). Thus, it is crucial when delivering a feature (following a successful pitch) to ensure that you get the content right and that your article has a strong structure. As when making a cake, assembling the right ingredients for an article, then adding each part in its necessary order, is a core part of the process.

For example, let us assume you've pitched an idea which has been accepted. This is a complex project of 1,500 words and the commissioning editor has offered some advice on the approach or has provided a clear briefing of the required content. Although you may know what you want to say in the article, it will help to first compose a provisional title (a working headline) that reflects your pitch as well as any briefing given. While you will have made some notes and collected other research material, it would be unwise to start writing a draft until you have first:

- checked you have researched all the necessary key elements;
- put all your notes in the right order;
- written a brief outline including a few well-chosen sub-headings;
- approached at least three relevant interviewees.

Often at this stage there might be a slight deviation to your original idea, at which point it would be advisable to get back to the editor and make sure any modification of the original idea is acceptable.

The right components

You will want to consider which of the following five components are both necessary and available:

1. a premise or point of view;
2. a strategy, concept or theme;
3. the descriptions, story, points, facts, explanations, arguments that are largely confined to the body, the core of the feature;

4 supporting material: anecdotes, case studies, quotes, mainly for the body;
5 images such as photos and if feasible an appropriate infographic.

When dealing with an investigative or in-depth feature, the intro and conclusion are likely to need much more attention than that of a standard feature as cited in Chapter 3. The intro for a complex article should provide a hook plus some briefing or orientation to make the reader's journey hassle-free, while the conclusion must bring all the preceding teamwork of (provisional) title, intro and body to a satisfying fulfilment.

Moreover, an intro may have as many as three parts to it, as outlined in the example below, in which case the full armoury would then be:

- **An angle:** either a provisional title or a working headline will keep the writer on track.
- **Stand-first:** will provide a clear summary or overview of the article.
- **Intro (part one):** a hook – the teaser or beginning.
- **Intro (part two):** a bridge or context, which gives any necessary background, or raises the questions to be answered, leading the reader in.
- **Intro (part three):** text or pivot, which indicates what the feature is all about and engages readers.
- **Main body:** including case studies if applicable.
- **Conclusion:** where possible the writer should always try to end on a positive note.

So how do those ingredients fit into the structure of a published feature? There's no rigid formula of course as no two features are identical in either their structure or in any three sections of an intro. For example, there is often some overlapping of the roles mentioned and their order can sometimes be changed for different effects. To further illustrate how an investigative article might be constructed here's an example of a 1,000-word feature I was commissioned to write following a tweet I had posted on membership models.

The article was for *What's New In Publishing?* and was published in March 2018 with an audience demographic of mostly magazine and newspaper editors or publishers, plus a small minority of journalism students who are interesting in the business side of publishing. My brief was to write a short investigative piece on magazine membership models that would be "an explainer piece perhaps with some case studies looking at when they are and aren't a good idea for publishers to adopt". Table 8.1 demonstrates how a feature plan for this piece might look.

As I had not written for this online magazine before the first step was to research the site and its audience before planning the article. The six key stages of this feature plan take us from an overview of the target publication to the final stage – outlining the draft, at which point the writer, having undertaken the previous five stages, should be ready to write up a draft. In this instance the plan and subsequent research proved straightforward, therefore no changes to the original brief were required. Also, some of the article's content was based on my

Table 8.1 A feature plan for membership model article

Stage	Action
1	**Compile an overview of *What's New In Publishing?* and its audience** **Target market overview:** Founded in 2008, this online title is the B2B for the publishing industry and therefore is a key resource for independent magazine and newspaper publishers/editors. **Key editorial pillars include:** News, advice, technology and education across a range of relevant magazine publishing-related topics. **Audience demographic:** ABC1 industry professionals – mostly magazine and newspaper editors/publishers educated to degree level or above. **Style and tone:** Articles are mostly informative and educational, written in a formal, but engaging tone.
2	**The angle:** Are magazine membership models the way forward? **Potential/working headline:** *When should a publisher adopt a membership model?*
3	**Identify key research questions:** • *Which type of magazine is best suited to a membership model and why?* • *Who benefits from creating a membership model?* • *In what situation is a membership strategy unlikely to work?*
4	**Key research** Successful membership models i.e. *The Lawyer* and *The Economist*.
5	**Potential interviewees:** • Steve Newbold, Centaur Publishing • Henry Leveson-Gower, proprietor/founder of *The Mint* **Case study:** • *The Mint* magazine
6	**Outlining the draft** **Hook or stand-first:** *With many magazines struggling to maintain cash-flow and build a solid business model an ability to develop sustainable income streams is crucial. Mary Hogarth investigates where membership packages are the way forward.* **Potential sub-headings:** • **Introduction:** setting the scene. • **Making memberships work:** an overview on how and why a membership strategy is best employed. • **Case study:** *The Mint* to validate earlier points in the article and demonstrate how such a model might work with regards to a new title launch. **My verdict:** A brief summary of key points followed by a conclusion using my expertise and experience.

expertise and research for a book I had written a few months before titled, *Business Strategies For Magazine Publishing*. Those interested in the finished version can read my article, *When should a publisher adopt a membership model?*, in full at *What's New In Publishing?*

Organise your notes

While it is always prudent to take more notes than you need, taking too many can easily overwhelm. Once the research is complete, read through what you've got several times until you're familiar with it. Go for a walk and sleep on it and see if a clear theme falls into place, with the beginning, middle and end coming into focus. Select what you want from your notes and source materials but keep the rest just in case there's a change of plan later.

Where you have gathered extensive research, try dividing your notes into sections with headings: 1, 2, 3, 4, etc. Your source materials can be labelled A, B, C, D ... and put to the side. Notes might come from books, journalism (consult the indexes), literature of key organisations and from legwork/interviews involved in phone calls and/or visits. Once your notes have been compiled give them suitable headings then place them in order so they form a basic outline of the feature with sources noted in each one. For example, if you have been commissioned to write a feature on what treatments are available for alcoholics a starting point for research would be to first identify key sources, then compile some note headings.

Creating a table, map or diagram is useful as demonstrated in Figure 8.1, which illustrates how potential sources can be labelled, then matched with your note headings.

As Figure 8.1 shows, creating a map not only organises the essential sources as well as identifying with eight essential points to cover, it also enables the writer to create links and form a basic structure. The next step would be to write an outline using this map to ensure all eight points are addressed, this will then highlight where additional research is needed as well as ideal points to include quotes, relevant anecdotes or a case study.

Once all your research and interviews are complete it's time to write an outline before attempting the first draft. It's worth noting that a detailed outline of this kind can also become the framework for a book.

Why write an outline? As stated in Chapter 5, most commissioning editors like to see a basic outline of a proposed article with research sources and potential interviewees indicated in a pitch, plus a proposed headline, stand-first and intro. Therefore, it's always useful to develop a basic framework prior to the pitch, this should contain some initial research into your subject.

An engaging feature

You may have sensational material but if you depend solely on its quality rather than following the style of your target market when writing up the story you can

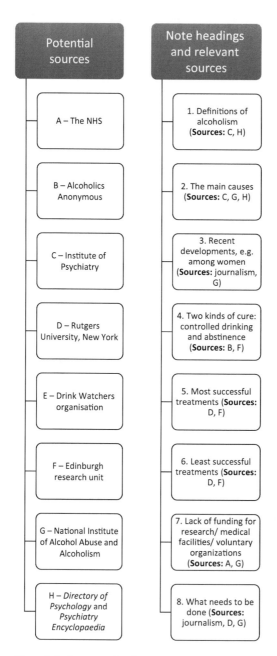

Figure 8.1 An example of mapping sources to note headings

end up with flat copy that fails to fully engage the intended audience. But what is style? Essentially it is a way of writing that is unique to each publication with prose written in a particular tone, or inflection.

Answering the question "What is style?" in his book *Newspaper Style*, Keith Waterhouse states: "Good newspaper style does not only mean writing seriously about serious matters. Bringing a light touch to a light-hearted story requires the same sure touch" (Waterhouse, 1993, p244). However, discussing differentials of style between stories in tabloids he goes on to explain why style is somewhat hard to define:

> What is this style? Why do some stories, captions and headlines have it and others not? It would be fruitless to try to define it – as Fats Waller said when asked for a definition of Jazz, "Lady, if you have to ask, I can't tell you." Obviously it demands flair, plus professionalism – two commodities that have never been in short supply in popular journalism. It demands experience, a quality that may have been taken for granted in Fleet Street. For the rest, it consists simply of choosing a handful of words from the half a million or so samples available, and arranging them in the best order. Neither this manual nor any other can show anyone how to do that, but for those who wish to be reminded of the ground-rules of what they do by instinct, the following notes may prove useful.
>
> (Waterhouse, 1993, p246)

The key to achieving the right style for any target market is to read the content vicariously – including back issues – and analyse its methodology of story treatments to deepen your understanding. But how do you find the right order for an effective body of description, narration, exposition (analysis/explanation/demonstration), argument? Each of these skills demands its own patterns, and a feature will normally require two or more different patterns. Narration usually needs some description and much narration (history, for example) is expository in purpose. Argument of any substance needs exposition to support it as well as straight facts as evidence. For the sake of clarity and convenience we'll deal with each order separately.

Focus on the readers' interests

But first, because we're talking about journalism, any order must take account of where your readers' interest will lie, so let's start with that. Readers' interest prevents any order from becoming too predictable or too rigid. The order required for a *how-to* feature on cookery or gardening is likely to be firmly dictated by the subject but there are features whose structure is not going to be at all obvious.

Features that require different kinds of material may need all or most of the patterns mentioned above. Then the main criterion determining structure is often readers' interest. Profiles often depend on it.

An example of this can be found in a profile by journalist and true crime writer, Geoffrey Wansell, published in the *Daily Mail* that revealed the story of the famous train robber, Ronnie Biggs. Titled, *A Nasty Little Thug to the End*, Wansell's obituary profile tells how Ronny, a self-confessed serial womaniser, lived life on the run following his part in the Great Train Robbery – first in Australia, then Brazil, until penniless and in need of medical treatment he returned to the UK.

Wansell begins with Biggs's death, skilfully interweaving the recent past with distance facts to document life following his escape from prison 15 months after being convicted while serving a 30-year sentence. The piece includes analysis as well as anecdotal evidence with the following key points:

- a summary of Biggs's life leading up to the Great Train Robbery;
- anecdotes about the reality of his life on the run;
- the truth about Biggs's family, his lifestyle and finances;
- how he exploited his fame to finance his lifestyle in Brazil;
- events leading to Biggs's return to the UK for medical treatment following a stroke;
- life post his release from prison in 2009 on compassionate grounds.

It is a colourful profile, which achieves an equally engaging intro and conclusion, ending by challenging Biggs's heroic identity – stating that: "Ronnie Biggs was no glamorous star, no modern Robin Hood robbing the rich to give to the poor" (Wansell, 2013).

The order of content begins with current events then goes back to the robbery then follows a chronological order. True to *Daily Mail* style, there's some linking, summarising and of course a moral, judgemental tone throughout. Could the article have been enhanced? Yes, probably. Though Wansell is a strong writer who easily engages his audience, including some background on Biggs's childhood along with interviews of one or two key associates may have given the article more depth as well as an investigative element.

Get the order right

Exposition is about being clear, concise and telling the story in logical order. Showing something clearly is what all your ordering and outlining aims to achieve. In its simplest form, when explaining how to do or achieve something (writing a book or setting up your own business, for example), getting the order wrong could do your readers severe damage were they to act on your advice.

Taking a how-to approach

Straightforward *how-to* features sell magazines, therefore in recent years they have become a staple in magazines as well as newspaper lifestyle supplements. Often produced in-house, you will find all kinds of subjects from how to cook healthy food to managing your finances, losing weight or going from coach potato to running 5K.

While content for *how-to* articles generally follows a logical order, freelances should study the prospects for any freelance contributions carefully to work out which have scope for freelance features and then what sort of treatments they want. For example, how do magazines use images, illustrations, fact boxes, infographics/charts, etc, in the layout? However, these types of articles are not as easy as they sound. Why? Because a strong *how-to* feature must include appropriate expertise – and that means sourcing then interviewing appropriate experts. Such experts need a strong profile, particularly if being featured in a national magazine or newspaper. Moreover, this type of article must be directly relevant to the readership if a writer is going to convince an editor to publish it.

Writing detailed, descriptive articles

This style of article provides a detailed account of a person, an object, a place or situation. However, be careful not to write the kind of essay, blog-style post or comment piece where you try to evoke something for its own sake – or use it as an opportunity to demonstrate your store of adjectives and adverbs. It is also essential to avoid giving a lengthy account of the make-up of something or the process of some activity, as an essay in biology might do for example. For these types of articles your narrative must be concise, the rationale being that description offers some background detail to help develop a story in an interesting way.

Such an article requires a clear and strong structure with the writer using logical order to develop the content. For example, Deborah Reynolds' feature about junk food in *Running* magazine is a well-research article detailing how poor diet impacts on energy levels and well-being. Starting with the headline *Junk Mood or Junk Food* this nutrition feature summarises the premise in the stand-first then the intro offers an overview, followed by these six carefully chosen – and ordered – sub-headings to help readers improve their performance:

- Mediterranean diet;
- selenium;
- blood sugar levels;
- serotonin;
- water;
- gut microbiota.

This in-depth piece, which includes expert quotes plus a study by researchers at University College, London, has been carefully structured to maximise impact on the reader while avoiding over description and jargon. Advice on dietary changes and health-enhancing tips are clearly linked to improving a runner's performance. Therefore, this detailed advice feature is likely to have a high success rate with its target audience.

Taking care of the narrative

Some features might need more ambitious kinds of description and narration where the writer uses his or her creative ability to transport the reader to fill the mind with imagery. A landscape can be easy enough if it's: to the north ... to the south ..., etc. But it's important to set the scene by describing a landscape as seen from a plane, moving train, or a riot in a marketplace where you would employ all the senses, and you might need to describe the effects of time passing. Your best guides to acquiring these skills are to study a few good fiction writers. However, it might be best to avoid following the style of Charles Dickens, as it contains too much description for many of today's readers.

Travel articles perhaps provide the best example of this type of narrative. Done well a piece can transport a reader to the said destination. Unfortunately, in today's cash-strapped economy many travel pieces often tend to be written from press releases. However, magazines such as *Wanderlust*, *National Geographic Traveller* and *Traveller* produce some great work in both long- and short-form travel journalism.

An example of such writing can be found in *Traveller Magazine*, which publishes three editions a year. In Volume 48, Guy Everton's piece on Saigon uses a clever structure combining description and some narrative to fully immerse the reader. Everton takes the reader on a tour of this exotic city by using a show not tell approach setting the scene of his adventure with the following, somewhat unusual, intro:

> "Just twist and go," instructs the Motorbike Angel with characteristic Vietnamese directness. Standing barely five feet off the ground and clad in a full tracksuit and hooded top in spite of the humidity, she has just pulled up outside my building on a scuffed-up Honda Airblade, which will be mine for the foreseeable future. "You have licence?" I withdraw the pink photocard that permits me to drive on four wheels in the UK. "Good." Moments later, I am signing a scruffy contract, using the bike seat for support. "If you have problem, call me, I come."
>
> "Thanks."
>
> With that, she is off, hopping on a Yamaha behind her shy, masked assistant, riding side-saddle. Only then do I think about a helmet. Lifting the seat, I expect to find one, but instead, the Motorbike Angel's handbag is tucked away inside. I send her a message and ten minutes later, she bustles back. "Sorry, I forget something."
>
> "And my helmet?"
>
> "Ah, yes. Here." She passes me a navy, baseball cap-shaped eggshell with a loose chinstrap. It will have to do.
>
> (Everton, 2018)

Those who have travelled to less safety-conscious countries will know that this is a typical exchange between a rental owner and tourist. However, using it as the introduction sets the scene well – telling the reader more about the heart and culture of the city as well as its somewhat liberal approach to driving laws.

The feature goes on to explore the city, using the said scooter as a focal point, which is a creative strategy as it sets the writer free to set off on an adventure and map the rich vista from a rider's perspective. Thus, blending in with the city's hustle and bustle as opposed to a more typical scenic tour one might expect. Everton states his intentions early in the feature stating: "I have not a clear plan but to explore, to follow my nose." What follows is a plethora of description, yet it is written with such creative flair that it creates a rich imagery in the mind of the reader.

So how do you end such a feature without disappointment? Everton keeps it simple returning to his starting point:

> When I met the Motorbike Angel earlier, I had feared I too might not survive the day. Snacking on a dragonfruit by the canal in the fading light, I now feel fully familiarised. Bring it on, Saigon.
>
> (Everton, 2018)

However, those novice writers who might think that such skill is beyond their reams should take heart – it takes practice and experience to become such an accomplished writer. Read widely and variously. That said, it is a given that analysis must also form part of your reading otherwise prose are simply words on a page.

Structuring arguments

While writing this chapter, Britain is in the middle of the Brexit crisis as no deal for the country's departure has yet been reached. Therefore, it seems appropriate to use this scenario to demonstrate how to construct a strong for-and-against style feature. To do this successfully a writer first needs to find an argument where both sides make valid points, then must put sufficient evidence forward using facts and quotes to offer the reader a full perspective, to deliver an evidence-based conclusion.

To write a first-class feature in this style the writer must be objective as the point is to let the reader make up his or her mind. To define objectivity, Edgar in *Ethical Issues in Journalism And The Media* cites Richard Rorty's definition of: "characterizing the view which would be agreed upon as a result of argument un-deflected by irrelevant considerations" (Edgar, 1992). What Edgar means is that where possible a writer must present the situation or facts as they are without injecting any personal bias into the mix.

In May 2018, *The Week* published a straightforward for-and-against feature entitled, *Brexit: The Pros and Cons of Leaving the EU* – which to date it is one of the best pieces on this subject I have read in terms of clarity. Although this 2,000-word plus piece is an amalgam of content from various reliable news sources, it has been carefully yet simply constructed. And yes, sometimes simplicity, in terms of structure, is the best approach. The intro begins by going back to the referendum in 2016 when 52 per cent voted to leave the EU, followed by a background summary of how Brexit developed. This is followed by both sides of the argument presented in key sections defined by the following clear sub-headings:

- Membership fee
- Trade
- Investment
- Sovereignty
- Immigration
- Jobs
- Britain's place in the world
- Security

The article ends without drawing a conclusion favouring either for or against. Surmise to say that with clear evidence presented – which clearly sets out both sides of the argument in a well-structured, jargon-free feature – the reader is left to decide as they should.

First drafts and the feature package

Once an outline is complete, the next stage is writing the first draft, ensuring that all elements – such as the title (or headline), stand-first, intro, main body and ending – all work together. Anecdotes and quotes, examples, case studies, figures, pictures, charts, boxes and suchlike can bring clarity, resonance, relevance and humanity. Key terms and other kinds of links keep the theme focused. It has to be a juggling act, and the components you're juggling with have to be the best you can find, within the time available. But do exercise careful judgement, as such components should not necessarily be the first that you find.

To get to this point will have involved in-depth research, collecting and verifying facts as well as representing ("interpreting") interviews accurately from which you will have written up an outline, which includes a few sub-headings to keep you on track. Also, your research has resulted in one or two anecdotes and quotes and you now know what you want to say – surely that's enough? Not necessarily, your words must convey a clear meaning.

A *Guardian* article by Peter Cole on news writing quotes former editor and journalist, Sir Harold Evans, author of *Essential English for Journalists, Editors and Writers*, on the essentials of good news writing:

> It is not enough to get the news. We must be able to put it across. Meaning must be unmistakable, and it must also be succinct. Readers have not the time and newspapers have not the space for elaborate reiteration. This imposes decisive requirements. In protecting the reader from incomprehension and boredom, the text editor has to insist on language which is specific, emphatic

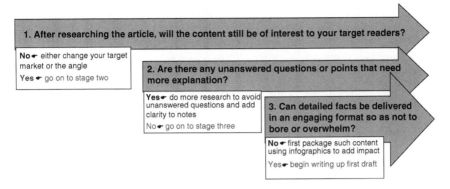

Figure 8.2 Three-stage map of a first draft (Hogarth, 2018)

and concise. Every word must be understood by the ordinary reader, every sentence must be clear at one glance, and every story must say something about people. There must never be a doubt about its relevance to our daily life. There must be no abstractions.

(Cole, 2008)

This quote is well worth some thought when writing articles. Its content is as relevant in today's fast-paced newspaper and magazine editorial offices as it was ten years ago. Keeping this in mind, it's a good idea to follow all the stages detailed in my three-stage map of a first draft (see Figure 8.2) – which I developed while teaching featuring to undergraduates. To maximise their chance of success, the writer must answer all three questions before writing up the first draft.

By answering the questions listed in Figure 8.2's map, writers will be ready to produce a strong first draft that is likely to engage the commissioning editor and more importantly the target audience. It's worth noting that your ability to interest an audience may well be easier if you're addressing like-minded people, for example, if it is your interest or specialism in trains that has encouraged you to write a feature for *Trainspotting Magazine*. Otherwise, if you're writing for a general market, you will be wise to assume that many of them will be coming to your subject cold. Remember that all of the aforementioned components must be written in a compelling way to achieve a strong, informative and engaging piece from start to finish.

A word about style and packaging

When writing up the first draft it's important to capture your target magazine's or newspaper's style and tone identified when researching the market – as some publications, such as those telling dramatic true-life stories, use a set formula for headings, intros and endings. If you work for a publication as a staff writer or sub-editor, or write for one regularly, your understanding of what's required will be finely tuned. However, freelances should give special attention to these articles if targeting such publications as the commissioning editors will have particular likes and dislikes in terms of format.

When researching your first draft, it would be wise to think about material to form a complete feature package as explored earlier in this chapter. A package should include an audio and/or video clip as well as an online piece – all of which must use a different angle to the print article so that content is not repeated.

With such packages the rule is generally 80/20, that's 80 per cent fresh content and 20 per cent repetition with the latter (repetition) used to signpost the whole package. Developing a complete package enables a writer to offer a feature with added value for the reader, while adding to their skillset. It also can widen audience participation and ensure that readers are fully engaged across platforms. Thus, this makes the writer more valuable to the publication as a staffer or freelance.

Get the structure right

Any feature – whether its focus is an investigative piece, a *how-to* or profile article – needs to be carefully structured. As with developing a news story the pyramid rules still apply, although for features these are somewhat elongated as features generally have more depth. To further illustrate the differences between news stories and features has led me to adapt the traditional pyramid-style news structure, which can be seen in Figure 8.3.

My inverted feature pyramid model (Hogarth, 2018) shown in Figure 8.3, demonstrates how to structure an article putting the most important content first followed by less primary material. Also – more importantly – this model contains four elements instead of the usual three used in other news pyramids. Years of

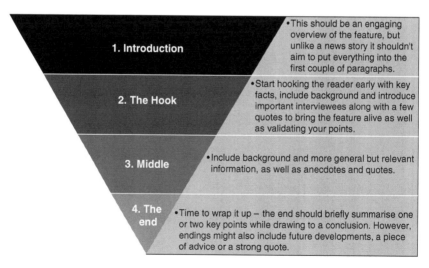

Figure 8.3 An interpretation of the inverted feature pyramid model (Hogarth, 2018)

experience as both a freelance and a staff writer has taught me that it is essential to elongate the structure as shown in Figure 8.3. Why? Because this enables the writer to produce a stronger story and engage the reader at every level. Ultimately, it's like painting a picture, only you are composing a factual story which – if done correctly – should have many layers.

How many quotes?

Quotes are not optional but essential as they validate your content, provided, of course, that you have interviewed the relevant people or experts in their field. While there are no specifics on how many interviewees and quotes should be used in a feature, I have compiled the following as a general guide:

- **500-word short article:** at least two good quotes from different sources plus statistical data.
- **800 words:** use three to four strong quotes mostly from different sources, plus anecdotes (if appropriate) and statistical data.
- **1,000 words:** this should contain about five quotes from three different sources as well as necessary data and a couple of anecdotes and perhaps a case study to add more depth and weight to your content.
- **1,500–2,000 words:** around eight to ten quotes from at least four sources with anecdotes, relevant data plus a case study or expert opinion.

Remember this is only a rough guide, there are many variants to consider including the type of article a *how-to* piece or profile for example and, of course, your target publication's style.

Key components of the draft

When writing the first draft of any feature it is essential to give careful thought to the headline (title) as well as your intro and of course the ending. Novice writers often seem to struggle with one or all of these elements. To perfect these elements wide reading of a range of features together with lots of practice is a must.

When teaching feature writing to undergraduates for the first time I advise them to write the intro and ending together first – before attempting to write up the full draft. This technique not only enables students to focus on how to hook the reader with a strong intro, but also to think about how the piece is going to end. Such a strategy will strengthen structure while serving to avoid the fatigue that many novices experience after writing the draft, then trying to come up with a definitive and engaging ending.

Headlines

Even though freelances' titles are often changed to fit the layout of the story, a provisional headline can help to define the angle and keep the writer on track.

However, it's important to remember a headline must make a big impact to fully get the reader's attention – it is not a label. Furthermore, it should charm, amuse, intrigue or spark the reader's curiosity in some way.

However, following the digital revolution, the style of headlines has changed. Some have become more dramatic, while others focus on clarity as sub-editors develop stronger skillsets with regards to online styles that require clear writing in order to achieve the best SEO (search engine optimisation). A former editor once referred me to the KISS theory – keep it simple, stupid – to improve my headline writing. It was sage advice and I still relay the advice to my students.

To demonstrate headline possibilities, here are three different examples taken from an online news story, a newspaper lead and a cover-line magazine:

- **Online:** taken from *The Independent* – an online story as the Brexit drama unfolds.
  BREXIT: WHAT HAPPENS IF TALKS COLLAPSE AND THERE'S NO DEAL?
  'Wh' phrases get straight to the point, and when combined with a question this can make a strong impact.
- **A newspaper story:** *The Sunday Express* uses facts and figures to make a statement with its front page:
  £600M A WEEK BREXIT BONUS FOR NHS
  Taken from the front page of the *Sunday Express*, this powerful use of facts and figures is designed to have maximum impact by using two very emotive words for readers in the current political climate – Brexit and NHS.
- **A magazine feature:** from *Woman & Home* magazine this headline aims to inspire its readers.
  WE'RE LIVING THE MAMMA MIA DREAM!
  This article is a cover story and can be assigned under the magazine's "In my experience" editorial pillar. It is an example of how lifestyle titles are now building features around reader experiences to develop a closer link with the audience thus widening participation and engagement.

Using a pun in a headline can also work well – but only in newspapers. Do steer away from using puns for online stories as this goes against SEO techniques and could result in a story not being easily found online, therefore unlikely to achieve good traffic data stats.

Intros that make an impact

Like the headline and stand-first, the intro is one of the most important parts of the feature, get it wrong and your reader will move on to the next article. A good intro should be between one to two paragraphs, although the length will depend on your target magazine or newspaper as will the style. However, it must not repeat the stand-first.

While there are several styles of introduction the main ones are as follows – each taken from a feature I have written:

- **The man who:** focuses on a person who has done something significant, this is particularly useful for profile pieces. This is the intro I wrote for a mini profile piece on novelist Freya North for Lovereading.co.uk (Hogarth, 2016b):

  It took four years to become established as an author, admits Freya who has since penned 13 best-selling novels. Her latest story, The Turning Point, revolves around chance events – reminding us you can't take anything for granted. As with all good fiction, this book leaves a mark on the reader. Can any of us really plan the future? Reading Freya's latest novel might just make you take another look at that five-year plan …

- **How-to:** this starts off with a statement that makes an impact then offers a starting point on how to do something – be it lose weight or write a novel. Here's an intro I wrote for a feature on how to get an agent, published in *Self Publishing* magazine under the pseudonym of Eleanor Norford.

  Getting an agent to take you on can be near on impossible. New authors who take this route face a huge challenge. Yet there are some fantastic new writers out there who have been brave enough to invest in their dream of getting published. So how can they get an agent?

  I spoke to three publishing experts – literary consultant Helen Bryant of Cornerstones, Literary agent Andrew Lownie, and Alison Baverstock, Associate Professor of Publishing at Kingston University – who each have their own perspective.

- **The comparative statement:** focuses on using an initial comparison to lead into the story. For example, this intro written for my interview with Alexandra Shulman published in *InPublishing*, September/October 2016, begins with a brief comparison.

  Like many magazines, Vogue's circulation has declined in recent years. The difference is that Vogue looks set to remain on the newsstands long after other titles have died. Why? Because Alexandra Shulman believes in innovation and is obsessive in her quest to engage the readers, all of whom love the magazine – as do the team who produce it.

- **Advice intros:** similar to a *how-to*, this intro focuses on a specific issue. An example of this can be found in the intro of a feature I wrote for *Writing Magazine*, advising on writing biographies, which was published in March 2016.

  Writing a biography is difficult. It requires painstaking research, attention to detail plus the ability to get people to talk. Biographers also need a nose for a good story as well as a fascination for human nature to capture those quirky characteristics of their subject. Without memoirs we would lack valuable insights into those lives that have shaped the future. But what makes a good biographer? And how can new writers learn their craft?

While there are many ways to write an intro, it is essential to keep in mind that you are setting the scene for the rest of the article, while aiming to hook the reader to invest their time in reading your article. Good intros take time to perfect, analysing a range of content – across platform – will help you hone your skills. For all writers, voracious reading is a must.

Get the right ending

Like intros, endings can be quite hard for novices to get right as, in my experience, new writers often run out of steam. To overcome this issue, I advise students to write a draft of the intro and the ending together before writing up the article as this then provides a basic structure thus taking some of the pressure off. However, it's important to keep an open mind as should a stronger ending present itself at a later stage then the writer can revise the earlier ending.

However, unlike an essay, generally it is best to avoid using a summary to end your feature. Also, do try to end on a positive note. But remember endings must be clearly defined. Good opportunities include:

- **Future developments**: this can work well for investigative articles. For example, if you are writing a feature on the impact of changes to state education then a paragraph or two on outlining future proposals will keep the reader engaged while also facilitating an opportunity for a follow-on piece.
- **Advice**: a good strategy for specialist pieces, particularly *how-to* features as you are giving the reader even more added value in the last paragraph they read by offering that extra nugget to take away.
- **A quote**: ending on a well-chosen quote such as a person's viewpoint, perspective or their ideas for the future can round up an article nicely and enables the writer to continue the pace while adding impact.
- **Suitable anecdote**: while ending on a relevant, short and amusing story can add drama, this strategy should be used sparingly as too many anecdotes can detract from the main purpose of the feature. Therefore, perhaps it is best left for profile pieces.
- **A call to action**: another useful device, which can work well for a variety of features – from political and business to investigative and healthy-living articles.

Lastly, an ending must be definitive. Yet, while clearly marking the end of the article, it should not leave the reader disappointed, let down or flat. It takes practice to perfect endings and is advisable that novices analyse a variety of features – noting great endings as well as identifying damp squids.

Turn your feature into a package

As explained in Chapter 3, feature articles are no longer solo components for a magazine or newspaper. More and more, in both my role as a lecturer and magazine consultant, I am seeing features evolve into packages as publishers develop more strategies to engage their readers on a multi-platform level. But what is a feature package and how should one be compiled?

A feature package can be defined as follows. Instead of starting with the old method of coming up with an idea which has been developed into an angle, a new way is to first think of a theme, then cultivate angles for each of these four components:

1. The print article
2. Digital adaption
3. The online story
4. Social media post

To produce a successful package the writer must ensure that each angle is intrinsically linked to the next so that there is a common thread. An example has been constructed in Table 8.2 to illustrate how a feature package might evolve from a single theme. In this instance, I have taken this theme from a recent global news story, which at the time of writing had gone viral. It is of course, the story of

Table 8.2 Turning a theme into a feature package

Output	Potential angle and content
Theme: Cave rescue of Wild Boars in Thailand	
Print article	*A daring rescue mission: what we can learn* • An in-depth analysis of how the preparations and rescue took place. • Interviews with key experts. • Infographic in the form of a timeline showing how events unfolded.
Digital adaptation	*A daring rescue mission: what we can learn* • This is an extension of the print piece, but should include hyperlinks to experts and other relevant aspects of the content. • An interactive, infographic map and a timeline to illustrate the key stages of the rescue together with a photo slideshow should also be included.
Online story	*My story* • A first-person experience interview with one of the dive team who tells his/her side of events, lessons learned and how the knowledge might be used in future rescue missions. • Extras: a two-minute video telling the story in clips. Plus, a short audio interview with an expert cave diver outlining potential perils and the key to planning rescues.
Social media post	**This should signpost the print, digital and online components** • To add further engagement and boost traffic, extra content should be included such as a slideshow and preview. Don't forget to link to all three of the above components as you want readers to engage across platform.

the Thai cave incident when all 12 members of the Wild Boars football team and their coach were rescued after being trapped deep in a cave system for 17 days in Northern Thailand.

Using the theme of Cave rescue of the Wild Boars, Table 8.2 shows how a feature package might look for a specialist magazine such as *Dive*.

As you can see from Table 8.2 each component is carefully linked to deliver a complete story package in an imaginative format as opposed to regurgitating content across the key platforms. Today's writers must be multi-skilled to deliver such a package. At this point, it would be useful for writers to develop key skills in software packages such as Adobe Spark's one-stop video and text software, as well as an audio recording facility (audacity, for example). It is also useful to have the ability to put key facts into an engaging visual format using infographics or an interactive map.

Case study: the cross-platform storyteller

Tyler Moss, Editor-in-Chief of Writer's Digest magazine (Figure 8.4), describes himself as a "cross-platform storyteller". He writes with passion and humour, "in that order". Below he shares his thoughts on what makes a good article, and how writers should be evolving in terms of digital content.

Good features are immersive. They pull readers in from the first paragraph and provide an informative experience that embodies the tone and style of the overall magazine. I hesitate to be too prescriptive about what format or structure a feature should have, because I think it can vary widely depending on the topic being covered.

Really, it's all in the detail. When commissioning a feature, the level of detail I provide in the brief can vary. In some instances, I get extremely thorough pitches that give a pretty extensive overview of the piece, so am less likely to have significant follow-up questions. Other times I'll be sent a strong nugget of an idea, but need to know more about how that concept would play out at a length of 2,000 or 3,000 words. It also depends on my past working relationship with the writer. If it's a contributor who has done a lot of work for us in the past, we've established a certain level of trust and I know what to expect from their writing. If it's someone I haven't worked with before, I'm likely to ask more questions in advance, and may request a rough outline.

Although there are now myriad ways to tell stories in the Digital Age, I firmly believe readers still appreciate long-form journalism. For a while it seemed as if there was a movement toward shorter features, as it seemed like there was this perception that readers no longer had the attention span to sit through a longer piece. I feel like in the past few years that's been disproven. There is still a robust audience for long-form articles (even

Figure 8.4 Writer's Digest cover July/August 2018. Credit: Saunders's photo – Chloe Aftel/cover design – Dean Abatemarco

online), as long as the feature is immersive and well-written. That's just a testament to the power of strong storytelling.

That said, I do think that editors today must have more of a 360-degree mindset. Instead of just thinking about commissioning a feature for print, I'm thinking about how it's going to look online, whether there's an associated idea we could make into a video, or audio we could turn into a podcast, and so on. The term "content" gets a bad rap, but that's really what a feature becomes when you start to think about it across platforms and mediums, and I don't necessarily think that's a bad thing.

An example of taking a "360-degree" approach can be found in our July/August issue. I interviewed George Saunders for our cover feature, the "WD Interview". Saunders and I talked for a long time, more than an hour, so I had a lot of content to work with. We published a shorter, curated version in the magazine, an extended Q&A online, and because I'd recorded our conversation, Saunders gave us permission to take some quotes for the interview and animate them for distribution via social media. We also published some "Bonus Questions" in the following issue.

Novices often struggle with intros and endings. I think that there's this notion sometimes that you have to write a piece from start to finish, in exactly that order. When struggling with an introduction, a more effective approach is often to hash out the body sections first, which can provide insight into what might make for an effective introduction. In my opinion, conclusions are always easier with an intro in place, because then you can look for ways to sort of circle back to the thesis presented in the opening, which will bring it all together in a cohesive way.

With regards to structure, there are a lot of different approaches that can be effective. And frankly, I think that writers who rely too heavily on a set structure before getting any words down can run the risk of having their piece seem formulaic and stilted. A very rough outline is useful in figuring out how to get from Point A to Point B, but the best writing is organic, with each paragraph flowing into the next.

While I'm not sure that I can pinpoint a single quote or bit of advice that informed my own early development as a writer, I can instead share this terrific quote from the venerable long-time *New Yorker* writer John McPhee: "A lead is good not because it dances, fires cannons, or whistles like a train but because it is absolute to what follows."

It's crucial for writers to learn from their mistakes and to keep striving for excellence. However, I think the most important lesson is this: ideas can come from anywhere, as long as your mind is open to the possibilities. An off-handed remark in a documentary, a snippet of conversation, a sidebar in a magazine – there's no shortage of fodder for good ideas. It's all in the execution.

My advice to new writers? Be persistent in pitching and reporting, resilient to rejection and receptive to editors' feedback.

Action plan

It is now time to put into action the skills you have learned in the previous chapters and develop a draft of your feature together with a plan for the rest of the package. Following on from Chapter 7's action plan, objectively review your research, then write up a draft of the print feature while planning the other components of your package using the following five stages as a guide.

1. **Stage 1:** write up an outline of your print/digital feature in note form covering all the basic points – and plan the other elements to produce a complete feature package. Now is the time to think about imagery and infographics, etc.
2. **Stage 2:** if you haven't already done so develop angles for the online component of the article. Do also contact potential interviewees to build audio and video content. Do also ensure you have sourced relevant images for the print, digital and online pieces.
3. **Stage 3:** now evaluate your outline objectively, this will help you to identify content that may need more research or additional quotes.
4. **Stage 4:** undertake any additional research or interviews to address gaps identified at the previous stage, then firm up your angles for each of the package components. Note there might be some subtle changes to these if additional research has provided more options to be explored.
5. **Stage 5:** write the first draft of your print/digital feature and then begin to develop the rest of the package.

9 How to develop a strong style

We have identified several qualities that reflect a writer's skill in previous chapters: notably rhythm, pace and euphony. In this chapter, we ask what sort of style is effective in description, narration, exposition and argument, by evaluating some good examples. These may also reveal the less definable quality – the writer's originality – which can mean the difference between mediocrity and excellence.

Get the description right

In the previous chapter, I demonstrated how Guy Everton effortlessly transports the reader to the streets of Saigon by taking a different approach. Such descriptions, plunging the reader into the whole experience, depend on sharp observation and the ability to include precise detail (which animals, what kind of food, what sort of old woman's face?) and the occasional figure of speech in the middle of "woop woop" for example if in Australia.

When doing legwork research, if you know that a description of a place or a person will be required, it's wise to take plenty of notes, of measurements and other precise details. "Big", "short", "comfortable", "beautiful" and suchlike adjectives are vague if you're trying to create a picture in the reader's mind. For a travel article, you might take pictures and video footage to record sights but to get the essence of a place the writer must also describe it well. For those with the latest technology (phones or tablets) it might be useful to record some notes and thoughts, plus, if appropriate, interesting sounds. But don't get too absorbed with tech or you'll forget to use your imagination and miss the essence of what you're trying to capture.

Description typically moves from the general or larger, to the particular or smaller detail. Consider the difference between a scene described from a plane and a vista depicted from a train. However, avoid including description just because you feel you should. To be effective it must have a purpose and add impact to your work.

An in-depth article also needs verve and a strong pace as well as factual content that contains necessary description. A good example is this excerpt from Dr Lesley Hulonce's article, published as the cover story in BBC *History Magazine*. It is titled *Paupers' brave new world*.

It's one of the most enduring scenes in all of the 19th-century literature. The pauper Oliver Twist – nine years old, orphaned and consigned to the workhouse – approaches the pompous parish beadle Mr Bumble and begs him for an extra helping of gruel. "Please, sir," he pleads, "I want some more."

Thanks to his pitiless response, Mr Bumble has secured himself a place in literary infamy. Yet so too has the institution in which Oliver uttered his famous request: the workhouse.

By charting Oliver Twist's travails, his creator, Charles Dickens, perhaps did more than anyone to highlight the neglect and crippling hunger that faced so many children consigned to Britain's workhouses. And, by the time Dickens wrote his famous novel in the late 1830s, this fate awaited more and more real-life Olivers.

(Hulonce, 2017)

Note that Dr Hulonce, who is also a lecturer in health humanities at Swansea University, takes a somewhat unconventional approach to the introduction by using this famous scene. By doing so she is able to show rather than tell the reader how bad the plight of paupers was in this era. Good writing is also about developing creative ways to tell a story. A narrative should seek to engage the reader, so that despite being time-poor they are willing to invest time and energy in reading the article. However, caution should be heeded, because while description is important in some pieces, it should always be used purposefully. Remember too much of anything tends to have a negative effect so care should be taken not to bore the audience.

Compelling narration

A story must intrigue the reader to the point where they need to know what happens next. A good technique is to use short, vigorous sentences around meaningful, active verbs. Aidan Hartley in *The Spectator* ('Me Frodo, You Jane') tells how one of Dr Jane Goodall's chimp study groups in Tanzania murdered a child:

The story begins on a morning in May. The wife and toddler son of Moshi Sadiqi, a park attendant, were collecting firewood in Gombe, on the shores of Lake Tanganyika. Like many staff families, they lived inside the park. The pair ventured into the rainforest. Frodo struck without warning. He swung out of the jungle, snatched up the boy and, as the distraught mother looked on, retreated into the trees. Here, Frodo flung his prey against the branches repeatedly, until the boy was as limp as a rag doll. The mother ran for help and park rangers rushed to the scene. Frodo had by this time disembowelled the boy and eaten part of his head.

(Hartley, 2002)

A graphic example of compelling copy with most of the description needed supplied by the verbs – "swung", "snatched", "disembowelled".

When your story is an expository narrative which needs historical context a writer must use devices that facilitate leaping through the years. An example of this can be found in an excerpt taken from a *Radio Times* article by Justin Webb. Titled, *The spy who hates Trump*, it reveals why former CIA director John Brennan and President Trump are sworn enemies:

> When I was 16, I told my uncle Oliver that I wanted to be a spy. He looked at me with kindly concern. "Not sure you're cut out for it really," he said. "It's rather private work, and they tend to look for people who are, well, discreet. And able to look after themselves."
>
> Oliver was right: I was not obviously cut out for, ahem, "government service".
>
> But he was. Oliver was a former soldier who spoke fluent Arabic and travelled around the Middle East before working for a time for GCHQ in Cheltenham and at various dingy Government buildings in London. That was what spies did in the Cold War. They kept an eye on people.
>
> Fast forward to the modern era, to the world of digital communications. A world of metadata. Or fake news. Of Edward Snowden and WikiLeaks. A world in which Russia, which my uncle and his pals kept in check, is able to seize territory in Europe and employ people to muddy online waters. A world in which spy agencies and the President of the United States are at war: a direct, loud, aggressive open war.
>
> (Webb, 2017)

This is indeed an interesting piece to analyse as it works using both narration and timelines. Note how the article begins when Webb is on the cusp of manhood, keeping the reader in that Cold War era to set the scene while offering background information. To move into the present day the term "Fast forward" is used, skilfully navigating readers back to the present.

It should be noted that such skill takes time and practice. While some have a natural talent, all writers must learn their craft, through hard work, in order to progress – and that means over many years and hundreds of articles. There is no shortcut.

A thorough explanation

A great deal of feature writing is exposition, illustrations of this can be found in newspapers' background and supplement features, which put the daily news into perspective by explaining the significance of the facts. Such features may make forecasts, anticipate problems, suggest solutions. In fact, much of a foreign correspondent's work is putting into perspective the events of the country reported from, making sure that everything that needs explaining – customs, ethnic balance, the governing system – is explained clearly.

How-to features also require articulate explanation and have many opportunities for angles across numerous subjects from gardening, cookery and fashion, to DIY, sport and business, etc. Such a straightforward *how-to* piece as following a recipe is not as easy to get right as it looks. It is easy to forget to say what you do with a particular ingredient, and putting the instructions in the best order requires careful thought if disaster is to be avoided.

Supplements are the bread and butter of national newspapers providing expertise on a range of subjects. Money, for example, is a particularly contentious subject as many people get confused when it comes to their finances, often finding the small print somewhat hard to decipher thus valuing clear copy which gets to the crux of the matter. Sam Barker, a personal finance reporter at *The Daily Telegraph*, regularly writes for the paper's *Money* supplement. Her article, *Should you downsize to a retirement development?* explores a possibility that many retirees have considered or are in the process of doing so – thus demonstrating the necessary skill of clear explanation.

> As people age, their housing needs change: children have flown the nest and the stairs may start to present a challenge.
>
> Those looking to downsize may find the idea of buying a home in a retirement development appealing. But is it really worth it?
>
> Retirement villages are custom-built communities designed with older people in mind. Homes are made accessible, maintenance may be taken care of and some sites offer medical care. These developments also allow retirees to live among their peers, with communal areas and social events.
>
> As the population ages – 18pc of Britons are over 65, according to the 2016 census, up from 15.9pc a decade earlier – one would expect retirement communities to be becoming more popular. But the British seem less interested than other nations in living in retirement homes.
>
> (Barker, 2018)

As the article focuses on the question from a financial perspective it goes on to explain the pros and cons of such a move in financial terms, giving examples of likely charges and potential losses. It is an authoritative piece, with each aspect clearly explained to the reader and more importantly it is jargon-free. Such explanatory articles must be written with knowledge and the understanding that readers don't have perhaps the same insight. A lack of reader knowledge or insight is a crucial point that some new writers fail to take into account. Such an oversight often results in a piece that cannot engage its target audience as they are put off by assumed knowledge.

Years ago, in my early days at *Writer's Forum*, I started to write a web column which not only covered websites but also touched on the latest technology – which in those days included desktops and early models of digital cameras. Aware that I had an in-depth knowledge of this subject I would always show a draft to my publisher's wife.

The multi-talented Mrs Jenkins was incredibly sharp, but had little knowledge of emerging technology, therefore she realistically represented my audience – as many of our readers had a somewhat limited knowledge of such matters. Alas, she always found at least one point that needed further explanation where I had used "assumed knowledge" and this taught me a valuable lesson. While it's essential to write with expertise and authority on a subject, it's crucial to first check that it makes sense to the audience. So always to find a suitable person to read such a draft.

All of the extracts cited contain the essential qualities of good expository writing: comprehensiveness (as far as it goes), logical order and, as always, clarity. However, the key techniques to achieve these are:

- **Analysis:** first see what the key elements of your subject are, then decide the best order of these elements to engage (rather than confuse) the reader. Think of a feature as a micro version of a book, an article is material divided into a headline, sub-headings and content.
- **Definition:** above, "caste", "Dahlit" and "Vedas" had to be defined. Obvious enough. Special care needs to be taken with words that have more than one field or register. It's probably clear when you're referring to a geological depression but not a psychological one. Many legal terms, like "plead", "contempt" and "prejudice", have different meanings outside the law and you may have to point out which field you're in. You use "cool" in a mention of an open-air concert: do you mean it was successful or that you should have taken a woolly? By "homeless" do you mean staying with Mum between selling and moving to a new house, or sleeping rough? A feature about the effects of divorce on children, for example, would need to make it clear what the difference is between care and custody.
- **From abstract to concrete:** use analogy, illustration, examples, anecdotes and figures to help you explain points.

Remember, clarity in writing is an essential skill, not an optional one. A good article must not leave the reader with any unanswered questions nor should it include unexplained jargon or technical terms.

Arguing convincingly

You are engaged in a debate about the Holocaust and Mr A says, "All right, there were concentration camps, and reportedly, a number of Jews and other unfortunates were exterminated, but six million is just propaganda." You might try to move the argument forward by asking:

- What do you mean by *reportedly*?
- How many people do you think were exterminated?

I don't think you'll get satisfactory answers. First, because the evidence is against Mr A. Sorry, no space to elaborate here. As a reminder though: to be convincing, arguments must be backed up by good evidence, facts or figures, or both. Keep in mind the gap between the facts and the truth that faces the deadline-pressured journalist, the problems that can make verification difficult and the limitations of different kinds of sources, matters that are spelt out in Chapter 7.

Second, Mr A doesn't convince because his language (*reportedly ... just*) doesn't inspire confidence. To argue convincingly means leaving no doubt about what you mean by your use of language. Your language demonstrates how clearly you're thinking as well as how clearly you're expressing yourself.

Defining your terms is crucial, and not only your own terms but those technical terms or jargon that you're confronted with by your subject.

The *Reader's Digest* feature, "Outrageous! Now we can't defend ourselves against burglars" (March 2003) by Alan Judd has at its core what exactly the Crown Prosecution Service means by allowing the use of "reasonable force" to defend ourselves. Judd cites similar cases of killing or seriously injuring intruders into family homes, where it is hard to see why some defenders were prosecuted and some not.

The feature follows a classical structure of argument. It starts by getting the reader emotionally involved. Two burglaries are described in which householders were injured yet refrained from fighting back and had long waits for the police. We then get the For and Against arguments, concluding with the view that the emphasis of the law needs to be changed.

Judd wants "a shift of emphasis for the courts to make it clear that there's a strong presumption against prosecuting any householder who injures an intruder". He counters the anti-gun argument by noting that in the US "where the law is more robustly on the side of the victim the rate of burglary is less than half of ours". (No comparisons are made about the rates of murders in the two countries, but we'll leave that aside.)

Emotion comes into the discussion again. As well as the phrase "reasonable force" leading to confusion it is also "a question of attitude ... Increasingly, our legal and judicial officials seem more concerned with covering their own backs in this rights-based culture, turning victims into perpetrators and perpetrators into victims."

Emotion used appropriately is needed to persuade. It helps you to get past readers' indifference, to encourage an attitude or mood and make readers receptive. But reason must be in control as emotion used dishonestly or carelessly can lead to the following common flaws in argument:

- **Emotionally weighted language:** an often used illustration of emotionally weighted language that prevents us from thinking objectively is: "I am firm, you are obstinate, he is pig-headed." Such terms are called "witch words": they may be used either cunningly or unconsciously (by the prejudiced). "Freedom fighter" or "terrorist", "staunch Conservative" or "hidebound Tory", "unemployed" or "work-shy": whose side are you on?
- **Non-sequiturs:** points that don't make sense as illustrated by the following sentence: "More children in this country are becoming obese. The main

reason is that they're eating the wrong kind of food." This excerpt doesn't make sense as there are too many other reasons to be sure that "the wrong kind of food" is the main reason.
- **Begging the question:** "More police on the streets will reduce crime." You assume to be true what you're supposed to be proving. Never make a sweeping statement without key facts or bona fide statistics to back it up.
- **Sweeping generalisation (or bias):** it's best to avoid generalisation or bias. An example of such phrases include: "The Labour Party are purely interested in getting elected" or "The Conservatives are only interested in ensuring that the rich stay rich." In practice, such faults appear in more subtle statements – go through the draft of your feature and ensure all such statements/phrases are deleted.

Essays, think pieces and polemics

The Op Ed (opposite the editorial or leader) pages of the national papers, the political weeklies and some magazines offer homes for features referred to as "think pieces". These are journalistic essays or opinion pieces, and may be designated as such. Some take up controversial topics of the moment and express a personal viewpoint that can vary from the publication's stance.

The style may approach that of the deliberately provocative pundits who use their personal columns to stir up debate, but they are more respectful, on the whole, of their content. Today these will include the writer's social media identity to encourage readers to respond – thus starting a conversation.

To further demonstrate what these involve in these types of articles, Table 9.1 – Analysis of writing styles – offers a few examples. These are short excerpts from a range of stories taken from the print editions of newspapers and magazines – illustrating the differences in style between each one.

Note the tone and style of language used in the examples shown in Table 9.1 – this demonstrates that each publication has its own voice. Therefore, to be able to achieve this, a freelance writer must study the target publication carefully before attempting to write a feature for it. And – when writing the said feature – should always have a copy of an article from the title close to hand to check that they have correctly reflected its house-style.

Find your own style

In addition to being able to reflect a house-style and tone, it is equally important to develop your own voice. This must develop naturally out of who you are and what you're interested in. It's integral to your outlook on life and comes from inside. It's your tone of voice. You can develop your own style as you go and if it has some originality, some distinction, editors will detect and value it. Extracts without attribution from feature writers with inimitable styles (the great columnists being obvious examples) can be recognised just as great novelists

Table 9.1 Analysis of writing styles

Publication	Example	Style
Daily Express 13 August 2018 (Tabloid)	*Year of the three popes* by Neil Clark **Intro:** *Forty years on, have questions surrounding the death of Pope John Paul I, who served for just 33 days, finally been answered?*	An interesting headline followed by a clearer intro. More sophisticated than the traditional tabloid style, the writer aims to intrigue readers – hooking them with curiosity.
The Times 13 August 2018 (Broadsheet)	*Workplace equality targets undermine women* by Clare Foges **Intro:** *The Conservatives' ambition for 50 per cent of candidates to be female is patronising, regressive and smacks of tokenism.*	A hard-hitting headline. The intro's language indicates a surprising bias here, while the style of language targets an educated reader.
The Guardian 13 August 2018 (Broadsheet)	*Acting is now a job for the well-off, says head of Equity* by Mark Brown **Intro:** *Working class youngsters who dream of becoming actors or performers are increasingly being kept out of the profession because of the cost and failures in the education system, the new president of Equity has warned.*	A statement style headline followed by a hard-hitting intro suggesting a bias towards a socialist perspective.
Western Gazette 9 August 2018 (Local newspaper)	*'It's a great quality of life here, why wouldn't you want to stay if the work was available?'* by Daniel Mumby **Intro:** *If you asked 100 people what a local enterprise partnership is, the chances are that only a handful would be able to tell you what it does.*	This headline reflects the paper's community feel. The intro follows through with a clear, concise style of writing.
TIME magazine 20 August 2018 (Political title)	*Democracy's aging problem* by David Runciman **Stand-first:** *Images of suffering children have a unique power in politics. They forced the Trump Administration to end its policy of ripping migrant children from their parents at the southwest border. In 2015 a photo of a dead 3-year-old who drowned trying to reach Greece also inspired policy changes across Europe. But the goodwill did not last.*	With a longer stand-first than many titles, this reflects the essay-style content of long-form journalism. Here the writer aims to form a picture in the reader's mind.

(continued)

Table 9.1 (continued)

Publication	Example	Style
Vogue May 2018 (Fashion/consumer)	***The power of the muse*** by Robin Muir **Stand-first:** *Robin Muir looks back at an anomalous shoot.*	Vogue opts for a headline acknowledging the power of imagery followed by a short stand-first – indicating less is more.
National Geographic August 2018 (Specialist)	***Are We as Awful as We Act Online?*** by Agustín Fuentes **Stand-first:** *It's not brutish human nature that prompts nasty posts and tweets, the author says. But how we evolved does play a role.*	A powerful headline followed by a thought-provoking stand-first in a style that reflects NG with its choice of words such as 'brutish' and 'nature'.

can. Meanwhile, you must let your style develop (improve?) naturally: you don't consciously cultivate a tone of voice.

Here are five points worth considering.

1. **Content must almost always come first**, however recognisable your writing is. Don't get too personal. Use the impersonal "you" rather than the personal "have you ever locked yourself out of your house?" Edit your features rigorously to weed out where you're too self-absorbed.
2. **Get on your readers' wavelength:** avoid (a) overestimating or (b) underestimating them:
   (a) You may be knowledgeable about how chromosomes work and it may be an aspect of your subject. You'll have to explain it without talking down (unless you're writing for *Lancet* or suchlike). If you're not sure how much your readers know, you can say something like: *The Parliamentary procedure, of course, is …*
   (b) Few readers will need to be told what a café latte or a chicken en croute is.
3. **Be natural:** if your writing is based on the assumption that it's leaking wisdom or great humour and it isn't, the article won't be used. Avoid showing off in any form. Don't name-drop.
4. **Keep it fresh:** "Against the orange glow of the setting sun the towers of the council estate were sharply etched …". So begins a newspaper feature. "Sharply etched" – haven't you heard that somewhere before? Didn't you put that in a school essay more than once? Find fresh figurative language and use it sparingly.
5. **Read voraciously:** study the great writers and learn from them. Take a wide approach reading a range of material by journalists, novelists, playwrights and poets.

Case study: a freelance shares her secrets

Dr Lily Canter, a senior lecturer at Sheffield Hallam University and freelance money, health and lifestyle journalist (lilycanter.co.uk) has written for numerous publications including The Guardian, The Telegraph, The Times, This is Money, Vegan Living *and* Local Living Magazines. *An expert in style with a strong voice, Lily shares the secret of her success and gives an example of her work,* Ink Redible *published in* Vegan Living *(Figure 9.1).*

My first break as a feature writer came while working as a news reporter in local papers, which I had been doing for about four years. A features editor position came up at my paper the *Northampton Chronicle & Echo* and I got the job, jumping straight from writing news to writing features as well as editing and commissioning articles.

It was a steep learning curve but loads of fun. A few years later I got a break as a freelance, which happened when I had a strong idea and decided to aim high. By that time, I had been teaching journalism to undergraduates for about five years while doing some blogging for an academic job site, but I was desperate to get back into journalism.

Most opportunities in journalism start with a good idea and mine came when I had an idea about my son's nursery and decided to pitch it to my ideal publication – *The Guardian*. I thought why not just go for it and see what happens. I had nothing to lose.

Originally I pitched it to the education section as it was a behind the scenes piece but they said a money story might work better. So I re-angled it to "I spend £9,000 a year on childcare – where does it all go?" then pitched it to *The Guardian Online Money* editor and they commissioned it.

It was published as the lead story in the Saturday Money section of the newspaper and on the website. This gave me a huge confidence boost followed by the belief that my ideas, research and writing could be published in a national publication. And, more importantly, that I shouldn't be afraid of pitching to anyone. This was three-and-a-half years ago and I haven't looked back since. Since then I have been commissioned by numerous national newspapers, magazines and websites and I'm always seeking new publications to write for.

All writers need a strong voice. I think the key is to develop a voice which speaks with authority and confidence which takes time. I have never deliberately set out to find "my voice" or writing style but I always approach stories in the same methodical way – from an informed point of view, even when crafting opinion pieces. I do research, know my facts and make sure these are used to back up what I am writing about.

Of course, it is different for all writers. Some will use humour and wordplay to great effect but for me it is about writing in a simple, straightforward way where the facts or interviewees can speak for themselves. When it

146 *How to develop a strong style*

Figure 9.1 Vegan Living *spread. Credit:* Vegan Living Magazine

comes to style and content, I think the two go hand-in-hand, although in some ways style is more important. You can have great content but if it is packaged terribly it will make no sense and no one will finish reading it and it will have no authority or authenticity. That said, you could have a brilliant piece of writing with very little content and people would still read it – so the best combination is excellent content written in an engaging, accessible style.

Writing for a publication for the first time, there are two key things that will help a writer get to grips with its style and tone. First, ask if there is a house-style guide; if there is, this will give you a sense of the tone and vocabulary that the publication uses. The second thing is to read features in your target magazine. When writing a feature, I read stories from that publication first and have them up on my web browser or the pages of the printed issue in front of me. I will always buy the magazine and read it cover to cover before writing for it, aiming to emulate what has gone before but in my own voice, so it doesn't come across as awkward or forced, or just plain copying.

Getting sufficient but not too much description (or colour) in copy is always difficult, writers need to find a balance that engages but doesn't bore or irritate readers. I tend to sprinkle it lightly throughout. I don't like long stand-firsts or excessively long drop intros as these days content tends to be quite tight. Most pieces I write are about 1,000 words and with a lot of information and case studies included. I remember one piece I wrote for *Telegraph Women* – "Meet the women trying to cure cancer with breast

Figure 9.1 (continued)

milk" – where I agonised over the intro as I wanted it to stand out and have a strong sense of colour. To achieve this I had an intro of two paragraphs full of description, the rest of the story was more of a straight news style with the odd bit of colour, which worked well.

The ability to give a clear explanation is also an important factor, particularly when writing specialist content such as finance, money matters or health pieces. Assume that the reader knows nothing. Even if they are reading a financial magazine it may be the first time they have bought it. I use simple language and explain all acronyms. For example, often I will start a story and not understand the specialist detail myself, like what a protein-lipid complex is or what a defined benefit pension is for example. It is only through research and talking to people that it begins to come clear, I can then put it into words that make sense to me and my readers.

Feature writing is always challenging. My most challenging brief to-date was a piece on veganism in the tattoo industry which I had pitched to *Vegan Living* magazine. What I didn't predict was how difficult it would be to get tattoo artists to speak to me and how antagonistic some people can be. There was also the added dimension that tattoo artists are extremely busy and work long hours in the studio so rarely pick up the phone or respond quickly to emails. It took a lot of perseverance and digging to find people to interview and I used Instagram a lot to track down artists. It all worked out well in the end and the people I did speak to were lovely but the research took much longer than I anticipated. Quite often the biggest challenge is tracking down people and then convincing them to speak to you.

The most important advice I was given when starting is KISS – Keep It Simple, Stupid – and I definitely live by this mantra. Short sentences, simple vocabulary and a clear structure. Starting in news ensured that I have always been a disciplined writer who writes in a conventional structure. I believe that to be a good feature you must know the rules of news writing before you can learn how to break them. Moreover, a feature writer needs to develop strong research and interviewing skills as well as the ability to write with clarity.

Good research skills are crucial so don't skimp when researching your subject. Read up on the subject matter, know what sources of information are reliable and up to date and where to find information. Get good at tracking people down and find new ways of contacting potential interviews, social media and LinkedIn are excellent resources.

A good interview style is essential, but it takes practice. Prepare well before an interview, ask open questions but leave any difficult or awkward ones till last, that way if someone clams up you still have some quotes. It's also important to focus on making people feel comfortable, try to develop a rapport as this will help an interviewee to open up.

Clarity is also key. A writer must make it clear to the reader what the feature is about and why it is important. Use facts to convey information clearly and quotes to convey emotions. A lot of people think feature writing is like creative writing but it is much closer to news writing – and involves a lot more discipline.

My advice to new feature writers/journalists is to aim high and don't give up. Never think such and such a publication will never commission me or hire me. Have loads of ideas and enthusiasm – demonstrate that you can come up with the goods. Being reliable this is important – because if you miss a deadline or fail to deliver a story it is unlikely the editor concerned will commission work from you again.

Lastly, don't be afraid to sell yourself and make a big deal out of every little thing you have ever written or had published. Have a clean, engaging social media profile particularly Twitter and LinkedIn (and increasingly Instagram). Do make sure you have a website, with the URL preferably in your own name.

Action plan

This chapter has covered style, looking at both the writer's own voice including description, narration and argument, as well as exploring those editorial formulas adopted by publications. The following two exercises will help you put the skills covered in this chapter into practice.

1   Write a short travel piece of around 800 words, which should be aimed at a specific travel magazine or Sunday supplement, about a place you visit regularly or remember vividly that seems to you dangerous, or mysterious or eerie or otherwise memorable. It may be a building (disused warehouse/rundown pub) or a street or a square, or uncultivated land (a wood/marsh). It must include the following components:
    - **Description:** describe the place and its atmosphere without story or explanation. Use imagery, and all the senses.
    - **Narration:** make up a story about the place that fits the description.
    - **Exposition:** give factual evidence that explains the nature of the place – is it isolated, vandalised, the scene of a murder or perhaps rumoured to be haunted?
    - **Argument:** the council have decided to change the place in some way. They plan to either repair it, destroy it or build on it. Include an argument which opts for a particular course of action.

2. Being able to capture a publication's style and tone is a crucial skill for any freelance. To practise your skills, select a feature that you've written recently that has a subject of wide interest – now rewrite the stand-first and intro for three of the following publications:
   - *Daily Express*
   - *The Daily Telegraph*
   - *YOU Magazine*
   - *GQ*
   - *Cosmopolitan*
   - *The Spectator*
   - A local paper or magazine of your choice

10 Images tell a story

Experienced feature writers and commissioning editors know that the right picture or graphic adds impact to a story. In today's digital age, where articles have gotten shorter and readers may scan content, imagery – be it pictures, infographics or illustrations – has become the linchpin of the feature be it an online, digital or print piece.

Morrish and Bradshaw (2012b) observe that "magazine design requires intelligent use of photographs, illustrations and colour" noting that that very few text-only publications exist. In my experience this is because readers like – and need – visual imagery to make sense of text. They also point out that: "every other editor, from the creator of a church newsletter to the editorial director of a major consumer magazine, must consider the visual aspects of the job" (Morrish and Bradshaw, 2012b, p162). Thus, it is important that the freelance considers visuals when pitching an idea, after all a picture is worth 1,000 words so it makes sense that good images can dramatically increase your chances of success.

The scope for such illustration has vastly increased as in print, digital and across online platforms visual imagery now takes many forms including:

- photographs;
- timelines;
- infographics;
- charts and flowcharts;
- maps;
- tables;
- diagrams;
- graphs;
- cartoons;
- line drawings and sketches;
- caricatures;
- old prints and engravings.

If not creating the image, obtaining it may involve negotiations with the image owners and/or a briefing of the experts, particularly if one picture is going to be used as a cover shot. In such instances fees, rights, image format and deadline will need to be negotiated, either by the editor or the freelance. Therefore, as a freelance you must decide when it's worth attempting to provide images or illustrations yourself.

Today's freelance needs basic photography skills and should also be able to create a reasonable infographic, as well as having sufficient competency in Word to develop a Smart Art chart. However, if a story requires a professional standard of photography, then writers need to learn how to source relevant images from picture libraries or agencies. For those who have either worked in-house for a publication or undertaken work experience, a stint on the picture desk learning how to source images for an editor or negotiate with a picture agency would have proved a valuable experience.

In this chapter, as well as gaining a comprehensive understanding of the value of imagery in features, you will also gain insight into how to obtain free pictures from the publicity departments of manufacturing or retail companies, or the press offices of institutions, agencies, charities and other non-profit-making organisations.

Early in my magazine career I was fortunate enough to end up with a staff job which incorporated a role as picture editor – a demanding hat that necessitated excellent negotiation skills and initiative because the magazine in question had very little budget. Back then photos arrived in the post, cover images were drum scanned and infographics had yet to be invented. Needless to say, this was a valuable experience. Not only did I learn how to source great images at little cost, including clip art, but also gained valuable insight into what makes a great cover shot and how to tell if an image is worthy of the centre spread.

Fast forward (quite) a few years and technology has made massive leaps facilitating great imagery, photos that can be sent in seconds and those expensive drum scanners consigned to the scrap heat.

Now freelances should be digitally savvy, and able to keep up with technology because publishers need content to fit across a range of ever-changing platforms. Therefore, a couple of photos are now unlikely to be deemed a sufficient illustration for a feature because infographics, maps and timelines as well as video content/slideshows might also be requested – whether a feature is written by a freelance or staffer.

This chapter will help you navigate the new rules, explore the market and choose appropriate illustrations for your work. There are also sections on essential skills and equipment, as well as starter points on the business aspects.

Images add impact

In my experience, most commissioning editors will value a freelance who can supply images to accompany their feature. Why? Because it saves the editor work – don't forget that the editorial teams on magazines and newspapers have substantially shrunk due to revenue problems – and furthermore the writer is perhaps best placed to understand what a story needs in terms of suitable imagery.

Therefore, it is important to do in-depth research with regards to your target markets.

As part of your market research, outlined in Chapter 4, analyse how a title illustrates its features before pitching an idea to the publication that you are targeting. To do this focus use the points set out in Figure 10.1 as a guide to understanding a publication's house-style in terms of feature illustrations.

Figure 10.1 demonstrates essential aspects that a writer should evaluate when thinking about how best to illustrate a feature. This needs as much thought as writing an article, because today it's not just about photos, cartoons or line drawings – the focus is on packaging information in an engaging and efficient format. This includes statistics, timings and geography, all of which can be neatly packaged in an eye-catching infographic, map or timeline.

It is important when pitching ideas that a writer includes details of potential images and/or pictures they either plan to source or shoot. Once commissioned, talk to the editor to get as much detail about image requirements as you can. If

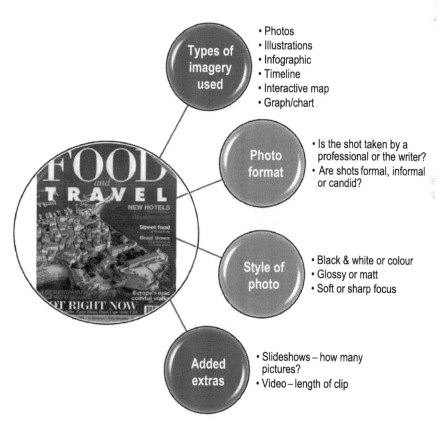

Figure 10.1 Mapping a publication's feature imagery

you become established as a writer/photojournalist then ideas for pictures may come first and can be pitched to picture-led publications.

Photos – relevance or art?

There are obvious places, such as photography and some travel or geographical magazines, where the art – meaning high-quality photographs – may be what sells them rather than the photos' actual relevance to the subject. But in the majority of cases, editors look for relevance first. Therefore, any photograph sold for publication should:

- Have enough impact to make the reader want to read the feature.
- Add visual impact to the story engaging the audience's attention and emotions more firmly than the words themselves could achieve.
- Conform to the format requirements of the publication as briefed – such as resolution and image type (jpeg, png, etc).
- Be of high quality, which usually means sharp detail, though special artistic effects such as fuzziness or graininess may occasionally be appropriate.

Pictures for features

Many freelances want to get into travel, fashion or sport, all of which provide a wealth of opportunities for imagery. But competition is fierce, with picture libraries/agencies groaning under the loads of excellent material supplied by professionals, photojournalists, students and amateur photographers. Therefore, editors may prefer to use those rather than commissioning you, even if you have a reasonable track record for pictures. So, if you are planning to building up a track record as photojournalist, it may be advisable to perhaps start nearer home.

Try to sell illustrated reports of local events that district or regional newspapers no longer have the time or budget to cover. While local and regional press budgets are tight, some will still pay a small fee for such reports, sports related picture stories are also favoured – particularly if a small club is on the rise.

Although it may be worth sending an article in on spec a phone call to the news desk is always a good idea as this helps to build a relationship. In addition to sports there are the numerous *how-to* subjects, hobbies, oddities, people in pictures that tell a funny or dramatic story, arts and antiques, inn-signs, strange animal behaviour (you might need a good zoom lens), and so on. These are well-worn subjects but still in demand by popular publications.

Build up experience

As an undergraduate, taking a photojournalism option as part of a journalism degree, I sold a couple of illustrated stories. Focusing on local crafts, my first photo story was about a blacksmith and farrier (a rare combination), which included an interview alongside a series of black and white photos taken at his forge in Hampshire. It was sold to what was then *Hampshire The County Magazine* and published in the 1997 August issue titled, *An ancient craft in modern times* (Hogarth, 1997a).

Buoyed by the success of my first piece, I then did another feature this time on a wood craftsman and hurdle-maker near Salisbury, titled *Is Mark's woodland craft doomed?* (Hogarth, 1997b) which was published in the *Andover Advertiser*. The former led to a relationship with the magazine and its editor at the time, Paul Cave, who commissioned me for a series of articles, which helped kick-start my career in features.

Relevant shots and getting permission

Unless targeting specific photography titles, only take photos relevant to the story. Try to avoid clichés such as Sydney Harbour or Big Ben unless they form part of the background scene or have relevance. The same goes for shots of crowded beaches or people lined up posing.

If you need to shoot a general scene – perhaps for an article on a topic such as the ever-more popular staycation for example – try to take candid or action shots – a scene in an open-air play, festival or parade for example. But in such instances permission may be required so always ask. If the person is under 18 you must get permission (in writing) from the parent or guardian. Remember too that pictures need captions and if appropriate tagging for social media shots, so do get the names of those involved – and check the spelling.

Some American magazines (see *Writer's Market*) demand signed permissions or email confirmation permissions from people you've photographed, particularly those who have recognisable faces.

Some English plane-spotters took pictures at a Greek airport and ended up in a Greek jail, accused of spying. In many countries, you need written permission before you photograph in art galleries, museums and archaeological sites. In the UK, you need permission to photograph properties or areas belong to organisations such as the National Trust, English Heritage and other places that attract tourists. However, be aware that most organisations, retailers and large businesses now have sophisticated PR/publicity departments which are willing to provide high-quality photos in return for a photo credit. More information on image copyright and permissions can be found in Chapter 16.

Specialist photography

For those who have developed strong photography skills there are many opportunities to sell your work across numerous markets particularly in sports, food and travel. However, if you also know about the technical side and image processing, then photography and some writing magazines could be good targets. Many such titles have a regular demand for *how-to* photographic or photojournalism features.

Ideas for such articles include:

- getting composition right;
- using different lenses effectively;
- making the most of flash;
- lighting tricks;
- the art of portrait shots;
- selling a photo essay;
- developing Photoshop skills.

For travel pieces landscape shots, while apparently easy, need particular skills but can often be taken with a good digital camera set on the appropriate programme. However, do consider getting free photographs of relevant scenery from tourist organisations in the UK and worldwide, as these generally are of a very high standard. If the scenery is merely a background to interesting people or animals then opting to take your own pictures might be better.

Whatever your subject, always take many more pictures than you need, that way you can illustrate more than one project, offering a different selection to each commissioning editor across a variety of platforms. Take different kinds of shots, then editors can choose those that best reflect the brand identity of their publication and have the composition they might favour such as vertical, horizontal, distant, middle distance, close-up images.

In addition, taking more images may provide some stock photos in preparation for similar, future assignments.

Cameras, tips and resources

There is a wide range of digital cameras to suit all abilities and price points. If just starting out opt for a medium-priced, compact digital camera, which is easy to use, and has various programmes that enable the user to point and shoot. Although photographic tech is fast evolving I would advise getting a model with the following spec:

- optical sensor resolution of at least 14MP;
- minimum 12xzoom lens;
- 3" LCD screen;
- built in WiFi – and GPS.

A camera with this basic spec is easy to use and should provide impressive image quality. Occasionally, I still take photos for articles and for most things I use my trusty Olympus Traveller SZ-11 which is light and compact.

However, more competent photographers should opt for either a DSLR model (Digital Single-Lens Reflex) or bridge camera. The latter, often less expensive, is a good all-rounder offering greater flexibility as they come with a fixed, but powerful zoom lens which is great for sports action or distance shots. Like their compact counterparts, bridge models have a range of automatic settings but also may include manual aperture and shutter speed options.

Most models – whether compact, bridge or DSLR – now have Bluetooth and Wi-Fi capacity which is useful for uploading photos directly to social media or sending directly to a newsdesk. In addition, most offer a video facility – useful if producing a feature package. When shopping for kit, it is also worth investing in a spare battery for back-up and a tripod. A large memory card of at least 32GB should also be a priority for your list.

While some journalists do use their phones to take pictures, I still prefer a camera as it offers photographers greater flexibility with the format. Plus, have you tried zooming in on an image with an iPhone? That said, phones can produce high-quality images if need be. They are also good for shooting short video clips and are often used by local sports reporters for this purpose.

Basic photo techniques

"Fill the frame" is essential advice. The eye should not be distracted by much space or fuzziness around the target, so that the target makes a sharp image and it's clear at once what the picture is all about. When taking photos of people, go for tight frames that flatter your subject. Avoid background unless it is needed for context and any kind of distracting features such as fussy wallpaper.

An illustrated feature generally needs three kinds of pictures: long shot, medium and close. Take these shots from various viewpoints and angles, and you may want to vary the lighting too. Once you have written up the feature, it will be easier to choose those shots that work best. When submitting an article with photos only send the editor three or four images unless he or she has specifically asked for more or requested a slideshow.

Sending/uploading images

Images can be sent via email but if the file size is too large or it's a video clip, there are a few cloud-based options, and many offer a basic free package. However, those users who need more capacity will have to sign up to a month subscription. Here are five good options.

1 **WeTransfer.com:** this is perhaps the preferred choice of many freelances as it enables users to upload and share image/video files for free and without creating a user identity.
2 **Dropbox.com:** this offers secure storage and sharing facilities, which can be used through the app or website. The free basic account includes 2GBs of storage space, if you need more there are various plans to choose from starting at £10 per month.
3 **iCloud:** this offers 5GB storage free and sharing. Plans for a higher capacity (50GB) start at around £0.79 per month.

4. **OneDrive:** 5GB free or 1TB for students. Non-students upgrading to the OneDrive 50GB will pay around £1.99 per month.
5. **Google Drive:** 15GB of free storage but all users must have a Google account. For more storage there is an option to upgrade to Google One at a cost of US$2.99 per month for a 200GB plan. At the time of writing Google One is currently priced only in US dollars.

From a personal perspective, I would use WeTransfer for sending images/video to editors. For storage, I have a Dropbox plan because it enables me to securely access files, documents and images from any device, anywhere in the world.

Working with a photographer

Whether you are a freelance, staffer or student journalist, collaboration is often a good way to pool resources, particularly if you are writing a piece that necessitates a high standard of photos or a professional photoshoot. In such instances working with a photographer is a good idea. To find one try the following sources – but always ask to see examples of published work before collaborating:

- **Press photographers:** who work on local publications, the names of photographers credited under their pictures in magazines.
- **Social media:** photographers can be found on Facebook and Instagram plus professional networking sites such as LinkedIn.
- **Photographers' associations:** such as AOP – The Association of Photographers.
- **Students:** contact the course leader of photography or photojournalism of under-/postgraduate courses at your nearest university.

Those taking under- or postgraduate journalism/magazine courses can usually find collaborative partners among their peers on other courses.

It is possible to arrange for an article and photographs to be paid for separately. If the fee is for a package, work out a division with the photographer. Be wary. For speculative projects the photographer may expect a fee whether the feature sells or not. Make sure you're going to get what your editor will want. Ideally, work with photographers who can produce exactly what you want and with whom you have built a rapport.

It's also worth noting that photographers who work regularly with journalists are also useful contacts as they are likely to hear of feature opportunities and let you know, or recommend you.

Getting pictures from other sources

Once commissioned, you may prefer simply to source images or pass on details of potential picture opportunities to the commissioning editor. If it's the latter, the question of permissions, copyright and credits will be taken out of your hands.

Free pictures can be obtained from tourist offices, PR companies and various organisations, including commercial companies, voluntary associations and research institutes. Museums and picture agencies normally charge a reproduction fee but BAPLA (The British Association of Picture Libraries and Agencies) will give advice. Do check copyright and licensing agreements for all images used. Photographs can often be downloaded with publishing permission through facilitated access to press pages on a company or organisation's website. In such instances always check if a photo credit applies and, if so, include it with the caption – and on the image file.

There are also numerous online picture and content agencies that have stock images for just about every subject. These include:

- **iStockphoto.com** – has millions of royalty-free images, illustrations, clip art as well as audio tracks and video clips.
- **Shutterstock.com** – a vast facility of footage, photos images and music libraries including some royalty-free photos.
- **Pixabay.com** – offers royalty-free images for commercial use.

Most agencies or libraries charge a fee, and therefore are best left for magazine/newspaper picture editors who have an account and budget.

Captions are essential

Captions anchor the pictures to the text. Therefore, a list of relevant captions for all accompanying photos should always be included at the end of your feature, clearly marked. Typically, the caption is in the present tense: it describes what the picture is saying, while providing context to the article.

It's important to remember to check the target publication's style and length of captions before creating one. However, the final form of the caption normally is the concern of the sub-editor or editor. With newspaper layouts and some magazines, the subs and photographers may get together at the final stage of page design.

Understand that a caption should add something to the picture, such as information that cannot be obtained from the picture alone, or provide a necessary explanation. It may have to answer some of those "wh" questions, identifying people and places without stating the obvious, while also identifying which meaning – out of many possible meanings – relates to the text. Captions can establish the required mood such as entertainment, amusement or even act as a call to action. Overall, remember it is a bridge between the title and the text – part of the teamwork of the various presentational elements.

Photos from a business perspective

Photos and illustrations can sell a feature so it's advisable to be well organised. Be professional in the way you do your negotiating, processing, submitting, storing and record keeping. Here are a few hints.

Negotiating fees

Since supplying photographs and graphics, either your own or from various sources, may entail expense, make sure you have been commissioned for an illustrated feature, establish exactly what is wanted and what the fee will be for supplying them.

Editors can assume the feature/pictures package is what is being discussed and may not offer a separate fee for pictures. Always make it clear that the copyright for your own pictures remains with you and that the fee is for one use. See the NUJ's website (www.nuj.org.uk) for guidance on fees.

Creating a digital library

When taking pictures, make notes on the subject matter as these will form the basis of your captions. If you regularly take your own pictures, it is essential to create a photo library with all images clearly catalogued detailing when taken, notes on names of people/places featured and when submitted and to which publication.

Most photo apps have such a facility including Apple's Photos or Windows' Photo Gallery. Do back up your photo library regularly using a data or cloud-based storage facility.

Infographics, charts, maps and timelines

Data has become a huge driver of stories. However, a list of statistics or solid facts doesn't always make great reading, neither does a couple of pages of solid text make an strong layout. Therefore, a writer must find a creative way to visualise such data and engage the reader, while adding value, depth and validity to the story. This is where infographics, charts, maps and timelines can transform such content, making it a valuable addition to the article.

Being multi-skilled is essential and that includes learning how to create infographics. I now include sessions on infographics, when teaching feature writing and layouts to undergraduates, because learning how to package data in an informative, visual way is vital. Whether your audience reads a feature from a print magazine, the digital edition or website, chances are they will be tempted to scan read if presented with columns of solid text – more so if reading from a screen. Also with digital or online content, such illustrations can be developed to feature interactive content, be it in the form of hyperlinks or buttons.

An infographic

This is a fantastic way of packaging data from statistics to explaining technical terms or how something works. When used to illustrate a feature, an infographic can bring data to life as well as having the ability to educate and inform – adding impact to the page and capturing the readers' attention.

Charts

It is relatively easy to create a range of charts and graphs using Microsoft Word, which also has Smart Art option. The latter facilitates a variety of charts including lists, hierarchical, matrix and relationship diagrams. These can be useful when writing a *how-to* piece and illustrating it with a series of steps. Figure 10.2 illustrates key steps for a successful interview.

Although used in this instance for the book, this concept can also be applied to features. For example, if I were writing an article on interviewing skills for a writing magazine then the Figure 10.2 diagram could also be utilised – albeit in a more colourful format – because it presents the five steps in a more memorable way than simply using bullet points or plain text.

Maps

These also have the potential to bring a feature to life, particularly if these are used with online posts or in digital editions. There are numerous ways that maps can add impact to a feature. Perhaps the most common use is for travel articles, where maps help the writer to clearly document a trail they have taken or travel adventure spanning hundreds of miles. They are also good for developing a new running or cycle trail.

Other uses might include environmental features, such as comparing rainfall in different areas, in this instance a map can highlight historical data such as the amount of rainfall in one specific area, add interactivity and the writer can expand that data. It can also be used for detailing important aspects of social

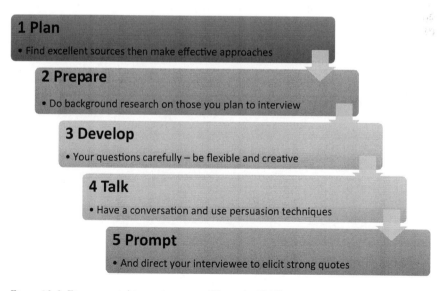

Figure 10.2 Five essential interview steps (Hogarth, 2018)

history – such as the highest priced districts for houses or the worst areas of poverty in the UK during certain eras.

Google NewsLab has a range of tools and training programmes for journalists, including how to tell your story with a map using their free Google My Maps tool. This tool enables users to make custom, interactive maps from a spreadsheet or from scratch, which include marker points and information – all of which that can then be embedded and uploaded on a digital platform with no programming required.

Timelines

These can be created using either Word's Smart Art or one of the online graphic resources outlined in the next section. Timelines are extremely useful in profile pieces for detailing your subject's lifetime achievements or demonstrating their route to success.

When writing an article, consider how best to package certain aspects of your content. For example, a timeline can also be used across most subjects – from mapping a range of historical events to charting the downfall of a business, not forgetting highlighting financial milestones, social history or the emergence of the digital revolution.

Resources

There are numerous online resources where you can create a range of illustrations from charts and maps, to timelines infographics and dashboards. Most offer a basic free package, but you may have to pay for more advanced options.

Here are a few to get you started, most run online video tutorials:

- **piktochart.com:** enables users to create a range of illustrations from infographics to maps. It has a basic free option, together with a range of priced packages including templates and custom colour schemes to suit different user needs. Download options include image files and PDFs.
- **canva.com:** offers thousands of templates, icons and stock photos to create a range of graphics – from social media posts, to CVs and infographics. The basic package is free, however, there is a monthly fee for more advanced features. A range of download options including transparent backgrounds is also available.
- **visme.co:** has options for presentations, infographics, web and social graphics. It has a basic free package which limits users to some charts and widgets plus a basic selection of templates. Images can be downloaded as a jpeg or PNG file.
- **Google NewsLab:** features a range of tools and resources backed up by tutorials to help journalists tell stories in a more engaging format.

Case study: what an editor wants

In this Q&A Pat Riddell, Editor and Chris Hudson, Art Director of National Geographic Traveller *(UK) (Figure 10.3) reveal what they look for when choosing photos for a spread and offer an insight into how to get your work published.*

Do you prefer to commission words and pictures from freelances or just the article?

Pat: We only really have a handful of writers who take photographs of a professional standard, so it's rare for somebody to be credited for both. It's much more likely we'll commission a photographer to shoot the piece after it's been written.

How much do you brief writers with regards to illustrating a story?

Pat: Generally, we ask for photos if the writer's taken any – more often than not it helps the designers in their picture search, rather than actually being published.

Is a freelance more likely to get published in *National Geographic Traveller* if they include ideas for images in their pitch?

Pat: Writers are commissioned primarily for their words – given the reputation *National Geographic* has for photography, it's something we take very seriously and we tend to consider the two disciplines separately.

What makes the perfect photo-essay?

Chris: The story must be focused and have a really unique angle. It can't just be a summary of a city or a country, it needs to really get under the skin of the culture and focus on a specific element of life that has a real impact on how that destination might be perceived. We want to educate our readers as much as we want to inspire them to travel and experience these stories themselves.

In terms of making an impact what elements do you look for when choosing photos for a spread?

Chris: Composition and construction is all important at layout stage – we obviously need that "wow" shot to open the story, which can be a scene-setter or an image that sums up the story. Beyond that, we need a good range of photographs that cover off everything. We advise our photographers to start big and end small – capture the town, the street, the front of the restaurant, the interior, the waiter, the table, the dish. That way you get a good sense of all of it and give us the best chance of telling the complete story.

Figure 10.3 National Geographic Traveller cover. Credit: National Geographic Traveller (UK)

Your favourite layout in the magazine to date?
Chris: There are so many different layouts and all have their merits, based on the style of photographer, or destination. A couple that have won us awards recently are Puglia and Namibia [see Figure 10.4]. Both are very considerate to the style of photography and, in the case of Namibia, the desolate nature of the location. We always try to keep our layouts simple for a better reading experience, but mainly to allow the fantastic photographs to tell the story in their own right.

Figure 10.4 National Geographic Traveller Namibia spread. Credit: *National Geographic Traveller* (UK)

Lastly, your advice to young writers or students whose goal it is to get published in *National Geographic Traveller*?
Pat: Don't aim too big, too fast! Read widely, understand a variety of publications inside-out and write, write, write … When you've got a feel for the type of stories that different magazines and newspapers are publishing, start pitching ideas for the smaller sections and establish a relationship with the appropriate editor.

We do occasionally commission new writers, but you'll need a good body of work and a killer idea before you're considered for the one of the main features.

Action plan

There is no doubt, being able to supply images – be it pictures, maps or an infographic – will dramatically improve your chances of getting published. Now it is time to put all the key points covered in this chapter into action.

1. Having written a short travel piece as directed in Chapter 9's Action Plan, source at least three pictures from PR companies and create an infographic plus map to further enhance the layout and add impact to your article.
2. Those who have knowledge of Adobe InDesign can lay out out their travel feature and images, in the style of the target publication. This will help develop a stronger understanding that the images will make on a page and how they can improve audience engagement.
3. Now come up with an idea for a 800-word picture essay on a subject that will require photography skills. This might be a piece on street style, a festival coverage or local crafts. Identify a local target market, then research the story and take some pictures to accompany the piece. Before pitching to an editor – think about whether you can package any of the text content in a more creative format using a map, chart or infographic.

11 Copywriting and PR

Opportunities for working or freelancing in media have tripled since the millennium. Now most companies, non-profit organisations and government bodies have a press office or communications department, if not they outsource to agencies. All of which are tasked with providing adverts, press releases, in-house publications, social media updates and web posts – usually on a daily basis. This, of course, is in addition to the rise of customer publishing, where companies provide media across a range of platforms for their clients.

As a result, there is a vast array of content marketing opportunities for copywriters to provide a range of content for:

- adverts;
- advertorials/content marketing;
- promotional features for newspapers and magazines;
- blog posts;
- leaflets;
- eNewsletters;
- brochures;
- instruction sheets or booklets;
- training manuals;
- scripts for corporate videos or broadcast adverts.

However, with so many platforms to populate a more visual approach is needed – as covered in the previous chapter. Because of this, PR companies and agencies commissioning copywriters now prefer multi-skilled writers who can package information in an appealing way using infographics, graphs/charts, maps or timelines.

Good writing skills are equally essential. Today's copywriter must be able to produce information in a clear, engaging format but also have an in-depth understanding of journalism. This chapter explores the divisions between PR and advertising while also covering the essential skills a copywriter needs to thrive either as a staffer or freelance.

From journalism to PR

In these somewhat uncertain times (particularly for local newspapers) journalists are often tempted into publicity. Their contacts will be highly valued as will their expertise on rewriting clumsy press releases. But this is no easy transition. Moving into PR, journalists must learn new skills as rather than having one editor there are various groups to please including executives and in some instances board members. That can mean a lot of compromises.

To adapt, the journalist-turned-publicity-writer has to develop a sharper focus on the audience too. Although journalists are used to having a definite age group/social class/professional group in their sights, a publicity writer has a much wider scope. For example, looking at content from the perspective of a younger sister or friend's 19-year-old daughter if a young woman's perfume is being promoted, or a 60-year-old uncle if the subject is an insurance policy for those about to retire.

Marketing is very much research-led with surveys often being used to identify a market before copywriting briefs are developed. The ABC scale of readership provided by the National Readership Survey (NRS) will indicate how to pitch the message. Using the correct language and tone for the target audience is also crucial. For example, a promotional feature aimed at a trade journal should contain the amount of technical jargon appropriate for that particular audience.

Unlike a journalist who writes articles for the readers of his or her newspaper or magazine, the copywriter may be asked to write several versions of a press release. For example, if writing a press release on a new car, there are likely to be numerous target markets each with a different set of audience profiles such as:

- technical audiences such as specialist car magazines;
- employee publications for sales teams at dealerships;
- middle-aged upmarket drivers;
- young professionals;
- parents;
- the lower end of the market.

Also, different media platforms may be used for one campaign which may include peak-hour TV to get the main message to as many people as possible, followed perhaps by adverts in the broadsheet and tabloid papers. Then the content may need to be reworked as a promotional feature for selected magazines and Sunday supplements as well as online and social media posts – all highlighting the attractions of the message for each audience.

Advertising and PR defined

In a publicity campaign it can be hard to distinguish advertising from PR. Advertising sells, while PR informs. But the informing part can often mean selling an image or lifestyle as part of the process of marketing products, services or promoting a business. Therefore, the starting point is to clearly define both categories.

First, advertising, according to the IPA (Institute of Practitioners in Advertising), it is defined by the following three points:

1. Identifies a current problem/opportunity for a product, service or corporate brand.
2. Identifies the consumers who can best solve/create that problem/opportunity.
3. Creates the most relevant and distinctive way of communicating to them in creative and media terms.

In his book, *Confessions of an Advertising Man*, David Ogilvy quotes Dr Charles Edwards, from the graduate School of Retailing at New York University who stated: "The more facts you tell, the more you sell. An advertisement's chance for success invariably increases as the number of pertinent merchandise facts included in the advertisement increases" (Ogilvy, 2011, p125). This is a useful point for copywriters to remember. When creating advertising copy a writer seeks direct action from the audience in terms of buying into something – be it a product, service or brand. Therefore, including sufficient facts to provoke such an action is key.

Next is the definition of PR – or public relations, which the CIPR (Chartered Institute of Public Relations) defines as follows:

> Public Relations is about reputation – the result of what you do, what you say and what others say about you. Public Relations is the discipline which looks after reputation, with the aim of earning understanding and support and influencing opinion and behaviour. It is the planned and sustained effort to establish and maintain goodwill and mutual understanding between an organisation and its publics.
>
> (CIPR)

Always define the category for which you are writing copy, because being a successful copywriter depends on keeping within those boundaries. To simplify, if it's advertising, you are selling, but with PR the focus should be on influencing or raising awareness.

Research is key

Whether it's advertising or PR work, the publicity writer needs to do the subject and market research that journalists do and often much more. The industry or activity being written about must be studied, which means accessing the right publications and online sources. It may also mean visiting trade fairs, factories or manufacturers and interviewing industrialists, managers, workers.

To get an advert or a press release or a promotional feature into a publication the writer must also research the target publications. It's crucial to understand the type of content a target publication wants and who its reader is. Media kits – often found on the publisher's website under the title's brand – are invaluable as they contain useful background information and sometimes an editorial calendar detailing timings of key or seasonal themes.

Advertising copywriting

An advertising agency seeking a commission will, after some research, pitch a "strategy". This identifies the essentials such as:

- the target audience;
- media outlets that will provide access to that audience (target publications, etc);
- an overview of a proposed advertising campaign;
- list of expenses (for example, any surveys that will be needed); together with an estimate of fees.

It's a sophisticated form of the journalist's pitch, to ensure that the agency and client are on the same wavelength. A copywriter's role in this situation is to provide the words for the campaign, whether it's a native advertising approach or the more traditional advert. With the range of platforms available that could be a short web banner ad, an advert for the print and digital edition of a magazine or newspaper, a post on social media or a native advertising script for a radio or TV advert. For the latter, the copywriter will need to be able to create a story – think Tesco Food Love Stories such as *Nana's Magic Soup* for example.

Whatever the platform, an advert must grab the reader's attention, arouse desire (or stimulate interest in the proposition), sustain interest, provoke to action – perhaps to buy something, join a society or club, vote or donate money. However, advertising space is expensive, so words must be used economically.

Slogans with impact

Creating a slogan that has impact requires a similar approach to writing a great headline. Inspiration can often be found in newspaper and magazine headlines. Alliteration, rhymes, puns, catchphrases, references to song or film titles are among the devices.

For a poster or full-page advert a slogan – or hashtag – with a picture is enough. Here are a few famous ones that have become embedded in society. From sports and insurance to beauty and politics, as well as being part of a high-profile advertising campaign these phrases have become part of a brand's DNA – even if it is a political party.

- Nike – *Just Do It*
- Zurich – *Because Change Happens*
- Tesco – *Every Little Helps*
- Always – *#LikeaGirl*
- L'Oreal – *Because You're Worth It*

Copywriting and PR

- Obama – *YES WE CAN*
- Labour Party – *FOR THE MANY NOT THE FEW*

So, what is the key to a successful slogan? First, it must reflect the era, some buzz words date quickly as journalists know. Avoid using an idea that can be held up for ridicule should things go wrong such as the 2017 Conservative Party's General Election campaign tag line of *Strong, stable leadership*. Also, don't use a slogan similar to that of rival brand as the advert may draw more attention to itself than the product.

The message in all advertising copywriting should be reduced as far as possible to the USP (unique selling point), the one concept or idea that will persuade the audience to buy.

Developing the idea

The process of composition, from knowledge about the product, through selection of subject matter, to proposition or image, has close parallels with the process of developing ideas for features described in Chapter 3. A slogan or catchphrase for an advert which neatly encapsulates the idea may come early, just as a title may come quickly to a feature writer.

However, research for a 200-word advert to identify the audience and gain an understanding of the subject may need to be more extensive than for that of a 1,000-word article. Copywriters might, where appropriate, visit factories – for example, to see the manufacturing of computers, cars, perfume or clothes if those are the products they are writing about.

It may be useful to adopt the five Ws approach to such research. For example, suppose you are given a brief to write a short advert to promote the launch of a new electric bicycle. The first task is to establish the key points of the campaign, which can be done by using Who, What, Why, Where and When as illustrated in Figure 11.1.

As Figure 11.1 demonstrates, by asking questions using those five Ws, a writer can quickly determine the essential components for advert copy.

From PR to journalism

Publicity writing that aims to get past editors into the editorial pages of newspapers and magazines must be regarded as journalism. Whether working on press

Figure 11.1 Processing the five Ws (Hogarth, 2018)

releases, specially written PR-orientated features, editorial of in-house journals promoting a company, writers must behave as journalists. Therefore, PR pieces need to contain news values and should also fulfil all the other requirements of good journalism.

Press releases

These should be divided into two categories: hard news and trade. A hard news release will contain news of value for a newspaper or magazine. For example, a new electric car company is launching in the UK. This will result in 2,000 new manufacturing jobs in the West Midlands, which – according to the Office for National Statistics – has one of the highest unemployment rates in the country.

Though the main purpose of the release will be to promote the product, the news value must be projected first. If the press release is aimed at local and national editors where there are employment gains which will have a significant impact on the area, then it must be adapted to reflect those gains. Whereas for a trade magazine, the innovatory qualities of the product may become the news value.

Getting copy past editors

To get published a good press release, whether it's for a national, regional or local market, must be angled as a valid news story with a good strapline to get the editor's attention. Avoid the hard sell in terms of the product, event or item, if you don't the press release will be passed to the advertising sales team as a lead.

I receive numerous press releases from members in my capacity as a communications specialist on the Executive Committee of the Dorchester Chamber for Business (a voluntary role). Many of these are poorly written plugs with little or no real news content, which would probably be binned or resigned to the slush pile if sent to a news desk of the local paper. It is worth noting that many small businesses have little knowledge of how to write for the media, meaning there are many opportunities out there for copywriters.

Furthermore, I suspect that many good stories buried in a poorly written press release are missed, which is a shame. Therefore, to minimise the chances of being consigned to the slush pile, writers should always: a) find out where and to whom to send the press release; and b) focus only on the news aspects relevant to that publication. Here are a few pointers for writing successful press releases:

- **Label it:** "Press Release" should be used in the email subject box. The Word document should also have "Press Release" at the top followed by the suggested headline underneath.
- **Make it relevant:** only target media outlets where the press release will be relevant to that audience.
- **Make an impact:** come up with a suitable newsworthy headline in the style of your target publication.

- **Follow a news story format:** use the pyramid format and *Who, What, Why, Where, When* and *How.*
- **Write a compelling intro:** put all the crucial information in the first two paragraphs.
- **Be accurate:** all content must be carefully fact-checked.
- **Include interviews and case studies:** with the right people, such as experts or those involved.
- **Use strong quotes:** a couple of carefully chosen quotes will add impact.
- **Keep to the facts:** the story must be tightly written with no waffle or opinion.
- **Don't forget pictures:** include high resolution (300dpi) images relating to the story where possible.
- **Note to the editor:** should be included at the end of the press release along with relevant contact details.

Example of a press release

Earlier this year, Dorchester Chamber for Business held a collaborative breakfast networking event at our local college to promote trade and enterprise. The Chamber was keen to get publicity following the event to raise its profile, so I compiled the following press release targeting the business section of our local newspaper, *The Daily Echo.*

PRESS RELEASE

Dorchester chamber focuses on employability

More than 60 members attended the Dorchester Chamber for Business July breakfast hosted by Kingston Maurward, which featured an educational theme, focusing on the Chamber's Retain & Retrain campaign.

Sponsored by Kingston Maurward and Keep 106, the event provided an opportunity for wider community to find out more about local initiatives underway to support young people.

During his speech to members, Steve Farnham, President of Dorchester Chamber for Business, reinforced how important education and the young workforce are to the future of Dorchester Chamber and Dorchester generally. "It was great to hear that Kingston Maurwood and the Dorset Studio School are leading initiatives to train the young who are looking for an alternative learning path with more focus on practical and land-based skills."

"We are also proud that one of our members can boast a National Apprenticeship Award winner and are delighted to congratulate Benji Reid on achieving that accolade," said Steve.

He added that we need to encourage young people demonstrating that they can achieve the best skills, qualifications, and training right here in Dorchester and that businesses in the town can fulfil their career aspirations. "It is not only the young that need training – with the ever-changing climate we are keen to help Dorchester Chamber members receive the training they need to stay afresh and ahead of the game."

Key speakers at the breakfast included Luke Rake, Principal, Kingston Maurward, Steve Bulley, Dorchester Chamber who reinforced the importance of the Chamber's Retain and Retrain campaign. Other speakers were DCCI's Young Chamber, Annetta Minard, Headteacher of Dorset Studio School, Christopher Moyse, Blueberry Wealth, Apprentice of the Year winner Benjamin Reid from Advanced Business Administration.

Exec Member Steve Bulley, who is also Head of Business Engagement at Dorset Chamber, said: "Dorchester Chamber for Business is keen to provide appropriate and relevant training for members and their staff – as we all have the ability to grow our knowledge base."

"As part of the affiliation with Dorset Chamber and on the theme of education there will be a major Careers Fair this September at the BIC in Bournemouth with over 4,000 students attending."

After a sumptuous breakfast, there was an extended networking period. In addition, both members and non-members had the opportunity to meet with Dorchester Chamber Executive members on a one-to-one basis to discuss requirements regarding training and any support they would like the Chamber to provide.

PHOTOS

Photo credit: Chamber's official photographer, SKC Photography. For captions please see image file names.

The story, *Business breakfast held at Kingston Maurward College*, was published in the business news section of the *Daily Echo* in print and online. It was deemed newsworthy by the editor for two reasons.

1 First, because the story mostly revolved around the Chamber's Retain & Retrain campaign encouraging local initiatives to support young people, who often in rural areas struggle to find meaningful employment and therefore often move away.
2 Second, the impact of growing local talent is newsworthy as it is likely to encourage economic growth in the long term.

Adapting to different markets

A new building company has been established to exploit a central heating system using solar energy. The system is about to be launched with demonstrations in newly built model houses in large towns throughout the country. Plastics and other materials are used that are cheaper than traditional building materials. Labour costs for building the average three-bedroom house will be greatly reduced.

For a national newspaper, the news peg is likely to be the prospect of a revolution (but be careful of that word: radical change?) in the house-building industry. The regional papers will want to cover the nearest demonstration in a town. Trade magazines that cover solar energy and plastics will expect the more technical information that will interest their readers.

This release could be adapted for several markets (after the necessary research) by changing only the heading and the first paragraph. The news value would be expressed in those places, and then the interesting facts ordered in a way that would suit all those different markets. The story must be of intrinsic interest to the general reader of the target publication, while the facts should be sufficient to highlight the merits of the product. Avoid superlatives ("excellent", "world-beating", "unique") and emotive adjectives ("lovely", "fabulous").

Writers of releases must think hard about what people need or want to know, no matter what the subject – whether it's a cycle to work pilot scheme or an initiative to encourage regeneration of the high street. But sometimes a news peg may have to be manufactured perhaps by tapping into celebrity culture using a picture of a celeb trying out the pilot scheme.

Trade releases

When writing a press release for a B2B or trade publication, it must be tailored to the publication's specific editorial news values and pillars. For example, some trade magazines will have an audience of garden equipment retailers serving owners of small gardens, while others have an audience of retailers of heavier equipment for parks.

Writers working for a manufacturer of garden equipment trying to get releases published may have to adapt them for those two markets or write two separate releases as each audience is likely to have a different set of needs. For example, readers with a small garden may be interested in extra-close mowing, while the council employee maintaining a park will be more focused in performance. In this instance those five W questions when compiling the press release might include:

- Who will benefit from a certain product?
- What questions are readers likely to ask about the product?

As with most aspects of writing, there isn't a one-size-fits-all method when writing press releases. To get the best results take an individual approach and think about the necessary information from the editor's perspective.

Obtaining publicity work

There are numerous copywriting courses for journalists including those run by the Press Association and Journalism.co.uk but you can train yourself too by analysing examples. There are many press release models from PR companies which are available online and can be found by going to the news or press page on a company's website. Study the format and have a go at rewriting them for different publications or markets.

Job opportunities for PR copywriting are posted online and in the press, but once you have an adequate portfolio, advertise your services. When offering writing services, find out the name and job title of the most appropriate person to talk to – Promotions director? Publicity director? Sales promotion manager? Marketing manager? Advertising manager? Titles vary greatly, however, make a great first impression by getting the right person and using their correct title.

Before making an approach, do your research. This will enable you to pitch your writing skills in a professional way by highlighting relevant specialisms that might be of value – if you have a background in IT or specialist knowledge of product development for example. *Campaign* and *Marketing Week* make good hunting grounds for pre-pitch background information as they give copious news about publicity firms and the key players.

Whether chasing a full-time staff job or seeking freelance assignments, increase your chances by providing a portfolio of published work such as promotional features, campaigns or adverts, etc., and building a professional profile on platforms such as LinkedIn. If seeking freelance work it might be worth approaching the promotions or publicity director of a business organisation or the director of an advertising agency. Websites such as *HollisPR* or *BRAD INSIGHT*, have a wealth of information and potential contacts. However, access to these resources is expensive and therefore is best accessed via a university or public library.

Try obtaining commissions from the agencies and consultancies rather than directly from client companies. That will save you time spent looking for work. The disadvantage is that you have lost some independence, you are further removed from the client – and have to depend on the agency briefing you well.

Building your portfolio

Develop an online portfolio and ask clients for testimonials. A strong portfolio should contain samples of various kinds of work across a range of platforms to demonstrate adaptability. It's worth investing in a basic website and domain name as this will provide a platform to advertise your services, showcase successful projects or campaigns and include client testimonials.

Once you become knowledgeable about a particular business or industry, organise your workload accordingly. Suppose you build up expertise in the hotel and catering business. You might then have such long-term projects as books, both general interest (*The World's Most Unusual Hotels*), with ideas for spin-off articles, and specialised (*New Ideas in Hotel Organization*). Shorter-term projects might include brief career guides in hospitality for publishers' series and educational texts on related subjects such as hotels for pets, elite customer service or a guide to understanding hotel management.

Specialist services

There is a wealth of opportunities for specialists. Many writers don't categorise themselves as having specialist knowledge, when in fact they do. For example, students often gain insights into a variety of industries such as hospitality or retail through part-time jobs to fund their studies. This provides an opportunity to develop expertise. For those with expert knowledge – be it on interior design, IT, finance, alternative therapies or sports – who have had articles published, there are corporate clients who might be interested to hear from you.

As a sideline, travel writers often obtain commissions to write brochures or blog posts for travel providers. Writers for trade – or B2B – magazines are likely to secure copywriting assignments aimed at those markets.

Fees are generally much higher for publicity work than for journalism and can produce a welcome additional income stream for the freelance feature writer. However, with regard to fees, it is worth considering whether to secure a contract for each assignment or work on a retainer basis. The latter of course offers a more regular income.

> ### Case study: a copywriter's career journey
>
> *Copywriter Jackie Barrie started out as a journalist but admitted finding a job was tough. "After training as a journalist, the only job I could get was writing product descriptions for Freemans catalogue. Every inch of space counts in the home shopping world, and this discipline taught me everything I needed to know about selling off the page or screen."*
>
> *After working her way up to senior management level, Jackie was seconded to the marketing department to head an internal communications and rebranding project and it was this that led to her freelance career.*
>
> "Once the secondment was over, my old job wasn't available, so I became a project manager in the creative department. I felt crushed that I wasn't writing anymore, so when the chance came to take redundancy, I grabbed it, but then struggled to find another writing job."
>
> As is so often the case, her struggle resulted in a successful freelance career in copywriting, specialising in marketing communications. She produces copy for websites, newsletters and blogs as well as brochures, sales letters and leaflets. After going freelance in 2001, Jackie – who has survived two recessions – expanded her business into training and speaking.
>
> When it comes to getting started, Jackie says writers need to "get out there, and get networking" as that is how she built her business. "Today, I get almost all my work through repeats, referrals and recommendations. I can trace over 90 per cent of new enquiries back to someone I once met, somewhere, sometime. The rest is thanks to SEO, my website and social media."
>
> Developing your personal brand, she says, is crucial, because when you're an expert, people choose you because you're you, not because of the business name you trade under. But how easy is it to get in front of the right people and where should a novice start?

"Attend your local breakfast networking meetings, Chamber of Commerce events, and/or business seminars. Make friends with web designers, graphic designers and printers – anyone who might share clients with you." However, she emphasises the importance of avoiding a hard sell, instead recommending building relationships with potential referrers where you get to know, like and trust each other.

"Once people understand the value you add, they'll refer you."

Jackie also suggests getting a pricing buddy as it's easy to undercharge when starting out, revealing that she used to put a quote together then email it to her buddy. "She would double it and email it back. I would then save the email as a draft, thinking: *I can't possibly send that quote, it's far too expensive.* The next morning, I would hit 'send and receive all' without realising, and the email would whoosh off to the prospective client. And … they would *always* accept."

Getting half the fee upfront is also a must and expected, says Jackie. "I don't write a word for any new client until I get their 50 per cent advance cleared in my bank account. This is a *normal* request for copywriters. Not one client has refused to pay. If a job is delayed over 30 days after the first draft is submitted, my T&Cs [Terms and Conditions] allow me to invoice another 25 per cent. Because – as we all know – most of the effort is in the first draft. Then, if a job never gets finished through no fault of my own, at least I've been paid three-quarters of my fee, which is a fair reflection of the work so far."

Refusing to discount your fees is not only good advice but sound business practice. "The only time it's worth giving a discount is when you are getting something in return such as a testimonial or payment in full upfront, otherwise you are just giving money away."

Freebies can often be a tricky area to navigate particularly for novices. It often requires a combination of care and skilled negotiating. However, Jackie's recommendation is to always invoice for any free advice or taster written for a potential client. "Send a zero-balance invoice quoting your usual price discounted by 100 per cent. That way, they appreciate the value of what they've received, and won't tell their friends and contacts that you'll help them for nothing."

What are her three pieces of advice she wishes she had been given when starting out?

1 Collect case studies and testimonials from day one, because third party endorsements sell you better than anything you can say about yourself.
2 Ask the source of every new enquiry. That way you'll know which bits of your marketing works (so you continue with those), and those that don't (you can drop those).
3 Understand the difference between turnover and profit. It may look as though you're making lots of money, but the only money that counts is what's left for you to spend.

Getting listed on copywriting directories is also prudent, says Jackie, who runs a Facebook copywriting group called Copywriter Club. She also recommends the following resources:

- **ProCopywriters (www.procopywriters.co.uk):** the UK's largest association for commercial writers, which offers support, networking and work-finding opportunities.
- **Copywriter Collective (www.copywritercollective.co.uk):** Europe's leading agency for freelance copywriters and creatives. However, to join, writers must have a minimum of five years' experience.
- **Social media:** there are numerous groups to support newbies on Facebook, and it's also worth joining professional groups on LinkedIn.

Techniques for publicity writing

Here are the four essential qualities of publicity writing. As with all aspects of writing the more you practise the better your copy will get.

1 **Descriptive:** avoid too many adjectives and adverbs and choose adjectives for precision. If you say a product is "truly amazing", the "truly" casts doubt on the "amazing", a word that has been drastically devalued anyway. Find one precise adjective that will convince. Give the burden of meaning to nouns and verbs. Description means making the reader see, hear, smell, taste, touch. Avoid abstractions.
2 **Narrative:** putting the meaning into verbs will help keep the story moving. Saying what happened is essential. Initial thoughts, plans, problems, how it began and how it progressed may not be.
3 **Exposition:** avoid over-long sentences. Planning your piece is essential when explaining something. Make a checklist to make sure no important fact has been omitted. What kind of order is required – chronological or logical? Who is the target audience? How readily will they understand? How technical can you be? What exactly is being explained? Does the audience have to understand how to carry out a procedure or merely have an idea as to how a machine works? Avoid a confusing mixture of pronouns: "one", "he", "you", etc. Consider using the passive. Punctuation is important: a comma in the wrong place can completely change the meaning.
4 **Argument/persuasion:** in news releases and persuasive articles the facts must be marshalled clearly and in good order to support the proposition. There's a tendency to "knock" the opposition simplistically in some releases. It's better to talk generally about the dangers or difficulties that have been surmounted by a new product or service, and concentrate on its positive virtues. In most writing aimed at persuasion it's useful to anticipate objections/criticisms before going on to the virtues. State improvements realistically. To repeat: the facts will convince if they are good enough. Superlatives rarely convince.

Action plan

Before attempting to land your first client it is essential to practise the copywriting skills outlined in this chapter by undertaking the following four steps. Only then will you be ready to embark on your journey as a freelance copywriter.

1. **Analyse and rewrite adverts:** choose a full-page advert in a newspaper or magazine that is quite wordy. Evaluate the content noting the main points then rewrite it. Come up with a strong tag line or USP and ensure the revised advert makes a strong impact. Practice makes perfect, so repeat the exercise a few times to improve your skills.
2. **Practise writing press releases:** for each of the following, targeting both your local paper and the county magazine:
   - The opening of a new shop and café specialising in sustainable local produce.
   - A council-led initiative to improve facilities in your town or village.
   - A talk and book signing with your favourite author in the nearest main bookshop.
   - The launch of a new literary or music festival.
3. **Get experience:** start developing a professional copywriting portfolio by offering to do some pro-bono work for a charity or voluntary organisation. Set up a website to showcase your growing portfolio and client testimonials.
4. **Build your profile:** start by developing a website to showcase your growing portfolio and client testimonials, also set up a LinkedIn profile to widen your network and register with professional networking sites and freelance groups.

12 Specialist features, columns and reviews

Most experienced writers will have a natural leaning towards a subject, for me it was profiles and interview pieces. At the time, I was working on a writing magazine and had a passion for fiction, soon a clear specialism began to evolve – profile pieces on high-profile authors. However, I also had another interest in websites, at a time when widespread awareness of the Internet was starting to emerge. Out of this interest came a regular monthly column in the magazine. I remember pitching the idea tentatively to the editor and publisher, who welcomed it but outlined a set of strict criteria for the first few pieces. Within a few months the column became successful and I was left to craft it how I chose.

Whether a writer's focus evolves into a specialist subject, column writing or reviews it is essential to learn the nuances of that particular specialism and hone your skills accordingly. Study successful journalists, columnists and reviewers, but make it an ongoing process. Simply reading one or two pieces is not enough. Read a variety of work every week across a range of publications, noting how writers keep their ideas relevant and fresh.

Wide reading is a must, no matter what area a writer focuses on. Columnists can become stale after a long series, while occasional bias may creep into reviewer's copy. But if you take time to understand the pitfalls of your chosen specialism from the start it is easier to avoid them. A natural curiosity – that essential journalistic trait – should keep a writer's mind fresh, without it stagnation will quickly set in. Keep your eyes open, as demonstrated in Chapter 3, ideas are everywhere – whether looking for angles for a column, comment piece or a specialist feature.

This chapter will guide you through the basics of developing a specialism, helping you to move forward, hone your skills and become a professional.

Part 1: Specialist features

Specialist feature writers will either have a wealth of knowledge in their chosen field from the start or develop it over time with experience and a database of experts. However, it's crucial to keep in mind that some expert professionals may have an agenda whether conceded or not. Therefore, regardless of who they are talking to, the writer must always fact-check and maintain a healthy scepticism. Of course, some specialists are experts who have turned to journalism, often as a part-time occupation. Such writers are highly valued by editors, especially if they have acquired journalistic skills and are able to write for the audience with a healthy mix of common sense, together with an avoidance of a narrow viewpoint and jargon.

Specialists are in demand to fill the regular slots, from the arts to zoology, across a range of publications and platforms. Some specialist writers may get their first break while working on a local paper perhaps covering for experts who are on annual leave then develop an interest. Over time such interest can often evolve into expertise. Once such expertise begins to emerge a writer may then opt to expand their market either by moving on to a staff job on a specialist title or by identifying coverage gaps elsewhere and pitching in a freelance capacity.

However, it is wise to remain versatile to some degree as specialisms (and those publications devoted to them) come and go because while some subjects remain constant such as politics and education for example, other areas can be more volatile. Over the years, various subjects have become fashionable from IT and alternative medicine to sports and nutrition only to fade when public interest moves on to the next trend. For this reason it is advisable to continue to write on other subjects from time to time so as not to become too pigeon-holed.

Whether a freelance or a staff writer developing the necessary skills to become a professional writer in your chosen specialism is crucial. Hence, while some of the techniques described in this chapter have been covered in previous chapters, the focus here is on how to adapt those skills with regards to specialist writing. This includes:

- finding opportunities;
- devising a publishing strategy;
- pitching to specialist or niche titles;
- research techniques;
- structure and style.

Finding opportunities

With a wealth of data continually bombarding social media and inboxes 24/7 – be it as emails, newsletters or links – many experts find it hard to manage the flood of information. This is where specialists come in as they have the skills to discard the dross and quickly get to those essential core points, then repackage the content in a clear, concise format ready to be disseminated to the audience.

However, there are also numerous other writing opportunities such as reports, eBooks, manuals, brochures and publicity materials for government departments, associations, business and non-profit organisations as well as producing material for PR companies.

Technology has also made it much easier for writers and journalists to work from anywhere, at any time. Networking and finding work has also been simplified with the help of professional online directories and of course LinkedIn. So look for other writing opportunities.

Keeping ahead in your field

Specialist writers keep up to date with the latest developments in their area of expertise. Those not teaching or actively engaged in the area must ensure that they keep ahead of developments. This can be done through following relevant organisations or figureheads on social media, keeping in touch with various networks or groups, listening to podcasts, documentaries, reading reports and other relevant literature.

Updates and developments can be found in newspaper supplements, specialist magazines, blogs as well as scripts of radio and TV documentaries if available. Always check on indexes to articles such as the Humanities Index, *The Times Index* and *Willing's Press Guide*, etc. These will guide you to recently published pieces.

It's also worth noting on which days the quality papers such as *The Times*, *The Guardian* and *The Telegraph* include a supplement covering your subject. For example, *The Times* has a daily supplement (*Times 2*) covering lifestyle, the arts and health, *The Guardian* also has a daily supplement (*G2*) with similar coverage to *T2*. The weekend (Saturday and Sunday) packages of the qualities are bulky, with a broad range of supplements from business, property and money to sport, travel, driving, food and gardening. *The Week*, published by Dennis Publishing Ltd, provides a weekly round-up of the features on the arts as well as providing a briefing on national and global news stories.

A publishing strategy

The research results or latest developments reported in specialist journals can form the core of features for mainstream newspapers, magazines or websites. A rule-of-thumb principle for finding information or a story in one kind of publication and adapting for another is to go more than one level up or down in the market. For example, medical specialists can more easily use the research material of *The Lancet* for an article in *Woman's Own* or their local paper than for such professional magazines as *GP*, *Pulse*, *Doctor* or *Modern Medicine*. For the middle-range professional magazines are likely to be aware of the contents of the more specialised journals.

Conversely, the same medical specialists will find interestingly angled stories in the popular markets that they will know how to develop with a little research. A story about an elderly person surviving laser surgery will send them through the specialised geriatric journals for detailed coverage of the subject. They may obtain material to rework in several ways – for a technical publication, one of the health magazines, or for magazines for the elderly like *Saga*, or for those who care for them.

To define your publishing strategy for specialist features make two lists:

1 The sort of features you think you could write.
2 The gaps you perceive in the market.

Pitching to specialist publications

Specialist publications have a clearly defined editorial policy for their audience – and that's why they need in-depth analysis. Ideas for specialist features are often developed in-house and may require careful briefing from the editor and even some reworking following the initial submission. Don't neglect to analyse the specialist pages of newspapers and general interest magazines.

Here are some dos and don'ts with regards to identifying gaps and pitching:

- Don't invade the territory of well-established contributors, unless you've identified a neglected aspect.
- Demonstrate that you have studied the target publication and know its editorial pillars.
- Angle your proposal specifically for the readership.
- Include an *About me* paragraph at the end of the pitch indicating your background, experience and subject expertise.
- Read through a few back issues of your target publication so that you don't pitch ideas that have been covered recently.

Do re-read Chapter 5 on pitching to maximise your chances of success. Remember first impressions count. If your pitch doesn't demonstrate that you have an in-depth understanding of the publication's editorial pillars and readership, the commissioning editor will reject it.

Producing specialist features

What are the special considerations, in terms of content, structure and style? How will you develop the content? First, your approach to content must take into account the vast differences in the needs of specialist markets. Business-to-business publications will be happy with features that can assume readers' interest for the subject's sake. However, for general and more popular publications the angle will need to impinge more practically on the lives of its readers.

While there are subtle differences between markets, the following approach to content should underlie any piece of specialist journalism:

- **Pitch information at the right level:** for example, suppose you are describing a solar plant in operation. At the popular level the aim will be to make the reader appreciate how the plant works, probably with the help of simple analogies, anecdotes and perhaps simple diagrams or other illustrations. If addressing solar plant engineers there will be complex scientific/technical explanations. Yet there are many levels in between. The level of discussion will determine which facts you select, which technical terms you use, which you will explain, which processes you describe.
- **Remove misconception:** sometimes it is necessary for definitions, fruitful explanation, argument and some discussion. An example of this can be found in an article published in the *Chicago Tribune* titled *Astronomer believes Aids*

has far-out origin by Sir Fred Hoyle and Professor Chandra Wickramsingh which listed some of the mythical origins of the Aids disease including Haitian pigs, African green monkeys, God and Russians in chemical warfare labs, in order to dispel such untruths.
- **Illustrate points in various ways:** a verbal explanation may not be enough. This is where an infographic or technical illustration can prove a valuable addition to an article by providing a visual explanation. Verbal illustration may also be necessary using a simple example, analogy, anecdote or quote, such as an endurance athlete needs to consume between 3,000 and 4,000 calories a day, or the lens aperture of a camera is like the pupil of an eye, dilating or contracting in proportion to the light, and so on.
- **Interpret information by relating it to people:** identify likely benefits but if appropriate warn about the possible dangers of discoveries, developments and processes. The education specialist, for instance, might consider the wider implications of the implementation of current education policies such as university tuition fees or the new GCSE grading. Writers on emerging technologies might warn of the hazards of driverless cars or the potential risks posed by 3-D printing.

Shape your copy

Specialist features are read by those eager for information, explanation or instruction in order to get ahead in their field. Information must be organised so that it's easy to take in, refer to and remember. Therefore, your approach should be to:

- **Select points and structure them carefully, using sub-headings if necessary:** don't make the text too dense. In *how-to* features of fair complexity readers will put up with some repetition (but not with digression) because it gives them breathers as they busily ingest all the information, so long as there's a steady progression.
- **Anticipate readers' questions:** create a list of potential questions readers might have, then put them in an order that will create a logical progression. This should provide a good outline to follow.
- **Suggest solutions to problems, or raise the most important questions:** make intelligent predictions about the future – this is often a good way to end a feature.

Use the right language

Take care to get the approach to content and structure right; however, avoid ineffective language as this can undermine your content. A way to do this is to check for the three "Cs":

1 clarity;
2 conciseness;
3 coherence.

Words:
- Is every word necessary, immediately comprehensible? Will any of the jargon need to be explained? Would a glossary be useful?

Sentences:
- Is every sentence relevant, comprehensible at first reading?

Structure:
- Are the sentences and paragraphs in the best order for effective description, explanation or instruction?

Figure 12.1 Words, sentences and structure grid

Note that the three Cs check should be undertaken at the editing stage and must be applied to your article as a whole – from individual words to sentences and paragraphs. Also use the words, sentences and structure grid in Figure 12.1 as a checklist when editing your work.

Beware of jargon

The Cambridge Dictionary defines jargon as *special words and phrases that are used by particular groups of people, especially in their work*. Explain a term, abbreviation or acronym if you think readers will not understand it, but do so unobtrusively so as not to bore others. However, for specialist audiences it is fine to assume they will be familiar with key industry terms. For example, readers of *InPublishing Magazine* will understand magazine publishing terms such as ABC1 (a readership of a magazine that falls in a certain category), CPM (cost per thousand) or the PPA (Professional Publisher's Association). However, if you are adapting the article for a general interest publication then it would be sensible to define such terms.

Other definitions of jargon are "debased language" and "gibberish". This refers to the unacceptable jargon developed by some trades or professions as a kind of slang with which only those initiated feel at ease, and which can keep others at a distance. Such examples can be found in the health sector – the NHS's "ACP" (advanced care plan), "ATO" (assistant theatre operator). Then of course, there's legal terminology such as "Bona vacantia" (goods or an estate belonging to nobody) or "Plenipotentiary" (a person given complete authority to act).

Always write with clarity – whatever the phase or terminology make sure your readers are familiar with it – if not provide a definition.

Research and fact-checking

The British Library's *Research in British Universities*, in several volumes, gives details of research projects being undertaken in the UK, together with the names of experts in specialist subjects. The various *Abstracts* (*Horticultural, Psychological*, etc.) summarise the most significant of recent academic texts. You should also have access to the directories listing members of your profession or trade, with details of their work, such as *The Medical Directory*.

Use constant legwork in terms of making and keeping up to date with a strong network of contacts to bring people into your expertise circle who you can contact for an update, chat or interview. This will avoid a rehashing of old themes from research materials.

Specialist features need scrupulous research and fact-checking. However much of a professional you are, you will depend at different times on interviews/quotes from experts in different disciplines that impinge on your subject, from the people in the middle (the care workers, for example) and from the people at the receiving end (the patients, for example). Always look for different angles to approach the truth. It's advisable to get significant interviewees to check your script (to ensure the facts are right, the quotes accurate).

The much-in-demand medical/health features can be a minefield. Readers will depend on the information and advice given, especially if you're a regular writer. Therefore, you need to be able to assess and verify the value to readers of information gathered online, from printed sources, new products publicity, interviews, and so on. Direct quotation may constitute a violation of medical ethics. Indirect speech and cautious summarising are sometimes advisable: "cure", "breakthrough" and suchlike words should be avoided.

Specialists new to journalism may not be sufficiently aware how much information from apparently reliable sources can be inaccurate. It's worth noting that errors are repeated in newspapers for years. Press releases and other materials from organisations may contain errors of fact and wrong spellings of names. Faulty grammar can also result in misleading content.

Thus, it is vital to develop a network of expert contacts and links with the relevant professional organisations in your subject area.

Case study: advice from a feature specialist

Chris Wheal is an award-winning freelance journalist, editor and trainer who specialises in business and finance features. He has written for numerous publications from mainstream, to B2B and specialist markets and says the main thing about having a specialism is that you can earn more money.

"There are fewer journalists in finance, for example," says Chris, adding that most journos come from arts backgrounds so anyone who can understand percentages and accounts and interest rates etc. is in demand. "The skills are the same — ask other people to explain things 'in a language our readers will understand' (which is code for 'in a language I might understand')."

Here he shares some of the secrets of his success and offers invaluable advice on avoiding the pitfalls.

Despite a degree in Modern European Studies and a thesis on the influence of the Spanish Civil war on three artists, Picasso, Dali and Miro, my first job was on *Electronics Weekly*. With no experience, instead of sending a CV I produced a four-page magazine about myself, which got me the interview.

After that, I was set a test to rewrite two press releases into stories. Not understanding VLSI (very large scale integrated circuit boards), I found an electronics engineer and offered to buy him drinks if he would explain all the technical terms, give me some background information as well as tell me about other competitors in the sector. There was no Google or Internet back then, so this had to be done in person.

And so began my career in specialist features. I won my first award on *The Engineer*; since then I have won awards for features in *The Guardian*, plus business and consumer magazines, as well as websites. After being made redundant from *The Engineer* magazine I became features editor of *Public Finance*, covering local government, NHS, education, housing and utilities' finances — their accounts, their spending, government funding and the markets. One of the first things I did was get a big financial firm to lay on a morning of training on financial terms.

The key is to explain what you don't know to people then to get them to explain it to you. Jargon should always be explained. When interviewing experts, a favourite of mine was to say: "Our readers come from all different backgrounds and sectors so may not be familiar with all the terms and jargon so please try to explain it in a language all our readers would understand." That usually got people to simplify it enough.

Having left *Public Finance* to be editor of *European Chemical News* I was sacked before starting. And so began my freelance career, since then I have edited three magazines, including *Insurance Times*, supplements in *The Guardian* and several websites, including *AOL Money*. Writing for online markets is different — you need to consider listicles and more direct intros that work for search engines and clickbait and SEO etc. There can be no delay drop intros, for example.

The skills in specialist journalism are the same as in any other form of reporting or feature writing. However, being an expert it's essential to keep up to date with developments, the best way to do this is to meet people. Go to events, conferences and awards because there is no substitute for meeting people, shaking their hand and swapping business cards as when you call or email them they will know who you are. Make contacts on

LinkedIn immediately even if you think that contact may never be useful – at some point in the future they might be.

So what have I learned along the way?

It's useful to meet other journalists and bounce ideas off them. Call, email, What'sApp or Facebook contacts often just so you are always in the loop when something new happens. Read what other people are writing. Use RSS feeds and Twitter to keep up – there may be a specific social media platform, group or page for your sector. For example, Telegram and Reddit for Blockchain and cryptocurrency news. Often new sites can contain huge amounts of great information not available from traditional publishers.

With specialist features, you need more sources than for lighter subjects. There will be differing perspectives on subjects within the industry so always seek out the differing voices. For example, there is a Charted Institute of Taxation and an Institute of Indirect Taxation and an Institute of Revenues Rating and Valuation, which covers the council tax and rates. Sometimes that means a trade association has no position on a subject because its members cannot agree. But, that does not mean there is nobody out there who will speak to you. The Bank of England Monetary Policy Committee rarely unanimously agrees on interest rates. Find the dissenting voices.

Statistics, a report or official data will often prove an invaluable addition to research. However, a specialist must be able to analyse, display and explain data. Crucially, data can be interpreted in many ways and some politicians will present data in a misleading way, so always be on guard. It's worth noting that you can even make money just from your data analysis. I did a piece for *Post Mag* where I came up with the data and rough idea for an infographic. I only wrote a few hundred words but was paid for more than a thousand.

Avoid mistakes by scrupulous fact-checking. Go to Wikipedia and edit an entry to make it wrong. Just try it. It is so easy. I seriously recommend everyone try it – you may get banned but only for a short while. You will never then trust Wikipedia as a reliable source. Misspell someone's name and it will still appear with that spelling on a Google search, so find that person's company or personal a site or their LinkedIn page to check names.

Nobody minds you ringing them back to check something, or emailing a follow-up question because you are not clear. That is not a sign of weakness but a sign of strength.

As a specialist, you still get to interview celebrities and politicians. I have interviewed two UK prime ministers (John Major and Tony Blair), several chancellors of the Exchequer and many other MPs and EU ministers and other foreign dignitaries, including Lech Wałęsa, the leader of the Polish Solidarity union. I also did a series for *Local Government Chronicle* asking celebrities what they thought of their local council, which included actors, England cricketers and footballers, TV stars and many more. I then successfully pitched the idea to *The Guardian*.

> Lastly, understand that your reputation isn't your best piece, it's your worst. People will conveniently forget all your good pieces if you make one huge foul-up. And in a smaller market, even a small foul-up will get around the sector. A PR who has got you to admit a mistake and make a correction will tell all their clients along with many other PRs in the sector.
>
> No matter what, always try to leave a workplace or client on good terms. The people you meet on the way up you will also meet on the way down. You will be surprised how many people you used to work with – and perhaps who you thought were not great at their jobs or not likable – will turn up later in your career as a boss or with a commissioning budget (or as a PR from whom you need information).
>
> The B2B press remains among the best places to work in my experience and certainly a good springboard. Struggling though they are, like all advertising-funded media, they still aim to provide detailed, intelligent and informed features to their readers and they want to challenge their readers and hold the industries they cover to account. The last two people I hired as editor of *Insurance Times* left to join *The Times* and *The Telegraph*, for example. My predecessor on *Electronics Weekly* is still the BBC's science correspondent, Pallab Ghosh.

Part 2: The art of columns

Writing in *The Rotarian*, Hallam Walker Davis (1927) captured the essence of a good columnist stating:

> The good reporter and the good feature writer do not encourage us to enquire into things. Even the editorial writer does not often ask us to look on both sides. But the columnist is ever flipping things upside down and wrong side out and inviting us to look and laugh – and think even.

This is a poignant description of the columnist, whose job it is to challenge preconceived ideas and thinking patterns, while sometimes putting forward new ideas. In this vein a columnist has a licence to be rude, funny, satirical, prejudiced, provocative or philosophical: in one word, different, depending on the publication's formula and the editor's interpretation of it.

Editors like columns. They provide the security that all regular features provide – at least those spaces will be filled. Moreover, a regular column can bring depth and perspective to a publication. Columns can provoke thought, move to action, inspire, uplift, amuse, to a greater degree than other kinds of articles. Content ranges from lifestyle pieces, through to humorists, specialists and pundits – all with a great variety of styles and formats.

What editors value above all in the regular column is an individual voice. But they also want a columnist who can engage readers and inspire a response, thereby starting a conversation thread with the potential to go viral. This could be via social media, online, email or even letters in the post. With a big drive towards active audience participation, some columnists are now paid on the size of the social media following.

This section covers different kinds of columns, techniques for finding a slot and ways of working, followed by an insight offered by award-winning columnist Suzette Martinez Standring who shares her expertise.

Learning from the best

The presses are currently groaning under the weight of columnists famed in non-journalistic fields. When those fields provide expert knowledge the specialist columns that result can be admirable. Those of former stars in athletics and various sports come to mind, and if they get a little more help than usual from subs the results are ample justification.

When that fame has been derived from exposure in an entertainment industry the resulting column is often based on trivia. Amusing for a while, but often lacking in staying power evoking a "so what, who cares?" response. That said, a clever columnist who can capture and identify with readers is a powerful weapon for widening audience participation. One such example is Liz Jones, whose column, *Liz Jones's Diary*, for *The Mail on Sunday's You* Magazine has run for more than 15 years. So popular is her column, according to *Press Gazette* (Ponsford, 2018), that it receives between 4,000 and 6,000 responses a week. Her no-holds-barred weekly rant about the trials of her life clearly strikes a chord with a loyal following of readers.

However, such a phenomenon is rare. A column must come from within. It stands or falls by how strongly attracted readers are to:

- a writer's voice;
- angle on life;
- what the writer has to say that is either individual or from a unique perspective.

Columnists not only need to be interested in a variety of subjects but must have the desire and the energy to share that interest. The best columns have an urgent inevitability about them. But that doesn't often come easily, often only after much reading, thinking and several painful drafts.

Notice that a sentence or two out of the best columns are usually enough to identify the author. Study the best columnists to develop your techniques until your medium and message are inseparable.

You will find your own ways of learning from star columnists, but here is a workshop method to try. Cut out, screen shot or download columns that impress, then cut and paste sections or paragraphs and write specific notes on those techniques with which you identify such as:

- **The angle:** do the columnist's topics usually revolve around their lives and experiences, political or specialist issues or do they take a more general approach such as key discussions trending?
- **Type of intro:** is it chatty and informal or perhaps it takes a more serious approach with a formal tone?
- **Structure:** consider how the main body of the column is structured, then analyse a few of the writer's previous columns to see if the structure follows a similar format for each edition.
- **Use of quotes:** does the columnist include any quotes such as brief chats or interview style quotes to reinforce his or her point?
- **Anecdotes:** these can provide useful examples in a column. Does the writer use this technique? If so, note the type of anecdotes cited.
- **Ending:** pay particular attention to how the writer ends the column. Is it with a question, call to action or simply an observation?

Have a look at a few anthologies, notably *The Penguin Book of Columnists* (1998), edited by Christopher Silvester, which includes American and Australian columnists as well as British; and Karl E. Meyer's collection, *Pundits, Poets and Wits: An Omnibus of American Newspaper Columns* (1991). The former is also overwhelmingly newspaper columns, though the *New Statesman* and *The Spectator* are represented. Both cover the ground from the birth of the newspaper column in the middle of the nineteenth century.

Securing a column

Getting a column is difficult, because coming up with relevant, insightful and engaging observations every day, week or month is hard even for the most experienced writers. Getting a column is the ultimate aim of many freelancers, as there are numerous benefits including some stability in income. Columns can also get writers noticed or may lead to a staff job. In some instances, it has even led to a book deal. Back in 2002, I interviewed Alison Pearson – who at the time had recently landed a book deal plus film rights for her debut novel *I Don't Know How She Does It*. My article, *First-timer lands major film deal*, for *Writer's Forum* magazine cited how Alison's debut novel had grown from her weekly column in *The Daily Telegraph* (Hogarth, 2002).

However, even if you have a good idea for a column getting an editor to commission you is no easy feat. Most likely you will need a portfolio of work and have to produce a few sample columns with indications of how you would continue for a few weeks/months after that. Today, in some ways developing column writing skills has been made easier with blogging. Therefore, if you are a strong writer with specialist knowledge or a passion, why not test the water with some blog posts then signpost your work to maximise audience reach? Once you have achieved a reasonable following, it is then easier to approach an editor as pitching the column can be made from a position of strength.

Maintaining continuity is key, especially for the more personal kind of column. This is where careful planning comes in as you may have six brilliant weekly columns in you, but what if your inspiration dries up? It's crucial to have sources for new material so that you continue to engage but don't become boring. For example, if producing three columns a week for *The Times* it will help if, like Bernard Levin, you have an office next to the editor's or, like Simon Jenkins, you're a former editor.

Often opportunities for staff writers can be plentiful and lucrative. If you are staff (writer or sub-editor), you'll be living and breathing the world of your publication therefore replacing your duties or adding to them by writing a column (assuming there's room for one or if a current incumbent is off sick) could be part of a good career strategy.

But if you're a freelance, before coming up with ideas undertake a forensic study of the market to find that opportunity.

Finding the gap

After completing a forensic analysis, list what you have found to be missing in the market. Would a general column fill the gap? Or can you see scope for a semi-specialist subject that you know something about and would enjoy exploring further such as a new sport, emerging technology, gender-bias, alternative therapy or perhaps a new take on an old theme?

Before making a formal approach it's usually worth a quick call to the editor first. Why? Because in today's digital world very few people pick up the telephone – and you can't beat that personal approach as it facilitates the chance to establish a rapport. But, always ask if it is a convenient time to talk, before going into detail about the proposed column idea. Should you be unfortunate enough to catch the editor on press day don't persist with your idea, instead say you will call back once the publication has gone to press.

If you succeed in securing even a vague interest, follow up immediately with an email giving more details about the proposed column together with a brief CV, plus links to your website and portfolio. Should you get a positive response then send over one to two sample columns and ask if you can discuss it further face-to-face or over the phone. Although it is unlikely you will secure a regular column immediately, you might get a commission for an initial feature or trial piece and from there you may be able to cross the bridge.

Types of columns

While there are numerous columnists, the stars are few. Some columnists have to know exactly what their discoveries are before starting to write, while others prefer to start sooner, with a germ of an idea, and discover as they go, freewheeling on their words that come. And there are all the degrees in between these two methods.

There are numerous formats in terms of general column writing. With regards to subject matter, structure and style, general columnists are more inclined to experiment with their content. No matter what the subject, accuracy is key to building an excellent reputation for knowledge and expertise. Therefore, always double-check your facts and sources – doing so will save you from embarrassment or worse still a potential law suit. In an article on *Why facts must figure* for *The Guardian* journalist Francis Wheen admits he has seen off potential litigants because he is scrupulous about fact-checking. He states:

> This isn't meant as a boast: I'm sure that minor errors creep in occasionally. It is merely a reflection of my old-fashioned belief that journalism involves telling people things they couldn't have found out for themselves – and that readers should be able to trust the essential accuracy of what I report. In the words of the 19th-century Times editor John Thaddeus Delane: "The business of the press is disclosure."
>
> (Wheen, 2002)

Table 12.1 illustrates the variations in format of general columns by dividing the main contents/styles into four key themes. Do bear in mind that any one column might exploit several kinds of content and techniques.

Although Table 12.1 only cites four main column themes and focuses on the general column, there are more to be explored. This includes the specialist column where the writer shares his or her perspective on the latest developments, events or news in their field.

However, before attempting to secure a column, it is best to get a few years' experience first. Aim to become an established writer with a good network of contacts. That said, there is no reason why you can't create your own column in the form of a blog or vlog.

How columnists work

Some columnists don't believe in much preparation and like to work an hour or two before the deadline, especially if they've already spent a good part of a lifetime as a newspaper reporter or journalist. Some may find it difficult to work in a quiet study and will prefer to produce their columns in the middle of a busy office.

Essentially, reporters turned columnists keep up with news and current trending stories, reading the papers, following relevant web posts, listening to podcasts or watching documentaries. Then when column day comes they will choose some news item that intrigues them, then write the column straight off. Well, they might need to do several drafts of the intro until they get that right, then the rest will follow. Because that's how they used to write their reports.

Others carry a notebook or use a voice recorder on their phones to record ideas as they occur. When decision time for the topic comes they evaluate their ideas and make a decision. Generally it's not finding the idea that's hard, it is having too many.

Table 12.1 Four key themes of a column

Column theme	Perspective
1 The world at large	Topics might include: politics, global or national events/disasters and key debates in society or the world from the writer's perspective i.e. a personal column. A writer needs their own standpoint, and must be well informed on each area they write about. Their own standpoint can then be used as a guide when researching new material. **Key examples:** • Peter Oborne, Political commentator and columnist in the *Daily Mail*. • David Brooks, politics, culture and social sciences columnist for *The New York Times*. **Pros and cons:** Such writers are generally encouraged to follow their publication's editorial codes and news values. However, if a columnist is well known and develops a good following then he or she may be given a free rein over their work.
2 Lifestyle	This type of column covers a range of topics – from fashion and relationships, to health living and interiors. It is designed to relate directly to an aspect of the reader's life. The aim is to identify with the readers' triumphs or tribulations and sometimes to inspire. **Key examples:** • Lorraine Candy's column in the *Daily Mail* titled, *I don't know how she does it*. • Baroness Karren Brady writes an inspiring monthly column for *Women & Home*. **Pros and cons:** It is easy to get pigeonholed, but on the plus side there may be a book deal waiting. Liz Jones, for example, has published numerous books on the back of her column.
3 Argument and provocation	Generally, this is an Op-Ed type of column that uses both logic and emotions to evoke a reaction from readers, encouraging them to participate in "the conversation". Recently Brexit has been among the trending topics. **Key examples:** • Matthew Parris in *The Times*. • Julie Burchill has written columns for numerous publications including *The Sunday Times* and *The Spectator*. **Pros and cons:** Those columnists who can provoke responses from their readers are highly valued by editors. However, as with lifestyle columnists there is a danger of becoming stereotyped.

(*continued*)

Table 12.1 (continued)

Column theme	Perspective
4 Humour and parody	A column combining humour and irony requires great skill on the part of the writer and as a result such columns are rarely edited. **Key examples:** • Andy Borowitz, a *New York Times* columnist who created *Borowitz Report*, the long-running satirical news column. • Acclaimed satirist and former *Telegraph* columnist Craig Brown who now writes for the *Daily Mail*. **Pros and cons:** Such a role demands natural talent and wit, as well as first-class writing skills. Having a flamboyant personality can also help.

A more leisurely approach – one that might work best for the columnist who produces weekly or monthly elegant essay – is to build up either digital or hardcopy files of cuttings or posts on subjects of interest. To these might be added correspondence or conversation threads coming from readers. Again there are likely to be several drafts before the column is ready to be sent.

Whichever preliminaries are preferred, and however good the columnist is at outlining or ordering the material, the key to a successful piece is the writer's ability to:

- interject humour at the right points;
- think laterally;
- enliven facts by linking them to your own experience.

Lastly, with column writing, surprise is the essential, and too much dependence on research can inhibit the gift.

Case study: a columnist shares her secrets

Suzette Martinez Standring (https://readsuzette.com) is an award-winning columnist based in the US and an Executive Director of the National Society of Newspaper Columnists. In addition to being a syndicated columnist, TV presenter and producer, Suzette is also a workshop presenter, speaker and author, who has written two acclaimed books on column writing, The Art of Column Writing *in 2008 followed by* Insider Secrets from Top Op-Ed Columnists *in 2014. Here she shares her journey from novice to acclaimed columnist.*

I lived in California and worked with lawyers for years, but when I relocated to the East Coast, I wanted to try a different career. On a lark, I took an adult ed class in journalism taught by the publisher of a regional paper. Over a six-week period, I wowed him with my mushroom hunting article and other features. He said I had a natural talent. Eventually, he offered me a job, first as a freelance features writer, then as the Hunterdon County Democrat's (New Jersey) county reporter. I added a weekly humour column to my duties as an antidote to the demands of county reporting, and that column became a popular feature.

After relocating to Massachusetts, I stretched my range by writing lifestyle columns for *The Boston Globe*, humour columns for various publications, and eventually getting syndicated with GateHouse Media for my spirituality column that runs twice a month in *The Patriot Ledger* (MA), one of its 400 plus national publications.

My first big break came in 2006. I call it "my Holy Ghost" moment because the editor of *Patriot Ledger* called me for some ideas to fill her weekend religion page. I blurted out, "You should make me your religion columnist. I bet I could fill the page." She said: "You know, I bet you could. I'll put you on rotation next week." Bam, suddenly I had a regular by-line, my own spirituality column, and a sudden case of the night terrors. I mean, who was I to write about religion? No divinity degree, no special expertise, and even though faith is a major underpinning in my life, that doesn't make me an expert, right? Religion can be very divisive, but it doesn't have to be that way. There is so much about faith that can be healing, inspirational, loving, and – doggone it – practical.

That's the kind of column I set out to write, and in 2007, *The Patriot Ledger's* parent company, GateHouse Media, picked me up for national syndication. It's 2018, and I'm still writing it. Gaining a national audience also led to authorship and public speaking.

What makes a column successful and how do you get readers to engage, are questions I'm often asked. American writer and journalist, Connie Schultz, once said that good writing, like cream, always rises to the top. Always work on your craft. Writing has a rhythm, cadence, and the distinct personality of the author. A successful column evokes a strong emotion from the reader. Too many writers rely on outrage or anger, but there's a range of feelings to tap into – surprise, a sense of belonging, joy, nostalgia, fear, shock, and much more. A fresh, novel perspective sets a column apart. Don't parrot the din. Instead, help folks to see an issue from a new angle.

Having gained so much experience over the years I wanted to share my knowledge and wrote *The Art of Column Writing* during which time I interviewed numerous well-known writers. This included Arianna Huffington, who had just launched the *Huffington Post*, which was a huge and novel undertaking bringing together reporters, columnists, and bloggers in one sweeping platform. That alone was memorable – what a role model for being an original.

That said, I am reminded also of a memorable piece of advice from Pete Hamill who said: "My goal is to make the reader say, 'I never thought of it that way before.' If I can make the reader say that, then I will have done my job."

But the most important lessons I've learned during my career have been from experience. These are:

Always tell the truth. Don't get sloppy with or fudge the facts because once you burn a reader's trust, you'll never get a second chance. Readers form relationships with columnists even though they've never met us. Because they consider us friends (or worthy adversaries) readers look to make sense of the world around them and help in forming their opinions. This must be done with facts and integrity.

Work on your style as vivid storytelling makes a column memorable in a reader's mind for a long, long time. Stories personalise a weighty topic, and humour, when appropriate, can lighten the reader's load when tackling painful issues.

You need company as being a columnist is unique in the field of journalism. As such, it can get lonely. I need to get re-energised, find inspiration to elevate my writing and like-minded spirits with whom to cry and whine, then to come roaring back better than before. The best thing I ever did to propel my own career forward was to join The National Society of Newspaper Columnists (www.columnists.com).

So, my advice to anyone aiming to become a columnist is that column writing is as unique as the writer. Think about what's important to you and what you bring to that table. Choose a genre (family, health, humour, politics, *how-to*, etc.) that gets your juices flowing. Without passion, the effort to write is not sustainable.

If you fear you have nothing to say because it's all been said before by the more qualified, then strike out on an original path. For example, Robin Givhan of *The Washington Post* was the first fashion columnist to win a Pulitzer Prize. Why? She writes about how politicians use clothing as symbolism, that what they wear is part of their message and identity. It's both compelling and captivating.

Columnists write because we are ever curious, ever questioning and so others may not feel alone. Columnists are front, center, and in-your-face personal, giving voice to the voiceless, especially now when freedom of the press is under attack.

And lastly ... frankly, I don't know any rich columnists, but if that doesn't bother you, then you belong in our tribe.

Part 3: The reviewer

The term covers a multitude of roles, from the arts and publishing to beauty products and tech. Reviewers have gotten a bad reputation on occasion. When Russian playwright Anton Chekhov stated "Critics are like horse-flies which prevent the horse from ploughing" (Boyd, 2008) the creator was mainly thinking of bad theatre reviewers, who didn't appreciate his new approach to playwriting.

While Goldwyn, the tycoon producer, could afford to rubbish film reviewers, in imitable style.

The two of them reinforce the point that the creator is essential but the reviewer isn't – however powerful a few of them can be in closing down expensively produced plays in London's West End and New York's Broadway. Yet Aristotle's quote reminds us that reviewers perform a useful task in helping the artist's audience to appreciate the art fully: "the guest will judge better of a feast than the cook" (Sofroniou, 2012, p43).

Thus, reviewers must be professional, avoid bias and develop a solid background knowledge of their chosen field. It's also true that reviewers can benefit from actively participating. For example, some successful novelists are also acclaimed reviewers of fiction, while theatre reviewers have gained insight from gaining some acting or directing experience, often at an amateur level.

The creators work from one premise; the producers, including directors and actors, work from another; the reviewers and the critics from another. Because of the differences in perspective it's often difficult to pin down what is fair and what is unfair comment. Mostly, each side is aware of this and refrains from joining battle, but occasionally war breaks out in a letters' page, on social media and in TV studios. Libel considerations mean in effect that the reviewer's comments should not directly threaten the ability of practitioners to earn their living, and must be written without malice.

In this section, we will look at the demands made on reviewers, while exploring opportunities to get started and how to develop the necessary skills.

How to get started

As with other by-line columns, general or specialist, reviewing is unlikely to be the first task a new writer will expect to be doing. Yet it's an obvious specialism for staff and those freelance writers interested in music, publishing, the arts, tech or health or beauty, and there are opportunities for beginners on local papers and small magazines. To demonstrate the basic process of a review, I have compiled the reviewer's map in Figure 12.2, which highlights the three essential stages when tasked with writing a review or taking on a new post. The basics of this map can be applied to all types of reviews – be it someone's work to a new product.

As Figure 12.2 shows, building a strong network of contacts is key, as is getting the press kit before undertaking further research. It might also be worth including a quote to two from well-chosen sources, particularly if there is an interesting backstory to be told.

Reviewers need a plethora of skills and traits, some of which are developed over many years. These include:

- good research skills;
- in-depth knowledge of their field;
- a passion to know and experience more;
- the desire to share your passion and knowledge with readers;

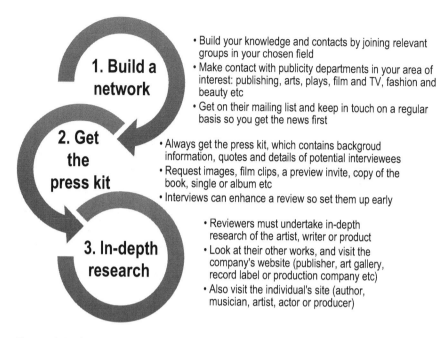

Figure 12.2 The reviewer's map (Hogarth, 2018)

- an ability to judge perceptively and avoid bias;
- the courage to stand by convictions against pressures to please those with other premises;
- excellent writing skills to communicate vividly and entertainingly.

Potential markets

Popular and quality markets are different in the way they cover the arts, so prospective reviewers must explore potential markets with care, collecting print and digital cuttings then analysing them before deciding where to pitch. Even within the same category of publication, arts or features editors can have varied demands.

Here is a selection of markets and their editorial preferences.

- **The tabloids:** editors often put an emphasis on lively, entertaining reading with arts coverage often merging into celebrity gossip.
- **Provincial papers:** these are a good place to start as they cover much amateur work, which requires a different approach and offers reviewers the chance to hone their skills.
- **Low circulation magazines:** another good place to start as arts editors tend to read these, along with students' magazines, in the quest to find new talented reviewers.

- **Mainstream consumer magazines:** will often give space to reviews on everything from books and music to beauty and tech.
- **Specialist magazines:** several magazines devoted to the arts including *The Stage* – most of which can be found listed in *Writer's & Artist's Yearbook* and *Willing's Press Guide*.

So how can a beginner get his or her first break? My advice is first to become established as a writer and build up a portfolio of work to demonstrate your skills. Decide which area you want to focus on – food, the arts, books, music or perhaps beauty or tech – then start small. Approach local magazines and newspapers in your area with a sample review written in their house style, plus ideas for further reviews.

While this won't make you money – indeed with budget cuts being what they are you may have to work for free – it will get you experience. It also could lead to a staff job in the future. After graduating from a journalism degree in the mid-1990s, my first reporting job was on a local weekly Advertiser series (*Avon Advertiser* and *Stour Valley Advertiser*), where I had to compile 35 to 40 news reports every week together with a front-page lead. Although it was poorly paid, with this role came an opportunity to do reviews of local amateur productions, books and gigs. It was a great starting point and my reviews later helped me land a job on a short story magazine.

Also, why not set up your own blog as this can also be a good way to hone your skills and get noticed. If you develop a large enough following you may start earning money from your posts and getting products to review for free. But be warned, there are numerous bloggers out there so it's crucial to find your own niche to stand out. Moreover, it's worth noting that successful fashion and beauty bloggers often get a mention in mainstream consumer titles – with the occasional one landing their own review page in a magazine.

As with most aspects of journalism, this is about learning on the job so if you want to be a reviewer then you must be proactive from the start. Don't restrict your market search to potential media outputs in your area, start your own reviews page as part of a blog or mini online magazine, then use social media to signpost your work and build a following.

On the job

Full-time reviewers have probably done a fair amount of subject research and have the time to prepare for what's coming up. Those who are part-time should at least have the latest reference books to hand, as well as subscriptions to relevant journals or newsletters. It's also crucial take time to make explore the artist, writer, playwright or musician's earlier works. Previous experience and reviews of the artist's (director's/actor's) work will add depth to your piece.

First reviewers must decide on the level of knowledge the readers of their publications are likely to have, and whether they may have read, seen or heard the work. Play and film reviews are often the result of attending previews in studios so generally assume readers haven't seen the works. However, TV reviews must take into account that while some readers might have seen the programmes, others haven't.

Table 12.2 sets out the core components of a review, from using basic reporting skills to developing your work and setting standards.

Writing up your copy

An advantage of book reviewing is that you can note passages that impress you together with page numbers and refer back to them as many times as you like. But when it comes to films and plays, it's not so easy. Therefore, it's sometimes better to keep your experience fresh, and write up the film or TV review immediately after the viewing. Furthermore, taking notes in any quantity while reviewing the performing arts can be distracting.

If the review of a performance can wait until the following day, you may be able to produce a more thoughtful and polished piece. However, some reviewers perform better when they have a deadline an hour or two after the performance. Practise doing reviews with both kinds of deadlines to see which works best. Here are a few pointers with regards to getting the content right.

- **Language and style:** strong, well-informed opinions go better with a distinctive style – a must for any reviewer. Readers want to read something that gives them a fair idea of the reviewer's experience, and they won't get it from a reviewer who's merely competent. A good reviewer can be memorably excited (in the angry sense of the word) by a bad work of art and have interesting things to say about it. That's one important test of the quality of a reviewer.
- **Conciseness and precision:** avoid clichés in reviews, particularly the clichés of approval and disapproval that don't give the reader a clear idea of how you arrived at your assessment.
- **Avoid unnecessary modifiers:** such as a grave emergency or an acute crisis and vague words, especially those recently overused to the point of exhaustion, used on their own, without explanation. Such words must be added to, exploited in some way, to indicate why they are being used: fascinating, interesting, amazing, beautiful, cool (in the newer sense), wonderful, marvellous, glorious, gorgeous, nice, feisty, funny, amusing, boring, uninteresting, ugly, awful, unfunny.
- **A strong structure:** it's helpful to report the main facts or the story of a book or play or film early in the review, so that there's a clear context for the judgements made.

Lastly, if appropriate, end with a verdict or perhaps star rating as this adds depth to your review offering a more personal perspective with which readers can identify.

Table 12.2 The core components of a review

Basic reporting skills	These form the basis of all reviews and involve answering a series of questions such as: • What is it called? • What's the genre (literary novel or thriller, tragedy or comedy, art-house film or blockbuster)? • What is it about? What does it mean and represent? • Is it any good? • Who created it? • Who produced/directed it? • Where is it showing, or can you buy it? • When and where does the action take place? • Why was it written/painted/composed? • How much is it?
Developing content	Your opinion must be informed and should be demonstrated by indicating the evidence for your statements and arguments. The evidence will be facts, examples and/or quotes. While it's good to have strong opinions, readers should feel they are being helped to make up their own minds and can disagree while still valuing your piece. Some important questions are: • What are the work's merits/defects? • Did I like it and is it worth my reader's time and money? • Is it informative/inspiring/interesting/entertaining? • What are the significant elements and how do they compare with other works in the genre (plot or characters, well-made play or postmodern experiment, message or slice of life, melody or in the raw)? • How does it compare with other works by this creator, producer, director, and that of their contemporaries? • How well has the work been served by those interpreters involved such as actors, directors, set designers, musicians, etc.? • If known (e.g. last night's theatre), how did the audience react to the work?
Setting standards	Don't pontificate – give an opinion about whether a work is good or bad, guiding your readers to the former. Remember that: • Your readers need to get to know where you stand on various aspects so that they can be guided by and interested in your piece even when they disagree on various points. • It's a question of integrity. React to the work, analyse your reaction, make an assessment then communicate it honestly, taking your readers' likely reaction into account. • Refuse to let your judgement be swayed by outside pressures; readers must feel they can trust you to tell the truth as you see it. • What outside pressures? Both the subsidised and commercial theatres, for example, depend heavily on PR and pre-production selling (interviews with the stars, lavish praise of the previews, and so on). • Be neutral. "The water is purer," as the late Hugo Young said about political columns. Don't become too friendly with the denizens of the world you're reacting to and assessing.

Book reviews

So many books are published that it's essential to choose wisely – that means only reviewing well-written texts or novels that will reflect your readers' interests. Book reviewers must be widely read, they should delve much deeper than the content covered in the publisher's press release and know something about other books by the author being reviewed, as well as previous profile pieces or interviews with the author. If time permits, a reviewer should read one or two of the writer's earlier books, while also finding out about similar books by contemporaries for the sake of comparison.

When reviewing a non-fiction text it often helps to explore the writer's expertise in their subject, ascertaining whether it includes case studies, real-world examples or interviews with experts in the field. It is also useful to measure how far the author has succeeded in avoiding the pitfalls of the genre and gaining its prizes. In such instances having some expertise in the field of the text you are reviewing is useful as it is then easier to spot inaccuracies, inconsistency or areas that haven't been sufficiently covered in the work.

However, with fiction – aside from good quality writing – a review is often more about a personal perspective. Therefore, it is worth noting the following elements that fiction reviewers may have to deal with:

- **The story:** what happens – the *plot* is the structure of what happens with the causality indicated.
- **The setting:** the place, ambience, atmosphere all need special attention when it's unusual. For example, if it's a little known or exotic place, such as an imaginary planet in a sci-fi novel.
- **The period or periods**: be clear on eras – is it set in today's world, 20 years ago or a century ago? When reviewing a historical novel a reviewer should pick up any anachronisms that damage the illusion.
- **The theme, or message:** behind the work may need to be carefully distinguished from the story. The immorality of characters must be set apart from the morality of the work.
- **Narrative technique:** should be discussed, such as how does the author use time? Is the sequence clear or confusing? Are flashbacks used and if so are they effective?
- **Characters:** may be caricatures as in Dickens, or true-to-life as in George Eliot or Jane Austen. They can also be symbolic, explore changes in society or represent the struggles people are facing in the modern world.
- **Style:** can be straightforward as to be hardly noticeable, a case of art concealing art, or perhaps simply an unobtrusive style that is more effective for what the author wants to do.

Note that a straightforward, clearly constructed review is required when the narrative is the key feature in a novel, especially when it's a historical novel.

However, when reviewing any work of fiction less is sometimes more as while it's important to give a compelling review, it is crucial not to reveal too much of the story. And should you not like the book in question? Then say so constructively, but keep to the point. Don't knit-pick for the sake of critiquing the work and avoid bringing in supposition or hearsay.

Music

In any form of art – including music – the work must rise to the challenge of how to interpret in words what is non-verbal. For example, a review of a Gilbert and Sullivan operetta by the local amateur operatic society won't cause too many problems. In fact, you might get away with giving something of the plot, referring to the performances of the leading singers and to the fun to be had by all. Therefore, reviewing concerts or releases of rap, pop, rock, soul, jazz or classical music needs good background knowledge plus an appreciation of what the sounds mean, and skill in translating that appreciation into an engaging piece. With concerts the writer must build in a sense of the atmosphere created and offer an insight into the audiences' reaction. A show-not-tell approach can work well as in this extract from a review of a Coldplay concert at Cardiff's Principality Stadium in 2017 written by Kitty Empire in *The Observer*.

> Bits of coloured confetti are stuck to Chris Martin's brow, giving him the air of a dad roped into a messy play session. In fact, the lead singer of Coldplay is banging away at the piano on Yellow, their career-defining love song, in front of a sell-out crowd.
>
> Martin is slick with sweat, as drenched as the crowd who have braved sodden queues outside the Principality Stadium for the band's first Welsh gig for 17 years. (Rumours swirled all day that the Cardiff landmark's roof would be left open to the elements; mercifully, it is shut.) Martin thanks us for "all the shit" fans had to go through to get in, noting how well things have turned out for the cagoule makers of Wales.
>
> The inside of the stadium is all aglow, thanks to Coldplay's signature light-up "xylobands", first used on the Mylo Xyloto tour of 2012. They are, yes, all yellow. It feels like the encore, the kind that sends you out into the night streets, hollering the chorus. We are just two songs in.
>
> (Empire, 2017)

It is a well-paced review, with Kitty Empire capturing the mood perfectly using just the right mix of description, first-hand experience and her personal perspective.

With classical music comparisons with other artists' work should be made, whether benchmark or just different, while opera requires a more peripheral approach. That means paying attention to all the usual elements of theatrical production, including set design, costumes, machinery and acting plus acoustics as well as the singing, the music playing and conducting. Reviews in *The Week* of theatre, films and opera are worth studying for the comparisons made between extracts from the quality papers.

Art exhibitions

Reviewing art exhibitions requires confident descriptive powers. It is a specialist subject – so much so that reviewers need the courage of their convictions more than other reviewers, such is the volatility of the visual arts.

As for the minefield of contemporary conceptual art – of which Damien Hirst's pickled sheep in a glass case is a well-known example – reviewers know they are walking through it on a tightrope. They have to say interesting things about the obscure, such as an empty gallery with its lights going on and off or a bit of a wall in white and pale blush-pink shades with a tiny smudge on it (a squished mosquito) shipped from Mexico, with the sound of another mosquito transcribed into musical notation displayed on a musical stand – a violinist occasionally playing the piece. The mosquito-inspired work is called "endemically chancy".

Often there is little criteria by which much conceptual art is being judged, this is because practitioners don't or can't explain. Consequently, reviewers can frequently be found in *Private Eye*'s Pseuds' Corner. But reviewers must be open to new kinds of art and must try to find ways of promoting what they find promising.

The theatre

Plays and films, like operas, need reviewers skilled at juggling and may share many of the concerns of the fiction reviewer. Genres are many, with different terms (or different connotations) from those used for novels: tragedy, comedy, straight play, farce and more. Various contributions to the staging and to the production, as with opera, need to be noted. The play reviewer is concerned almost entirely with how well the production is served in a particular performance, so allowances may be made if reporting an early performance and there are signs that it might get better. As the reviewer might want to discuss whether or not justice was done to the text, he or she will often read the text as preliminary research.

Skill at compression is a prequisite in reviews of plays since you have to juggle assessments of various aspects of the work. Here's an excerpt from Mark Lawson writing for *The Guardian* with his review of *Trial By Laughter* – *Private Eye team's tribute to embattled satirist*:

> Ian Hislop and Nick Newman, editor and lead cartoonist of *Private Eye* respectively, have developed a flourishing sideline in plays about forgotten heroes of speaking abuse to power. Their story of a British satirical newspaper printed in the first world war trenches, *The Wipers Times*, moved from Newbury's beguiling Watermill theatre to a UK tour and an impending second London run. The same production team now launches from the Watermill another fascinating excavation from the satire archives, which,

involving an editor and a cartoonist, comes very close to the day job for Hislop and Newman.

William Hone, a provocative pamphleteer, was subjected, in 1817, to a menacing legal triathlon. Tried for "blasphemous libel" – after publishing a series of spoofs of the Church of England liturgy – he was forced by penury to mount his own defence, assisted by the caricaturist George Cruikshank. Irritated by Hone's acquittal, the crown went, sub-legally, for a "best of three", dragging him to court twice more in 48 hours on escalating charges, which Hone rebutted in a style that might be called standup comedy if he had not been almost falling over from ill-health.

Structure and staging are conservative, the use of expositional scenes intercutting courtroom action recalling Agatha Christie's *The Witness for the Prosecution*. But, as Hislop and Newman know from their own fights with libel law and the taste police, the subject is hotly contemporary in a culture where definitions of offence and blasphemy are regularly tested. As is still frequently the case in repressive regimes, Hone was accused of offending God when his real sin was to have mocked a top man: in this case, the gluttonous, rutting Prince Regent.

Here Lawson gives away just the right amount of the play's content and background to give readers context. Moreover, although written for *The Guardian*, Lawson's review is personal, his own unique style and voice clearly coming through – and there lies the essence of a great review. It is that mix of having experience and confidence along with first-class writing skills which have been honed to perfection.

TV and films

If writing TV or film reviews regularly, then you will need to be on the publicity mailing list of film and production companies to obtain press releases or kits. These normally contain full cast details, potted biographies of actors, details of the production, etc. Keep in contact with publicists and make sure you are invited to the preview screenings of films being released.

Reviewers of films and TV plays need some knowledge of emerging technology and of the production techniques used inside and outside the studio. When starting out a reviewer should research this medium to gain a deeper understanding of techniques used, such as the difference between the montage of numerous short scenes and the slow build-up in the scenes of a televised drama series.

With films the pace is often much faster than that of a TV series, play or novel therefore it can take a while to get inside a character's head. Added to this there's the power of images and continually changing scenes. Ingenuity is called for in terms of flashbacks and voice-overs. Films have the great advantage in realism. Fast-paced films such as the Jason Bourne series might be set in Rome or London in one scene, the offices of the CIA in another, while character types are often portrayed by association. For example, a Rolls Royce or Aston Martin might be used to establish a character's wealth, while poverty is represented often through stereotyping in terms of attitude and type of clothes worn. On screen images tend to take precedence over the words.

There are numerous markets for both TV and film reviews including *The Radio Times*, *TV Times* as well as newspaper weekend supplements such as *Culture Magazine* (*Sunday Times* supplement). In addition, there are soap magazines and specialist film titles including the renowned *Empire* – a monthly magazine for film buffs.

Empire covers all aspects in general features, dissection of works in progress and news on the technology, as well as numerous reviews of current releases. Despite averaging 200 to 300 words, *Empire's* reviews manage to pack a lot in. For example, David Hughes' review of *The Wife*, published on the magazine's website, which starts off with a brief summary before exploring the impact of the film and comparing it to the book. Here's an extract from his review:

> The film, adapted from Meg Wolitzer's 2003 novel, opens in the 1990s with an epic eye-roll from Close's Joan as her husband Joe (Pryce) pesters her for sex, while they await the call from the Nobel committee that will seal his status as one of the greats. News of the award reinvigorates the ambitions of Joe's smooth-talking biographer (Slater on seductive form), who has been raking over the coals of their lives, and seems determined to expose not only Joe's many infidelities, but also other, far more damaging, secrets.
>
> This is teased out through flashbacks to the early 1960s, when young Joe (Harry Lloyd) and Joan (Annie Starke) meet for the first time. Back then, he was an unhappily married literature professor with a child and an unborn first novel, while Joan was his student and an aspiring writer. An affair was almost inevitable — and arguably vital in order for Joe to blossom into the writer he became, while Joan's own literary aspirations were ultimately eclipsed by Joe's success.
>
> Such archetypes could easily be the stuff of cliché or melodrama, but Wolitzer is much too clever to gravitate towards obvious tropes, etching characters of subtlety and nuance, and taking them in unexpected directions. Likewise, Emmy-winning screenwriter Jane Anderson (HBO's Olive Kitteridge) expertly navigates its narratively tricksy structure, while Swedish director Björn Runge does a good job of evoking the twin period settings (a shot of Concorde in flight proves surprisingly emotional) as well as the pomp and self-importance of the Nobel ceremony. And when Close and Pryce are going at it like Burton and Taylor in *Who's Afraid Of Virginia Woolf?*, he mostly has the good sense to sit back and give the actors room to shine.
>
> (Hughes, 2018)

Hughes' review has both authority and pace. Having clearly read the book on which the film is based Hughes is also able to demonstrate a wide knowledge of literature on which to make insightful comparisons. Added to that is his tone and style which, although reflective of *Empire's* house-style, reflects his own unique voice.

Whatever you are reviewing make sure that you have read the book, listened to the music, seen the play, film or TV series or tested the product. Remember, readers will be relying on you to guide them in their choices so provide an unbiased, honest and informative review.

Case study: it's a reviewer's life

Former Financial Times *journalist, Liisa Rohumaa is also an expert on reviews. During her career, she has worked for the* Radio Times *and was theatre and TV critic for* The Stage *before becoming a senior practitioner at Bournemouth University. Here she offers an insight into the craft, highlighting potential pitfalls and sharing her own experiences.*

Reviews have radically changed following the digital disruption era and for the better in my opinion. Critics used to be a cabal, an elite club where the best writers had huge followings and clout. Now we have bloggers, sponsored bloggers, podcasters, Metacritic and a host of aggregated sites with a ratings system produced by an algorithm. Readers can now contrast and compare and are becoming more savvy about sponsored bloggers paid to do a write up and therefore not independent.

Anyone can be a critic. Readers can join the conversation in the comments section. They can have a powerful voice, just look at Trip Advisor. My favourite website is rogerebert.com. Roger Ebert died years ago but you can still access his style of intelligent, punchy reviews on his website which continues with a core of contributors who keep his ethos alive.

My first review was *She Stoops to Conquer* at Leatherhead Theatre. I was 19, a reporter in my first job at the Surrey Comet, and after many heavy hints to the Entertainments Editor, Hilton Tims, he gave me my first break. It taught me to do the research first not afterwards. As you can imagine a restoration comedy by Oliver Goldsmith would not have been my first choice. I scribbled too much in my notebook and should have watched and listened more.

Like most journalists, I learned the craft by legwork, seeing as many shows in as many different genres as possible. You can't be a snob or say you don't like jazz. If the editor wants you to review a post-modern interpretative dance troupe's ballet about the meaning of life, you go. If you really don't want to go then you just don't have the passion for the job and that will tell in your writing which will become dull and repetitive.

Of course, there are highs and lows as with any job. As a reviewer, the most memorable gig was going to the first night of *Five Guys Named Moe* at Stratford East which was a smash hit. I enjoyed it so much I forgot I was there to do a job. And I probably used the cliché smash hit. I think you can get away with it at least once. But my worst experience was having to review a dismal production of *Joseph and his Amazing Technicolor Dreamcoat* – the cast were good but the show had been touring for so long it looked tired and Joseph's coat resembled a worn out bath mat. I said so and there were letters to the editor outraged that I should be so mean. One was addressed to "Miss Crab Apple".

Being fair is the hardest part of being a reviewer as it is easy to criticise. Reviewers shouldn't take the title critic too literally. The reader wants to be informed as well as entertained – they're not interested in your pet peeves. Never repeat yourself – even if you have seen 100 productions of *As You Like It*.

The best advice I was given when starting out was "go to see the shows no-one else wants to see and make contacts". That actor in a fringe show when only three people turned up could be an Oscar winner one day and you may be the journalist who spots that talent first. Read other reviewers. Take criticism on the chin – you've got to take it if you are dishing it.

How do you get started as a reviewer? I was lucky and someone gave me my first break. But it's a very competitive market so new writers must create their own break, which is much easier in the digital era. My advice would be to first set up your own blog or podcast. Second, specialise. Write about your passion, e.g. computer games, film, TV, tech gadgets. Go to everything and accept every invitation.

That's what Tom Beasley did and he now runs *The Popcorn Muncher* website as well as writing for *The Guardian* and *New Statesman*.

Action plan

No matter what aspect of journalism you want to specialise in it's important to first build subject knowledge and a strong network of contacts. Read widely, follow professional blogs and keep up to date with the latest developments.

Here are three exercises to help you put into practice the key points of this chapter – attempt all or just the one relating to your chosen pathway.

1. **The specialist feature:** research and write a specialist feature on a topic of your choice. It should be between 1,500–2,000 words, targeting either a specialist, B2B or mainstream title and must contain interviews with at least four sources two of which should be experts in their field. Once written, pitch the article as an idea to your target market.
2. **A column:** identify a market gap in your chosen area of expertise or interest, then research the topic and write a 1,000-word column piece. When you have written it then come up with ideas for a series of four

columns before pitching to your target editor. If unsuccessful don't give up – start a column blog and post on a regular basis.

3. **Reviews:** choose any one of the following items and send to the editor, alternatively start your own review-style blog and build a following:
   - A play or drama being shown at your local theatre, this could be a pitch to your paper or county (600 words).
   - A film for *Empire* magazine (350 words).
   - A concert or festival for a music magazine. This can be on any genre from classical to rock or pop (800 words).
   - A product or event – which, depending on your area of interest, can be anything from health and beauty to fashion and technology – for a mainstream magazine, newspaper or Sunday supplement (500 words).

13 Interviews vs profiles

To develop this specialism, writers must be able to differentiate between an interview and profile piece and be a highly skilled interviewer. Interviewing skills, as demonstrated in Chapter 7, form a core part of the information-gathering process. However, when the feature is based on the interview, then the process becomes a more complex operation.

As well as doing in-depth research, a writer should make the effort to meet his or her subject. However, if a face-to-face interview can't be done, then there are other options including Google Hangouts, Skype, a video or phone call. All of which can be run through a computer enabling the writer to record and type at the same time. The best method is undoubtedly the face-to-face – in person or using one of the technical options such as video-calling allows for a degree of personal interaction. Email is the least favourable method as there is little opportunity for such interaction.

Interviews and profile pieces are something of an art and subsequently demand a passionate interest in people. If this specialism appeals, then you must read widely and study the best interviewers such as Lynn Barber or acclaimed *Guardian* journalist, Simon Hattenstone, who recently interviewed Helena Bonham Carter for *The Guardian*. It is vital to read those regular interview slots across a range of publications, from highbrow newspapers to prominent national magazines – most of which have a regular interview slot such as *Empire* – *The Empire Interview* or *The RT Interview* in the *Radio Times*.

Don't restrict your quest to one medium, the more sources you can draw on the more skilled you will become. Watch Louis Theroux's documentaries, BBC1's *Newsnight* with Jeremy Paxman, or even Piers Morgan, who is adept at getting the most reluctant interviewee to open up. Listen to BBC Radio 4, pay attention to presenters such as Martha Kearney and John Humphrys. *Desert Island Discs* also has lessons to be learned. It is hosted by Kirsty Young, who has proved to be a maestro at revealing her guests' lesser-known personality traits.

Reading collective interviews is also helpful. *The Penguin Book of Interviews* (1993), edited by Christopher Silvester (republished in the USA as *The Norton Book of Interviews* in 1996), is a fascinating anthology from 1859 to 1992, taking in such luminaries as Karl Marx, Mark Twain (interviewed by Rudyard Kipling), Emile Zola, a taciturn Ibsen, a voluble young Greta Garbo, Freud, Hitler, Stalin (by H. G. Wells), a drunk Scott Fitzgerald, Marilyn Monroe,

Margaret Thatcher, Bette Davis and Mae West. A 43-page introduction charts the journalistic interview through its history and analyses some psychological subtexts. Interviewers who are almost celebrities in their own right have published collections.

This chapter aims to help you develop the necessary skills for this specialism. Whether the subject is famous or not, the trick is to discover how to guide the interviewee so they find their voice, while developing your own style. As well as literary skills, the interviewer must exhibit tact, warmth, intuition and rapport. Some interviewees ramble and need to be kept on track while others may be unforthcoming because they are worried about how you'll represent them. The more famous they are, the more difficult they can be. They may have been asked the same questions over and over, or have perhaps grown frustrated by too many interviewers having done too little preparation.

Interviewees: choose wisely

Decide who you want to profile or interview and why. Note that those who have an unusual backstory usually have interesting things to say. If your area of interest lies in fiction, then look for writers who have released a new or debut novel or have been nominated for a prize. Actors might have won an award or become patron of a charity, while high-profile business people or a politician might have launched a new enterprise or campaign. Above all, an interview or profile piece needs a timely, engaging and topical angle, which of course must be relevant to the target market's readership as discussed in Chapter 4.

Once you have chosen your interviewee, it's crucial to prepare for these challenges by researching previous interviews and finding new questions. Find out as much as you can about how your prospect performs at interviews (from agents, friends or acquaintances). Carefully examine the questions he or she have been asked and make sure you don't repeat them. Finding a TV, video or audio clip of your potential interviewee will help you to work out a friendly, professional, positive approach – as well as offering further insight into how he or she might respond under pressure.

When looking for a prospect, you will also need to consider suitable target markets. Think about how the audience can relate to your potential subject – why would they read a profile or interview piece? Subjects must be relatable. For example, if writing an interview piece for a local paper (perhaps while on a work placement) the focus will be on the community aspect, meaning the interviewee should either live in or be visiting the area. To clarify, the editor of a local newspaper might be interested in interviews with the:

- Head teacher retiring after 50 years.
- Businesses developing a new outlet or expanding an existing one.
- Councillor embroiled in a corruption allegation or involved with a major campaign on behalf constituents.
- Local teen who has won a part in a soap opera or secured a place on X Factor.
- Policeman awarded the CBE or a bravery award.

Offbeat, quirky characters can make good profile pieces. Accountants who have won a triathlon or iron man, a psychic who has a day job working for the NHS or perhaps the GP/surgeon who performs in amateur theatre productions.

Avoid locally-based celebrities as they have probably been done too often in the local press. But do keep an eye open for other celebs passing through. For example, former *Eastenders* star, Rita Simons, was interviewed by Lorelei Reddin at the *Daily Echo* prior to her stage debut at The Mayflower Theatre in Southampton.

When someone writes a book – be it a well-known author or a celebrity writing their autography – then they are seeking publicity so are more amenable to interviews. During my career I have interviewed numerous celebrity and high-profile authors including Cathy Lette, Katie Fforde, Tony Parson, Sir Arthur C. Clarke and Gordon Ramsey but to name a few. As I built my reputation it became easier to secure interviews. Make no mistake building a reputation as an interviewer or profile writer is hard. When starting on *Writer's Forum* I took every opportunity to meet potential subjects including attending numerous writing events and literary festivals. A few of my interviews were the result of approaching famous authors in the Writer's Room at the Cheltenham Festival while there to promote the magazine.

Acting is perhaps the hardest sector to gain interviews. Many stars hide behind their PR firms or managers who often dictate the terms and carefully screen questions prior to an interview. Unfortunately, such control usually results in a formulaic piece that rarely offers an insight into the essence of the person being interviewed.

Getting commissioned

Once you have a suitable interviewee in mind do some preliminary background research. Check their website, social media pages and look for news items such as a forthcoming book, tour dates, acting role or an award. Now read up all the recent interviews. This should help you find an angle or peg that will enable you to put together a strong pitch sufficient to pique the interest of the commissioning editor.

It's best to approach your interviewee before pitching to check that you can secure the interview. Such an approach can sometimes be difficult because you won't have a definite commission. In these instances, my advice is to say you are writing a feature for X magazine or newspaper as this is not a lie. However, at this point while you might imply otherwise don't say you have been commissioned if you haven't.

Before the pitch, read a few issues of your target publication noting their style and tone of interviews or profile articles. Go back to Chapter 4 to gain a comprehensive perspective of market research. This is crucial as an editor will know from your pitch whether you have researched the publication. If it's apparent you have not, then your pitch is likely to be binned. Lastly, when pitching, make it clear if you have an interview lined up as this will make your pitch more viable.

Setting up the interview

For reporters talking to people becomes second nature. They are used to barging into places, extracting a couple of juicy quotes and barging out again. However, setting up an in-depth interview to elicit substantial amounts of information is much harder. Interview and profile writers not only need the confidence to set up an interview, but they also must have the necessary skills to get the best out of their interviewee. Therefore, it may be wise to start modestly with a strategy for going up the scale, once your credentials in the eyes of both editors and interview prospects have been established.

Finding contact details and getting in touch with your prospect can be surprisingly easy. It requires mostly common sense and persistence. Figure 13.1 illustrates a few tried and test methods for contacting potential interviewees.

Should you be fortunate to have the interviewee's mobile or landline number, then call them to request/set-up an interview, but be mindful that they may not be able to talk. At the same do be ready with your questions just in case they say "yes, I have some time now", which has happened to me on more than one occasion.

If setting up the interview via a third party such as an agent, manager or publicist always ask for key data that will help you to prepare. For a musician, this might include a download of their latest album/song, an up-to-date biography, high resolution jpegs of the musician or group, plus artwork for their latest release – the latter being for illustration purposes. An in-depth online search

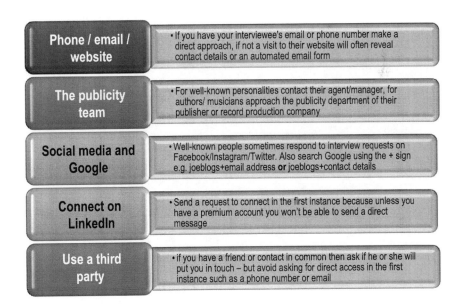

Figure 13.1 Contact methods

should also bring up some previous articles and interviews which will help you prepare insightful questions.

For those focusing on a particular field – actors, pop singers, authors, footballers, tennis players, IT experts – you can receive regular updates on their activities and whereabouts from either their website, intermediaries or social media. Actors, writers and others have their unions, guilds and societies, which will divulge agents' names. *Spotlight* directory (www.spotlight.com/contacts) lists a range of showbiz contacts including actors, agents, casting companies and photographers.

For writers who are serious about making a career in showbiz writing, it might be worth investing in a subscription to a service that keeps you informed of the movements of celebs in the entertainment business. *The Celebrity Bulletin* (www.celebrity-bulletin.co.uk/) published by FENS Information offers a range of services from news and celebrity to travel for a monthly fee dependent on the package but it offers a free, no obligation trial.

Getting past the minders

Without a track record you'll find it difficult to get past the minders. Even with a good reputation you may still be thwarted by agents, managers and publicists. In *Caution: Big Name Ahead*, an article published in *The Observer's Life and Style* section, Lynn Barber says that the "celeb war" between media outlets has got worse during her career. In the article Barber reveals interviews which were thwarted because the celeb or their publicists has taken against a line of questioning. She cites an interview with Nick Nolte for *Vanity Fair* which was pulled on "writer approval".

> Then there is "writer approval" – the chosen weapon of top Hollywood PR Pat Kingsley. She simply bans any writers who ever write anything nasty about one of her clients from ever interviewing any of her clients again. I got the black spot from Kingsley years ago when I interviewed Nick Nolte for *Vanity Fair*. He didn't like the tone of my questions and Kingsley pulled the plug, before I'd even written a word. Of course, Vanity Fair could have defied her and published my interview anyway – but then where would it have got its future cover stars?
>
> (Barber, 2002)

Unfortunately, the digital age has given celebs and high-profile personalities more power and their own voice, resulting in even tighter controls on interviews. Starting out you will confront obstacles at all levels and must be persistent. Here are six tactics to help you get that interview:

1 Aim to get agents, publicists and prospects on your side with a strong pitch highlighting the benefits of such publicity.
2 Sell yourself as someone who wants to "help" interviewees by getting their ideas, campaigns and message across. It's often worth stating that an "exclusive" can further raise their profile.

3   Ensure you say why the commissioning publication is interested in the interview, as well as stating your interest and knowledge. Flattery often works wonders, as does demonstrating that you have an in-depth knowledge of the person's work/achievements.
4   Arouse the subject's curiosity, especially if you have to encapsulate your request in a voice message. Don't be too precise as to what you have in mind if there's a chance that it may not appeal or that it may have been raised too often in previous interviews.
5   Take any opportunity to convey to your subject that you can correct any misrepresentations that have been unfavourable, which you will no doubt find in past interviews.
6   Be flexible. Offer to do the interview via Skype, phone, face-to-face or email. The more flexible you can be with the method, timings and dates, the more likely you are to get the interview.

Interview options

There are many options, as described in Chapter 7, subsequently there may be some repetition. However, this should serve as an important reminder to help you get the results you need.

Your choice of method will depend to some extent on distance and your interviewee's schedule. As well as being tooled up tech wise, always take a notebook for the face-to-face, with phone interviews notes can be made on a laptop if you have touch typing skills. It's advisable to record all interviews but do ask the interviewee's permission first.

Face-to-face

Be as considerate as possible about time and place of meeting. Avoid meeting people who keep late hours early in the day, and don't opt for a noisy venue such as – film sets, TV studios, bars, restaurants. After you've listened to a recording of an interview done over lunch in a busy restaurant seated near the kitchen you won't do it again. Steer clear of rooms with low ceilings where you'll tend to get poor acoustics, or offices overlooking main streets with busy traffic. Try not to be interrupted by mobiles or message alerts – particularly from your device.

Opt for a non-threatening seating position. For example, don't sit opposite the interviewee as if you're considering them for a job or suspecting them of a crime. Make it 90 degrees.

Face-to-face is the most favourable interview method for an in-depth piece as it enables the writer to play things by ear to some extent and have a conversation. The interviewer is also able to judge their subject's reactions to questions (or statements) by their body language and facial expressions, as well as their tone of voice. Correctly reading these signs will allow you to shape the interview accordingly, making the questions shorter and simpler or more demanding.

Once the interview is over, aim to write up a draft within a few hours of the meeting so that it remains fresh in your mind. This will enable you to capture those nuances that bring out personality traits – thus adding more depth and authenticity.

Recording face-to-face interviews

The digital disruption along with social media has meant that most people are more relaxed about being recorded. As previously stated, you must ask your interviewee for permission to record the interview – ideally this should be captured on the recording.

Make sure that your recording device – phone, tablet or dictaphone is placed sensitively on the table – sufficiently near to capture his or her voice, but not so near as to be intrusive. If it's a phone interview do a test run with a friend first to check it works and that the sound levels are good.

There are many pluses to recording interviews including the following:

- A recording provides an accurate replay of the interview, which can't then be disputed.
- It frees the writer up to pay more attention to the interviewee.
- Nuances such as intonations, the manner of speaking, the accent will be captured. Much of the personality can often come through these aspects.
- A recording can – with the interviewee's permission – also provide additional material as it can be made into a short audio clip to provide that added extra for a feature package.

Most editors expect recordings of interviews to be used for features so that the published version can be backed up should there be any complaints from the interviewee about misrepresentation or threats of libel action. Bear in mind that people can be astonished when they see their casually bestowed words in cold print. "Did I really say that?"

In an unobtrusive way make a note of the interview setting (venue), facial expressions, body language, clothes and so on. Perhaps take a few shots on your phone or a short video clip before getting started – though these shouldn't be used for publication unless you have the person's permission to do so. Transcribing will be easier if you make a note of the timings of key quotes/anecdotes on the recording device so that you can quickly locate the best bits.

Write down all names and figures clearly. They may not be clear on the tape. Ask for names to be spelled out and go back over any figures you are doubtful about. For example, "did you say 15,000 or 50,000?" Accuracy must be a priority.

A phone interview

Especially when time is short, a phone interview can be ideal. No longer are journalists reliant on a handset. For ease of use the interview can be done as a video call via Skype, Google Hangouts or Facetime if using a Mac. Alternatively, if Internet speeds are a problem you can also opt for voice-only calls with such apps.

Ideally you will want to record the interview so it would be best to use a mobile phone such as the iPhone – if you are working on a Mac – which can be run through your MacBook or desktop. The call can then be recorded using an app without plugging in additional equipment or trying to record using the speakerphone. With the latter, recordings tend to pick up lots of background noise which will impact on the quality of playback.

For a phone interview, it's sensible not to have too many questions. Having between seven and ten questions placed in a good order should work well, but place the least important at the end. This way if the interviewee gets chatty you can cut the last couple of questions if running short on time.

When not using a video link option, getting subtle or ironic on either side can be problematic as you can't see each other's faces. Do remember to smile as this will come through in your tone of voice.

The email interview

If your subject is unable to meet or is perhaps on tour, then an email interview is a good solution. Generally, if interviewing high-profile people or personalities, an email interview should only be undertaken where there is little alternative as often the essence of someone may not come across accurately in email correspondence. That said, it is a useful method for interviewing experts when you don't need to capture the sound or tone of their voice. In such instances, it is their expertise that is crucial, although some humanity should be allowed to creep in.

While you can't break in to follow up an interesting point raised, the email dialogue can easily continue allowing the journalist to come back with new questions that have resulted from previous answers. Furthermore, the situation is more relaxed because both parties choose the time when they want to contribute. But do make sure that the interviewee is aware of your deadline.

Preparing questions

You've been commissioned and have set up the interview. Now the hard work begins. A forensic approach should be taken to background research (and fact-checking). This will help you to prepare questions that will prompt insightful and intelligent responses – with perhaps an unexpected anecdote or two. Always know the direction of the article before an interview and keep the conversation on track. Never develop questions without having come up with a strong angle for the interview or profile.

Remember, first and foremost you are looking to tell the interview's story in their words. That involves doing some background research. For a profile this may involve talking to their friends, colleagues or family and exploring their work. It is important to allow sufficient time for preparation. Read one or two of an author's books, go see a playwright's latest productions or visit an artist's exhibition. Making time to walk around an architect's building, watch a footballer play a few times or pore over the annual accounts of the company will give your work that added depth.

Read previous interviews and collect digital or print cuttings. Such in-depth research should result in identifying a few lesser known facts or issues. Also, note any errors that have been lazily repeated in previous interviews and indicate that you're correcting them. This will ingratiate you with the interviewee and help to build a reputation for professionalism.

What questions, in which order?

Make sure you're on the same wavelength as your subject, building a rapport will help you get more detailed and unguarded responses. When developing questions, aim for them to be specific, open-ended and well ordered.

Joan Clayton's *Interviewing for Journalists* proved invaluable when I started out and I still have a copy of the book today, often referring my journalism students to it. In the introduction, Clayton (1994) makes an obvious, but nonetheless, important observation, a point which often can be missed by a novice, stating: "Readers want words out of people's mouths – the Big Name's anecdote or confession, the expert's opinion, the personal touch." And there lies the essence of a strong interview piece or profile. It is the writer's ability to convey that voice to the audience.

Therefore, questions need clarity. There can be no room for ambiguity and they should be asked one at a time. The formula of putting two questions in one sentence can be detracting so keep it simple and specific. Avoid closed questions or those which encourage brief answers. Here are a few examples:

- "Do you enjoy being a solicitor?" is too vague. What good to you is the answer "sometimes"? "Which of aspect of the profession do you enjoy most?" is more likely to encourage an articulate response, perhaps followed by "Which do you dislike most?"
- "Do you agree with the new Education Bill?" is unlikely to achieve a desirable response – instead try the open-ended "Do you agree with the criticism that the Bill is likely to be divisive?"
- "What would have happened if you'd succeeded in that business?" Likely answer: "I would have become prosperous." How boring, but with such a question what sort of answer did you expect?

Open questions develop a conversation. Encourage articulate answers by contributing to the subject. For example: "Your colleagues tell me that you're good at getting the best out of interns. How do you do that?" His or her answer should be followed up with "can you give me an example?" Anecdotes and examples will naturally build colour into an interview or profile piece.

Leading questions, which contain your assumption of what the answer is, whether the prompting is in your words, phrasing or tone of voice do not make for a convivial meeting and could result in the interview being terminated. For example, "You've had a lot of arguments with the players this season, haven't you?" might provoke an angry and non-committal response. Find a subtler way to approach the subject. If you know it's true ask, "I've heard from some fans [or I've read reports] that you've had a lot of arguments ... Is that a fair way of putting it? Do you want to comment on that?"

A structured approach

The value of a strong structure in features has been outlined in some of the previous chapters, with interviews it's no different. It is prudent to arrange your questions in an order you think will make a good conversation and elicit interesting answers. For example, you can place the awkward ones judiciously – immediately after a particularly welcome question might be a good place, or near the end.

An interview needs to be fluid, so structure your questions accordingly in a logical order. Avoid sudden jumps, lead up to the big challenges or life changes such as jobs, marriages or health issues. Moreover, if the interview is to be published as a Q&A then having the right structure at the start could substantially lessen your workload.

With regards to difficult questions, or ones that have been forbidden by the publicist, it's prudent to always bring these up last. That way if your interviewee walks out or hangs up you still have your answers to all the previous questions from which you should be able to write up a good piece.

Interviewing techniques

In this section, we will focus on the face-to-face techniques, although aspects can be adapted to phone and email interviews. The first step (after "hello") is establishing a rapport with your subject. Remember they are human too – and that means they are just as susceptible as the rest of us to a bad mood, anxiety, tiredness or the desire to be somewhere else.

There are also likely to be glitches. These might include technical difficulties relating to your recording device, noise levels in the venue or perhaps unwelcome interruptions although you've done your best to avoid them. Try to take such things in your stride: be charming, focused and avoid showing signs of stress.

If you have failed to establish a rapport, then look for some common ground. Turning the occasion into a conversation not only takes the pressure off, it also makes for a stronger interview. Reveal something of yourself. If you are seen to be friendly and trustworthy your subject will be more likely to confide. Find some warm-up, non-interview remarks/questions to start off with, and smile.

Be in control

This means creating a conversation in which the interviewee is encouraged to give the answers you require without feeling under pressure. Your list of prepared questions will be organised in a particular order by topic or chronology. However, as you get to know your interviewee you'll see how to adapt these to the shape the conversation takes, judging how best to phrase your questions to get the best response.

Listen carefully to the answers so that you can take advantage of any opportunity to follow a promising path. Without interrupting too often, you may want to challenge an argument or put the other point of view. Your interviewee might embark on themes or reveal information that you didn't anticipate.

However, be wary of potential diversions. In such instances, you must decide whether the diversion is sufficiently interesting and relevant to merit a follow-up, which might mean cutting out a few of your less interesting questions. But don't be deflected from your purpose. Return to your agenda.

Techniques for tough questions

Here are nine essential techniques for tough questions:

1 **The everybody approach:** "Many have been guilty of having an affair, might you have found yourself in this or a similar situation?"
2 **Other people approach:** (a) "Do you know anyone who has cheated on their partner?" (b) "How about yourself?"
3 **The Kinsey technique** (with an air of assuming that everyone has done everything): "As a matter of interest, did you cheat on your spouse/partner?"
4 **The people say that:** this tactic allows you to be unobtrusively tough in your approach. "There are people who say that putting X out of business was going too far ..." ("Perhaps they don't understand or know your motives ...").
5 **The separate questions:** this formula is used when a series of continuous questions (one after the other) put together would impede a frank answer. However, include other questions between to get confirmation such as "Are the regulations in your company about what can be claimed as expenses quite strict?" and "I suppose you'd feel freer to pursue those activities if your company could stretch the rules on expenses a little ...".
6 **Rephrasing a painful question:** when a question appears too difficult to answer, you might be able to return to it later, rephrasing it so that it sounds different.
7 **Switching off the recording device:** if your interviewee is going through a hard time and is finding it difficult to talk about it, try switching off the recorder. Alternatively, invite the person to "say something into the recording if you like", explaining that you must leave the room for a minute or two while the device is left on record.
8 **The question you should have thought of asking:** a possible last question could be "Is there anything you'd like to add to what you have said?" or "Is there anything I should have asked but didn't?"
9 **Using the "just one more thing" approach:** when you haven't got a reasonable answer to a question but it was difficult to pursue it, stop your recording device,

close your notebook, and get up to leave. Then on the way out, bring up the question again this time more casually, and this time you may get an unguarded answer. 'I suppose it's difficult to get on with a co-star when …?'

Difficult interviewees

Every interviewee is different, heed prior warnings but never assume everything you have been told is true. Go to the meeting with an open mind then determine your approach by reading your subject. Proceed with some caution, monitoring your subject's responses to keep one step ahead of them, should the conversation take a turn for the worse instinct will tell when it's time to leave.

In my experience, the most difficult interviewees are those who don't have a great deal to say. They may be anxious about failing to do justice to themselves or their ideas, or by the situation. Therefore, establishing rapport becomes more difficult. In such instances a solution is to get into a conversation where you do most of the talking, perhaps revealing things about yourself that the subject finds it easy to respond to then begins to exchange confidences. But don't finish a nervous interviewee's sentences as you may end up with an interview more with yourself than with the subject.

However, this tactic with other interviewees can have the reverse effect. Talking too much may make them clam up the more, in this situation restraint and judicious silences on your part are more likely to make the subject open up.

Encouraging revelations

If you're too friendly it will be easy for the interviewee to take control and hide the things you would prefer to know. Nancy Mitford, the English journalist who became a star interviewer in the US, was good at getting people to reveal themselves. She describes her techniques in the classic *The Making of a Muckraker*, which contains a collection of her articles.

The following extract from one of the articles, "Let us now appraise famous writers", first published in *Atlantic* (July 1970), illustrates her method. She interviewed Bennet Cerf, columnist, TV personality and Chairman of the Board of Random House Publishing Corporation, one of the "Fifteen Famous Writers" who, according to the advertisements, taught you "to write successfully at home". Ms Mitford has indicated that she is critical of the correspondence course:

> "I think mail-order sell has several built-in deficiencies," he said. "The crux of it is a very hard sales pitch, an appeal to the gullible. Of course, once somebody has signed a contract with Famous Writers he can't get out of it. But that's true with every business in the country." Noticing that I was writing this down, he said in alarm, "For God's sake, don't quote me on that 'gullible' business – you'll have all the mail-order businesses in the country down on my neck!" "Then would you like to paraphrase it?" I asked, suddenly getting very firm. "Well – you could say in general I don't like the hard sell, yet it's

the basis of all American business." "Sorry, I don't call that a paraphrase, I shall have to use both of them," I said in a positively governessy tone of voice. "Anyway, why do you lend your name to this hard-sell proposition?" Bennet Cerf (with his melting grin): "Frankly, if you must know, I'm an awful ham – I love to see my name in the papers!"

(Mitford, 2010, p156)

As illustrated Ms Mitford listens hard, has charm, good manners and firmness – all valuable assets for an interviewer. She wouldn't have got the admissions she wanted without them. Even so, it isn't always easy to analyse why a subject will talk to one interviewer and not another.

Mr Cerf's "don't quote me" raises the subject of what interviewees can expect to be "off the record" and what not. The journalist must be up to date with the law (see Chapter 16). An interviewee has a stronger claim to confidentiality if you are asked for a statement to be made "off the record" before the statement is made than if you're asked after it is made.

Prepare to follow up

At the end of the interview always thank the person for their time. At this point it is also prudent to ask if you can come back to them should there anything you need to clarify. The majority will agree. By doing this you have prepared the ground should you need to clarify a point or think of a crucial question after the interview.

Remember to exchange contact numbers at the end and – if you haven't already got it – ask for an email address too. Warn the interviewee if you or the editor will need to arrange for photographs to be taken later.

Editing the transcript

Jot down your immediate impressions of the event as soon as possible after the interview, while it's still fresh in your mind. With phone interviews, I always try to schedule in a couple of hours immediately afterward to write notes and begin the transcription. As soon as I've ended the call I then write the stand-first and a rough draft of the intro, before beginning to transcribe the interview.

It's important to remember that a transcription can take three times as long as the interview unless you have superb keyboard skills. I have audio typing skills, a bit rusty but sufficient for typing up much of the interview as we are chatting. Thus, for me transcribing is much quicker as I'm mostly checking that I have recorded the conversation accurately. There are some voice-to-text options too, such as Google Docs. When setting up a new document in Google Docs you can activate the voice typing tool (under tools), which should be able to transcribe a clear audio recording file (MPEG 3 or 4) with reasonable accuracy.

However, while this is much quicker than transcribing manually, caution is advised. To ensure accuracy you will need to check carefully against your recording that the voice tool has transcribed the interview accurately. The time spent either transcribing or listening to the playback should provide some thinking time with regards to structuring the interview or profile piece. This is an opportunity to assimilate the copy and edit out any rambling, while looking for hooks. There may, for example, be a hard-hitting quote that you can lead with or perhaps a revealing anecdote which could work as an apt ending.

In some instances, portraying your interviewee's unique way of speaking such as "to be honest with you", "the dog and bone" or "not me matey" – can provide additional colour to your piece. Use such inflections once or twice, but avoid a constant stream of phrases. Do indicate a person's accent at the start if it is interesting or distinctive, but don't produce slabs of incomprehensible dialect. Correct faulty grammar that leads to a lack of clarity but if it's a trivial matter then leave it in as this can also add colour.

Summarise parts

Writing up concise copy necessitates summarising some of the bigger chunks. For example, Table 13.1 demonstrates how 136 words of questions and answers can be reduced to a 25-word summary.

Be careful as you edit not to misrepresent with your compressions. When using quotes, it is safest to repeat the actual words said and always be completely faithful to the interviewee's intention. That said, you can correct grammar and edit out hesitations such as "eh" or "um" which tend to occur frequently in audio playbacks. When not using quote marks, ensure your summaries or paraphrases are comprehensible, and that they have sufficient context to be clearly understood without those statements you have edited out.

Table 13.1 Summarising quotes

Recorded quotes	Summarised version
Question: "Do you think your team will get into the First Division next year?" **Answer:** "I have no doubt whatsoever ..." (Here follows some history of how the club has gone in and out of the First Division for many years, but unfortunately you haven't got room for it.) **Question:** "What makes you so sure now?" **Answer:** "I'm sure because although they've had their ups and downs over the past few years – for example, last year ... Nevertheless, when you look at the record as a whole you see that there's improvement more or less in the course of time ... And if you look at what's happened in the last three or four games you can see that from all points of view the lads are showing a definite improvement ..."	He thought his team would get into the First Division next season because it has been constantly improving in the last four or five games.

Formats for writing up

The point of an interview or profile article (whatever the format) is to put the interviewee centre stage. More often than not, the interviewer remains discreetly in the background unless they are something of a celebrity or star writer. After all, how often do you note the by-line of the writer? And really that is the point – the writer is not the focus here.

There are many styles from straightforward Q&As to the more dramatic TOTs (triumph over tragedy) usually involving survival, deceit or immoral behaviour. Such stories can be described as "As Told To" or are written up in the first person with the writer remaining anonymous. There are also case studies formats, involving double-page spreads that cover such TOTs as an addiction to diet pills or food. In these formats the case studies are briefly introduced by the writer, with highly relevant statistics in boxes. Such styles allow the reader to feel they are being spoken to straight from the heart. Nevertheless, the input from the interviewer is likely to have been considerable.

The two most common formats that offer the most scope are the Q&A and the narrative. Whichever of these is used, there is room to experiment as well as the need to create a satisfying structure. The essential principle is to be fair to your subjects while being able to reveal what it is about them that your readers need or want to know.

Q&A

This has become more common since the digital disruption era, which has resulted in shorter articles in many mainstream titles. It is a versatile format able to lend itself to serious debate leaving out personalities, but it is also used for a mini interview. Often these begin with a short introduction to the interviewee with perhaps some backstory, descriptions of clothes, appearance, setting and writer's comments that would otherwise be difficult to incorporate in the dialogue.

Popular magazines use the Q&A for fast-moving, concise accounts of a person's views, often accompanied by a stand-first and brief intro. However, this format doesn't guarantee that the subject is represented more objectively or more fairly than any other format, although it appears to do so. There is also the misconception – particularly among novices – that this is an easier option than writing a narrative, straightforward interview or profile piece. It isn't.

Whether you are writing a Q&A as a direct interview or to show contrasting points of view between two eminent personalities or politicians, this style requires in-depth research and the skilful structuring of questions, which must follow a logical progression.

When I first began working in this style a few years ago (having previously avoided mistakenly thinking that it was a lazy option) I was surprised to learn that this was no mean feat. Like most things it takes practice to write an engaging Q&A which demonstrates the interviewees mannerisms and uniqueness – as opposed to telling the audience.

As one of the editorial experts for Lovereading.co.uk, I successfully pitched a series titled, *Five minutes with*. The series ran over a couple of years featuring well-known and celebrity authors using a Q&A style. Why opt for Q&A? Because I felt that this format worked particularly well for an online platform. As both the series and style were my idea, the editor mostly gave me a free reign with the series. Here is an excerpt from *Five Minutes with Tony Parsons*, which as you can see uses an intro prior to getting into the Q&A – thus setting the scene.

> Despite leaving school at 16 – and after a few years of unskilled, low-paid jobs – Tony Parsons got his first job in journalism at the *New Musical Express* (*NME*). For a few years he has juggled journalism with fiction achieving phenomenal success. Writing is, quite simply, his life.
>
> Author Tony Parsons talks to Mary Hogarth about writing his first book while working the night shift at a distillery, those wild years at *NME* and his dog, Stan.
>
> **How did you get that first job on NME?**
>
> By publishing a novel. It was called *The Kids* and it was not very good but when the *NME* advertised for new writers in the summer of 1976, they asked for a sample of work and I sent my novel. So that looked pretty impressive, I imagine.
>
> **Did this shape your work as a journalist?**
>
> I don't think I was really shaped as a journalist by the *NME*. There was too much sex, drugs and Rock & Roll – too many nights when I didn't go to bed. We were a weekly publication the pace was relentless so there wasn't much chance to learn more than the basics of journalism. It was only after I left the *NME* that I started to grow as a journalist and a writer.
>
> **Tell us about your first book, *The Kids*.**
>
> I left school at 16 and worked in a series of low-paid jobs. In my late teens, I got a job on the night shift at Gordon's Gin Distillery in Islington. They gave us free gin and left us alone from 8pm to 8am. While my colleagues slept, I wrote my novel. It took a year to write, another to find an agent, then a year to find a publisher. So that is how my first book evolved – by never giving up. I think that is how every first book evolves.
>
> (Hogarth, 2016c)

Note how my questions follow a natural progression, which results in a stronger structure thus hooking the reader. In preparation for this interview – which was done over the phone – I read a couple of Tony's books including *The Kids* and did a fair bit of background research on the author. This meant I could write a draft of the intro before developing my line of questions. It is also a good technique as it can help the writer to develop stronger questions. Knowing what you need in terms of answers prior to the interview will be more likely to result in a stronger Q&A or interview piece.

The narrative

Opting for the narrative interview also requires skill. It needs a fast pace just as a work of fiction does, interspersing quotes with the unfolding story while dropping in various insights into the subject. These insights come out of an interviewee's way of speaking, their mannerisms, appearance and the way he or she fits into the surroundings.

An example of this can be found in these extracts from an in-depth profile interview in *The New Yorker* titled, *Can Mark Zuckerberg fix Facebook before it breaks democracy?* The writer, Evan Osnos, first sets the scene with an intro which is both observational and descriptive:

> At ten o'clock on a weekday morning in August, Mark Zuckerberg, the chairman and C.E.O. of Facebook, opened the front door of his house in Palo Alto, California, wearing the tight smile of obligation. He does not enjoy interviews, especially after two years of ceaseless controversy. Having got his start as a programmer with a nocturnal bent, he is also not a morning person. Walking toward the kitchen, which has a long farmhouse table and cabinets painted forest green, he said, "I haven't eaten breakfast yet. Have you?"

As the interview continues Osnos offers more poignant insights, also including quotes from Zuckerberg's friend and former employee Dave Morin – which not only adds colour to the profile, but also demonstrates an unlikely trait.

> He and his wife prefer board games to television, and, within reach of the couch, I noticed a game called Ricochet Robots. "It gets extremely competitive," Zuckerberg said. "We play with these friends, and one of them is a genius at this. Playing with him is just infuriating." Dave Morin, a former Facebook employee who is the founder and C.E.O. of Sunrise Bio, a start-up seeking cures for depression, used to play Risk with Zuckerberg at the office. "He's not playing you in a game of Risk. He's playing you in a game of games," Morin told me. "The first game, he might amass all his armies on one property, and the next game he might spread them all over the place. He's trying to figure out the psychological way to beat you in all the games."

Finally, the article ends on the question of whether Zuckerberg can make good all the controversial issues currently threatening Facebook – leaving readers to draw their own conclusions.

> In some sense, the "Mark Zuckerberg production" – as he called Facebook in its early years – has only just begun. Zuckerberg is not yet thirty-five, and the ambition with which he built his empire could well be directed

toward shoring up his company, his country, and his name. The question is not whether Zuckerberg has the power to fix Facebook but whether he has the will; whether he will kick people out of his office – with the gusto that he once mustered for the pivot to mobile – if they don't bring him ideas for preventing violence in Myanmar, or protecting privacy, or mitigating the toxicity of social media. He succeeded, long ago, in making Facebook great. The challenge before him now is to make it good.

Osnos has written an excellent narrative. Despite weaving in core profile information, Osnos has managed to keep to the narrative, thus illustrating those aspects of Zuckerberg's character – through anecdote, quotes and observations – that may hold the answer to his headline question.

The profile

Having written numerous profile pieces over the years, this is perhaps my favourite type of article. Make no mistake, profiles are hard work. They need scrupulous attention to detail but also require the writer to illustrate rather than state their subject's characteristics – some of which will no doubt have contributed to their success or failure.

There are three basic types of profiles:

1 **The personal profile:** usually between 1,000 and 1,500 words, these are much like the typical interview feature but draw on various sources and sometimes require a few meetings rather than being based on a one-off meeting or phone call.
2 **Serious, overall assessments:** some may not have by-lines, thus putting the publication's authority behind it, although the majority do include a by-line. Typical examples that might feature high-profile public figures such as politicians, economists or entrepreneurs can be found in publications such as *The Observer, The Sunday Times* and *New Statesman*.
3 **The long literary profile:** notably done in *The Guardian* or a specialist publication is more akin to an essay than a piece of journalism.

Whether you are a staffer in a fast-paced editorial office or freelance juggling multiple submission deadlines, it can be tempting to produce a cut-and-paste profile with an overuse of material gathered from cuttings and publicists. Don't. While the profiler or interviewer isn't always remembered for their skills they will be noted for poor-quality pieces. As with any job, the journalist must take pride in their work – and that means no shortcuts.

Always follow up

After an interview, it is always good to follow up with a "thank you" note, after all he or she has given you their time. More importantly, if an interviewee is treated well then they are more likely to put you in touch with their friends or talk to you again.

Should the interview ask to see a draft of your article prior to it going to press, refuse politely saying it's against the publication's editorial policy. As mentioned previously in this chapter the only exception is if the person is an expert who has provided detailed and intricate facts in his or her answers.

Lastly, it is good manners to send your interviewee a digital or print copy of the article once it's published. And hopefully, they will help you publicise it on social media with a few tweets, likes and shares.

Case study: in the author's experience

When I first started writing profile pieces I was lucky enough to have a superb mentor and editor in the form of my former publisher and laterally friend, John Jenkins, editor of *World Wide Writers* and later *Writer's Forum*, where I was to become deputy editor. John, a former *Telegraph* night editor, had an amazing gift for writing. He could turn an ordinary intro into a form of poetic prose that not just hooked but fully immersed the reader. It is from him that I first learned the craft and developed a passion for it.

Throughout my career – which has become more varied – I have continued to write profiles and interview pieces, further honing those skills with each article. And that is the point. A writer's journey is a continual one. Your work stagnates the day you stop learning.

Why do I love interviews so much? Probably because at heart I'm a people person and continually curious. No matter who I'm interviewing – whether it's a high-profile editor for one of my books or a writer, celebrity or entrepreneur – I need to know what makes them tick. It's the whole process that fascinates me, from the initial groundwork, digging around asking questions to find out what it is that motivates my subject. Through that process, I can piece together the untold parts of a subject's story – in the same way a detective tries to solve a crime. Exploring how a person's past has impacted on their present will often add an extra layer and depth to the story.

Over the years I've had some fabulous interviews. My favourite was the Australian-born author, Kathy Lette, whom I have interviewed a couple of times over the years. Not only is she fabulously funny, but also very natural. During our first interview (for *Writer's Forum*), which lasted a lot longer than planned, we also talked about life, sharing a couple of confidences along the way. When it came to writing up the article – a first-person piece titled, *A writer never stops* – capturing her voice and essence was easy. Another enjoyable interview was with Alexandra Shulman, *Vogue's* former Editor-in-Chief, for *InPublishing* titled *Alexandra Shulman Interview*. A rapport was soon established when we shared a passion for magazines and valued the print format. Needless to say, that interview also overran.

Not all my interviews have gone so well. There have been those who have given little more than one-word answers, while others have gone wrong.

Many years ago, at the start of my journalism career, I managed to secure a face-to-face interview with the internationally-famed author, Sir Arthur C. Clarke, while on holiday in Sri Lanka. Unfortunately, I made the mistake of allowing a boyfriend to accompany me into the interview. The said boyfriend then proceeded to take over the conversation and I barely got a word in edgeways during our 45-minute audience. Thus, I left Sir Arthur's compound in Colombo with very little to write up. It was my first lesson in making something out of nothing and making sure you avoid possible distractions. What a valuable lesson it was.

Summing up, it is lessons such as these that have had the greatest impact on my work. When starting out it is important to understand that you shouldn't be afraid of making mistakes because failure has much to teach us. Learn from your errors and move on, making sure you don't make the same mistake twice.

Above all be driven by a passion for your work, combined with a dogged determination to get the back story. If you would choose to do this job without pay, then a profile writer/interviewer is the role for you.

Action plan

Practice is the best way to master the art of interviews and profiles. Start small both in terms of your subject and target publication, get comfortable with the process and develop your skills. Only once you have published a few articles in small-scale publications will you be ready to branch out.

The following exercise is designed to get you started. Remember to choose your interviewee and your target publication with care.

Write an 800-word interview or profile piece for a local publication of your choice. It's advisable to come up with three potential candidates in case of refusals.

1   **First choose your target market:** perhaps the student magazine published by your university or a local newspaper or magazine. Whichever title you choose, it must include interviews or profiles among its editorial pillars. Don't forget to research your target market as described in Chapter 4.
2   **Next find a suitable candidate to interview:** he or she will need to have some standing or be well known in the community. Alternatively, they might have achieved something outstanding. For example, if it's a student magazine then interviewing a student who has landed a top

internship or won a national award would be perfect. If writing for a local paper, then choose a local high-profile business person, councillor or perhaps someone who has been recognised for an outstanding achievement.

3   **Make an approach:** using the methods mentioned in this chapter, contact your potential interviewee to set up an interview.
4   **Make your pitch:** it's advisable to re-read Chapter 5 before approaching the editor of your target market.
5   **Research and plan your questions:** take a forensic approach. Obtain their biog details, look for any previous interviews and read up on their subject or area of specialism, etc. Now develop your questions based on the data gathered from your research.
6   **The interview:** before conducting the interview have a final run through of your questions then draft out a headline, stand-first (or strapline) followed by an intro. During the meeting, or phone call, try to be as relaxed as possible. The greater the rapport the better your interviewee's answers will be. Do ask if you can clarify any points at a later date, then should you forget a key question you can ask it later.
7   **The write up:** first read through previous interview/profile articles in your target market so you become familiar with the tone and style. When writing up the draft have one of those articles next to your computer to ensure you capture the tone and style of your target market.

NB: If you can't get the article published, then post it on your blog.

14 Worldwide markets

A key plus point of the digital age is that it has widened the horizons of feature writers, bringing numerous publishing opportunities for articles targeting English-speaking markets. Such markets include the USA, Canada, Australasia, South Africa, Ireland as well as those countries with a large ex-pat community. Moreover, some of the other markets are often keen to translate features. There are exciting prospects, both for the traditional print publications as well as digital and online mediums. However, there is a great deal of competition, so your market research must be at its sharpest.

If you're something of a traveller and also like print magazines, it may be worthwhile making a list of likely targets from the marketing guides then picking up copies while on holiday or visiting the area. Alternatively, you could ask relatives and friends living or travelling overseas to send you publications from various countries. However, if you don't travel much then getting copies of international titles is relatively easy. iPads and tablets allow writers to buy and download single issues of publications worldwide in a digital format while email allows instant communication when submitting pitches and articles.

But why sell your work overseas? Because multiple sales to overseas markets could greatly boost your income. Although, a feature that will sell without change to different publications overseas requires careful shaping to transcend all the cultural boundaries.

Increasingly, magazines are being reproduced in various countries in their own languages (sometimes with a new title) and they will translate from English, but few features can be marketed in this way without some rewriting. There are, on the other hand, numerous possibilities for rewriting a feature, especially if you've done a fair amount of research which has thrown up a few different angles which can be exploited.

If you are serious about becoming an international writer, then it might help to register with a syndication agency. However, such agencies are likely to take around 50 per cent of your article fee in commission.

This chapter will guide you through the necessary processes, demonstrating that all is required is initiative, research, good marketing skills and of course the ability to write.

Finding opportunities

There are excellent resources for finding such markets including marketing magazines, guidebooks such as *The Writers' & Artists' Yearbook* (UK) and *Writer's Market* (US) as well as websites. No matter which source you use, it is important to check the names of editors and other details as these could be out of date. A visit to the publication's website or a quick phone call may be necessary to confirm such details. It's also wise to check if the magazine's website has any submission guidelines.

From Michael Sedge's perspective, the digital age has enhanced his opportunities by widening his market. When the freelance journalist, author and entrepreneur first started, he had to ask friends to pick up magazines while on their travels or pour over pages from directories. "Now I can find markets in seconds," he says.

"For example, I just typed 'Iberia in-flight magazine' into Google and came up with, among others, Nexus Media Asia (http://nexusmedia.asia/). They appear to be an international advertising firm, which represents hundreds of publications in the travel, entertainment, luxury, and many, many other industries. Among their in-flight publications are those of Iberia, British Airways, Air France. They represent global hotel publications for Marriott and Ritz-Carlton."

In such instances, Michael advises spending time reviewing an agency's selection and then making an approach, "acting like you want to advertise". He also suggests asking such agencies to send you media kits, which are put together by advertising departments and frequently include a recent copy of the magazine.

During his search for international publications ISSUU (https://issuu.com) came up. This digital publishing platform has thousands of publications which can be viewed online. However, do make sure that these are bona fide titles as sometimes students publish their course magazines on this site.

In addition to digital publishing platforms, the following online sites have a range of useful resources:

- **Worldwide Freelance Writer** (www.worldwidefreelance.com): has a comprehensive database of worldwide markets listing more than 2,400 publications from across the globe.
- **Onlinenewspapers.com** (www.onlinenewspapers.com): is a worldwide newspaper directory which enables users to search for entries by country.
- **Writer's Contracts** (https://writerscontracts.com/syndication-agencies-for-feature-writers): lists numerous syndication agencies worldwide and has numerous resources for freelance writers and journalists.

When selling copy to media outlets, it's important to be clear about what rights you will be asked to sign over. Always check whether those rights will be for print, digital or online, or all three. Many publishers now ask for all rights. In general, the rights you are willing to grant and how the rights are offered are likely to determine the fee you can expect. Some overseas publications are not interested in features you've sold in the UK under an FBRO agreement, but many are, so long as you're offering a publication First Rights within its country.

Some overseas magazines will accept features in English then translate them. The German periodicals business, for example, will do this, charging you a fee for the service, but often paying well enough to make it worthwhile. Increasingly, magazines are syndicated around the world, produced at the same time in different European countries in their own languages. Again, they may translate your feature for a fee. Sometimes features that can be marketed in this way without some rewriting are relatively few. If you're going down this road opting for syndication would seem to be the answer.

Getting started

Although close analysis of a publication is the best kind of market research, editorial policies can be put into sharper focus by having the writers' guidelines that some magazines will send to you on request. Many American magazines, for example, provide this service.

Apart from the writers' guidebooks, writing magazines such as the American *Writer's Digest* and in the UK *Writer's Forum* and *Writing Magazine* often suggest likely markets for recycling material, including reselling in different countries. Examples of this are shared at the end of this chapter by Michael Sedge, who wrote a few features on this topic for *Writer's Forum* early in the 2000s. His feature on the sunken Roman city of Baiae off the coast of Italy had sold more than 20 times, in 12 countries.

Often, suitable publications can be found through search engines. For example, a Google search of writing magazines in New Zealand yielded a few prospects. It is worth investing time honing your search skills, this can be done by trial and error. Using the "+" in your search will narrow it. A search for international business magazines+freelance articles (note, no gaps between magazines+freelance) also produced numerous opportunities.

Once you have developed a global approach to selling your work, more international opportunities in English language publications may open up. The monthly magazine *New Internationalist*, for example, published in Oxford, devotes most of each issue with campaigning zeal to important world issues related to world poverty and inequality.

Getting your pitch right for such markets is crucial. First impressions count so each one must be carefully crafted. Avoid cut and paste jobs, as when pitching to several editors on similar titles errors such as the wrong name, or title of the publication, can easily occur. Instead opt for a personally tailored but professional approach and capture the editor's attention with a sharp subject line in your email.

Make sure your pitch demonstrates:

a) That you have read the magazine.
b) How the idea fits in with the title's editorial pillars and relates to the culture, etc.

c) Why their readers would be interested.
d) Your professional profile and why you are the best person to write this article.

Pay attention to your pitch metrics. How successful are you in getting ideas accepted? Editors everywhere receive numerous pitches daily. They may find it convenient to reply "No thanks" but it may be more convenient just to press delete. Experiment with follow-up emails when no reply is forthcoming within a week or so. Decide from the response, or lack of it, whether to keep that editor on your list.

It's important to understand that with the vast increase in opportunities comes a corresponding reduction in the proportion of pitches that are accepted. So, make sure your pitch is watertight.

Writing for different countries

When starting out choose countries you know something about, that interest you, that you can research reasonably quickly. If you have contacts (colleagues, friends or family, etc.) living there then this could help you keep up to date from a journalistic perspective. They may also be willing to send you magazines or newspapers and help you add a personal slant to your market research.

Study the culture

Market research when pitching to overseas markets must be extended. As well as the target publication, study the country – its culture and its people. For example, features about prison life in the UK or sailing around the coast of Britain may well be of interest to overseas markets. But the writer also needs to know what the prison life or the sailing is like in the target country – and what aspects a magazine's readers would be most interested to know.

Whether pitching or writing up the article, avoid any suggestion that your country is superior in the way it handles things. The exception to the rule here are column or comment pieces (and the editor has agreed to it), in which case ensure the facts stand up and that you do it tactfully. It will help if you know the different varieties of slang and the kinds of English used overseas. A feature sent to the US must use American spelling and watch those cultural references such as referring to baseball rather than a cricket match or soccer as opposed to football as in the US the latter is a different game.

Guidebooks, encyclopedias, online tourist and government sites are all good starting points for your research. Read, if you can, what your target audience is likely to read. If you're aiming at the US, for example, get acquainted with *Time Magazine*, *The New Yorker* and *The New York Times*. Also, have a look at local papers and magazines if targeting a specific area or town in the US.

When writing a pitch, demonstrate that you're clued up on the cultural aspects – and that you have something to offer that might be more difficult to obtain from the natives. This could be a different angle or perspective that will intrigue or arouse curiosity. Second, reveal that you know the audience both in terms of demographics and the culture.

Gaining an understanding of the cultural differences is vital. For example, if pitching to an Islamic country it would be wise to avoid mentioning women in bikinis, human body parts, alcohol, dogs and pigs due to the strictness of the religion and its interpretation. Moreover, features are rejected in some European countries because they suggest readers can buy goods at international chain stores such as Wal-Mart or can visit a McDonald's when these establishments haven't arrived yet.

Finding opportunities

In the first instance, many of your opportunities for writing internationally are likely to come from travelling. Freelances have an advantage because they can find more time for it and have greater freedom to publish in a range of publications. Even travelling without a specific purpose or for a holiday has many benefits such as seeing how other people live, and broadening your horizons.

Although the art of writing travel articles was explored in Chapter 6, the focus here is on features that come out of travel, whatever your interests. Whether writing about the catering industry, art, architecture, agriculture, sport, banking, zoos or whatever, you can find subjects, ideas and angles for features in English-language publications worldwide.

Of course, travel writing can be expensive, but with luck and experience it is sometimes possible to get your travel expenses covered. That said, editorial budgets are rapidly decreasing along with fees for articles. Therefore, it is prudent to consider other options to fund your trips, these might include:

- **Writing numerous articles:** rather than just one for every area visited, thus generating sufficient income to cover your expenses and make a decent profit.
- **Producing a travel article:** for each trip to facilitate free accommodation (and sometimes travel) from travel companies, hotels, tourist offices or international trade associations.
- **Press trips:** getting invited on a press trip then using that trip as a basis for also writing other articles for multiple markets.
- **Using part of your holiday:** to research potential articles. That way you should cover all your holiday expenses and perhaps will make a small profit.

The last is also a good way for new writers to get started as it helps to build a portfolio. Without one, or an established reputation, it is very difficult to get decent rates of pay for your work, reasonable expenses or free press trips.

Apart from the US the other English-speaking or post-colonial nations are a good bet. Many of their media organisations have editorial offices in London such as ACP Magazines, formerly the Australian Consolidated Press. Having acquired samples of those magazines produced by such an organisation, it is often possible to pitch to their London office. Spain with its English-speaking tourists and expats has several English-language publications, and so does the Netherlands where English is widely understood.

Syndication

If you are an established writer, or have had a few articles published in national newspapers or magazines, then syndication agencies can help achieve an international status. However, undertake an in-depth research of potential agencies before approaching them. Their requirements (and efficiency) can vary greatly. Some will buy your work outright, others will pay between 25 and 50 per cent commission from the sales. Some deal with translation fees, others don't.

Writing for journalism.co.uk Sarah Marshall points out that it's important for writers to understand their earning potential. In her article, *How To: Syndicate Freelance Articles Abroad*, Marshall cites the IFA (International Features Agency) when giving example on earnings. "The International Features Agency has a simple formula: the journalist and agency get a 50–50 split of the revenue generated. If the IFA commissions a writer, the split is 80–20 in the favour if the journalist" (Marshall, 2011).

However, syndication isn't just for features, columns can be sold worldwide too. If you can keep a regular column going that becomes eagerly awaited in many different areas, you may be catching sight of substantial rewards. The masters are mainly American, such as Art Buchwald, an American humourist known for his column in *The Washington Post* which was syndicated around the world. Although, with column writing, agencies are unlikely to be interested in taking you on until you have become well established. Even then, you will need to convince the agency that you can produce a column of *international* quality indefinitely. Not an easy feat.

So how does a writer identify a potential international quality in a column? Although it is hard to pin down precisely, such a column should have a unique style with the depth, breadth and humour to appeal to readers across the globe as demonstrated with Art Buchwald. Writing about Buchwald for *The New York Times*, Mitchell Martin reveals how Art began his career as a columnist at 23 writing a column for the European edition of the *New York Herald Tribune*. This excerpt from Martin's article titled, *Art Buchwald: He'll Always Have Paris*, demonstrates the power of being able to adapt to circumstances.

> It seems like it was a pretty good job, squiring the likes of Bogart and Bacall, Lena Horne and Elvis Presley around Paris. But it began badly, he said, largely because his newspaper experience consisted solely of some unpaid work for Variety.
>
> With those credentials and some questionable early writing, he said, "I figured I was going to get canned, so I started being funny. I was funny about international stuff, I was funny about the Aga Khan, the Duchess of Windsor."

Eventually, he said, his ineptitude at writing and the dealing with the daily difficulties of Parisian life, worked to his advantage and he built a following: "I have been described — and I don't object to it — as a Charlie Chaplin figure. Everything happened to me, and it also happened to all the tourists and they identified with it."

(Martin, 1999)

In the excerpt, we see how Buchwald embraced his identity and adapted his style instead of trying to change who he was to fit in. By taking this somewhat brave approach, Buchwald forged a unique style in his work thus giving his columns that global appeal throughout his career which spanned several decades. And in that is a good lesson – writers must embrace their sense of self and forge their own identity if they want to stand out.

Some syndication agencies want a series of columns that will continue indefinitely, and are already being published. When the field is specialised (food, architecture, health, science, etc.) illustrations, photographs, cartoons or infographics will also help sell your work.

Agencies may also be interested in finding book publishers to consider putting a writer's work into a book.

Case study: the expert in selling articles multiple times

Michael Sedge is a prolific American journalist, author, marketing specialist and entrepreneur. He is credited in more than 4,000 articles, several audiotape scripts, children's plays, some 30 books (combined collaborations as well as solely authored) and four television documentaries.

His diverse scale of topics range from expatriate affairs, US and NATO military and archaeology, to the London theatre beat, the business of freelance writing and Italy. Here he shares his experience, revealing how he once sold one article more than 20 times, in 12 countries.

I was unique in that I became a writer after four years in the United States Navy, stationed in Italy. When I left the service, my wife asked: "What are you going to do now?" "I think I will be a journalist," I replied, which was strange given that I had worked in accounting and administration. "As long as you make the same amount of money, great," was her immediate response.

A steep learning curve followed. My total income for the next 12 months was $82 – I learned that good writing was not enough – you had to know how to sell those words. So, I spent the next five years becoming perhaps the top "sales" writer in the world. On average, I sold 27 articles a month to 42 clients around the world in several languages. This was pre-Internet and each day I would send no less than 15 queries (pitches) and editorial packages (article/photo).

The fact that I travel a great deal makes it is easier to find new markets. I find international publications – in English – at airports, train stations, hotels, restaurants, and many other places. Writers who are not so fortunate but live near a large airport should spend a few hours there going through the newsstands and bookstores.

The Internet has made things much easier as writers no longer have the expense of shipping their work to media around the world. Today anyone can do exactly what I used to do – which used to take up a full day – in just 30 minutes. Digital images and articles in Word are standard around the world. And they arrive in minutes. Moreover, you get replies usually within a day or two, whereas I used to wait up to three months.

Perhaps my steepest learning curve was that major media, whether it be an online or print newspaper, magazine or even television, radio or podcast, runs on advertising. I learned to reach out NOT to editors, but to the advertising departments of these potential clients and ask them for a media kit. This not only gave me their distribution data (such as the circulation plus readership figures, geographical reach, reader demographics and profiles), but also the publication's editorial pillars together with a detailed list of the key topics they would be covering in the next year or more. Armed with this information I could focus my ideas only sending editors targeted pitches on topics I knew they were seeking.

One of my biggest successes early on was selling the same article 20 times in 12 countries. It's important to realise that there is a world of good writers, but only a handful of good marketers. To be a successful writer you need to be both.

Early in my career, I realised that an editor working with a magazine distributed in the United Kingdom, did not require or desire worldwide publishing rights. When I pitched an article, after researching their distribution, I would then offer them ONLY the rights within their distribution area. And sometimes I would even narrow that. For instance, I would pitch to a magazine that deals with gardening and suggest, "Exclusive Serial Rights to a Gardening Magazine in the United Kingdom." This then becomes part of the pitch – and you should always get some form of a written agreement. This would leave me free, say, to sell the article to a weekly newspaper magazine. Or I might sell it to *high life*, the in-flight magazine of British Airways.

Taking such an approach, a writer can sell the same story to hundreds even thousands of publications around the world. For instance, I have one evergreen (can be published anytime of the year in any publications that use general interest articles) on an Italian archaeological discovery for which I have sold exclusive in-flight magazine rights, exclusive rights in the Italian, Spanish, Arabic and Korean languages (each separate sales), first serial rights in the USA, second serial rights in the USA, etc.

To thrive writers must tell editors what is for sale, not the other way around. But in the digital age, selling to Internet publications GREATLY limits your right to sell. So you may want to start with traditional print media and then offer second and third serial rights to Internet publications because you can say, "However, you are getting exclusive internet serial right."

In this vein, other successes include *The Lost Ships of Pisa*, sold 37 times. It also became a book and a *Discovery Channel Book Club Selection*. Second in line was *Baiae: The Sunken Roman City*, which sold 26 times in several languages.

What is the secret of my success? Without a doubt the fact that I spend 70 per cent of my time marketing and selling. Let me give you the math behind this decision: I worked for The Associated Press as a stringer for three years. I would write three to four articles a week and get $100 each and at the end of the month I'd get a cheque for $1,600. And that was for 16 articles. Then I realised if I dedicated more time to selling my work around the world, I could write two articles a month and get, say, $250 for each one. But if I sold each of them to eight publications, I would make $4,000. By monitoring the rights I was selling, I would keep sending out these same articles to other publications if they were rejected.

Ultimately, I was producing 24 articles a year, but had over 800 packages out circulating and my annual income was into the hundreds-of-thousands of dollars. Less work, greater income is the key to success.

When working this way, unless the article is really specific to a geographical region, little or no adaptation is usually required. I have published over 4,200 articles (you see, I said have "publish" not have "written") and less than 1% were rewritten to fit a market.

Pitching – albeit by email in today's digital age – is still the best way to get published. A professional pitch must include: a potential headline, first paragraph, a paragraph on what the article will cover, any experts you will interview/quote, and finally who you are and why you are the perfect person for this assignment.

My advice to those just starting out is to be resilient and keep going. For example, in the last 48 hours, I have been traveling through the Italian region of Tuscany with friend and author Joel Jacobs. We wrote the novel, *Death Watch*, back in 1995. The story was about an American special forces soldier turned terrorist. He gets hold of the Ebola virus and puts it on to a US aircraft carrier in the Mediterranean and then runs through Europe with an NCIS agent on his heels. Remember, in 1995, before the 9/11 attack in the United States, terrorism was something between the American military and some group in the Middle East. The TV show *NCIS* was not even an idea, so no one, except people in the US Navy, knew who they were. And the Ebola virus had not become a household name.

We were, one might say, ahead of our time. As a result Columbia Pictures option the work for a movie, and actors were being selected, a major, global publisher was preparing to launch the book just ahead of the film ... Then comes 9/11 and all of the deals were cancelled. No one could touch the subject of terrorism.

The point is not to get discouraged. Three years ago, a Los Angeles publisher called and asked, "Did you ever sell that book about Ebola." "No," I told him. It was released a year later in English and a short time ago in Italy, which is why we were enjoying the country's great food and wine while autographing books.

So, the best advice I can give is to write, every day. It can be a poem, short story, an article, or three to five pages of a book, but write. Writing is one of the hardest disciplines I know. Persistence, however, is the key to success.

Although writing is a hard career, it can be a beautiful one if you only have the discipline to do it every day.

Action plan

After undertaking in-depth market research outlined in this chapter and having read at least a couple of issues of that magazine or newspaper, put together some pitches.

The ideas should be an adaptation of any of the three feature proposals you have produced while working through this book. Your pitch to overseas editors – and make sure you have the right details for the commissioning editor – should contain the following:

1 A headline and stand-first written in the style of the publication.
2 Sell your article by including why this is suitable for readers of the magazine/newspaper and demonstrating some local/national knowledge.
3 Give a summary of the content along with details of interviewees, etc.
4 Now sell yourself, include an "About me" paragraphs setting out your credentials.
5 Do cite publications you have been published in or attach a sample or two of your published work.

Then follow up any commission or write the feature that is based on what you think was the most promising pitch.

15 A career in magazines and newspapers

Miriam Phillips

Whether you work for newspapers, magazines or online, the fundamental core journalism skills are the same. You must be good with people, you must have a thirst for news, the truth or just writing the best article on any given subject. I have to admit, I was one of those really annoying people who knew exactly what I wanted to do from about the age of four. At the age of four it started with making family newspapers, then on to the dizzy heights of my primary school newspaper, comprehensive school newspapers, college radio and then on to train to be a multimedia journalist at Bournemouth University. All that time I had this unwavering vision that the end goal was to be a journalist, there was simply no other option.

During those early days, taking advice from peers I volunteered for pretty much every work experience or media platform available. Timing has played a big part in my career. While at work experience at the small weekly newspaper *The Western Gazette* in Somerset I was assigned to cover the protests ahead of the Iraq war in London. This was the very first time I felt like a real journalist. The day was powerful, emotional and completely eye opening in every way. I realised the true power of interviewing people and bringing their opinions to the people. From that point onwards I wanted to cover every possible news story.

During my time at university I also went on various work placements that really put me in good stead for the future. I was at BBC Northampton the day of the 7/7 bombings in London in 2005 and that day, for many journalists, was the day everything shifted. It was the day that user-generated content made the front pages of newspapers, mobile videos of the bombing were on every TV news channel and the traumatic event was covered in real time, in a way the UK had never experienced.

Stuart Allen, Professor of Journalism at Cardiff University, said the fateful London attack "was the day that news reporting was redefined" stating:

> Viewed with the benefit of hindsight, the London attacks signalled a decisive turning point in the emergence of a new, collaborative ethos for journalism, at least where the reporting of crisis events unfolding in real-time was concerned.
>
> (Allen, 2017)

Colleagues of mine reflect that it was a very symbolic day for journalism in the UK and ever since that day, obtaining the right user-generated copy, mobile and video has become a fundamental part of our job.

My career path

Starting my career on daily newspapers, it was quite a traditional route in journalism. From the first day, I loved the variety that each day would bring. One moment you'd be in court reporting on petty crime, to high-level abuse cases and the next running around my patch trying to report on community stories. Crime reporting became my passion and I moved around from paper to paper to experience different places and to work in London. Working for *Trinity Mirror* at a time when the London weekly papers became free, the role was to be a roving multimedia reporter covering the huge boroughs of Kensington and Chelsea. All these roles required you to become embedded in the community. This was an essential experience and actually, at the very heart of it, building contacts and knowing what's going on in your community, be that geographical or online, are the absolute fundamental skills for any journalist.

Eventually I returned to Dorset to work as a Chief Reporter for Newsquest and there I started writing longer features for magazines and soon found this was a passion to take further. Soon after that I left to set up my own publishing company and launched a high-end hyperlocal magazine. Of course, these two types of journalism are very different. Magazine stories are nearly always positive for one thing, but the skills of networking and understanding your community are key to both. I now also teach journalism to students at on the Multimedia Journalism BA (Hons) degree at Bournemouth University, returning full circle to the place where I learnt my craft. There, my news and feature colleagues and I teach that writing stories is always down to research, the interview and the writing.

It doesn't matter what discipline or platform, be it social media, newspapers or magazines, the basics are the same. Journalism has not changed, just the way we display it. That, to me, is what makes the future so exciting.

Publishing from a business perspective

In newsrooms, job roles used to be clearly defined. You were a reporter or a sub-editor, designer or editor and it wasn't until being promoted to a senior position that you had to worry about the business side of things. Now, more than ever it is important that even as a trainee journalist you understand the business model.

Consider the following questions:

- Are you working for a newspaper whose priority is newspaper sales or website visits?
- Does your editor want people to stay on the website for as long as possible or click through to lots of other stories?
- Does your magazine's revenue rely on repeated sales, subscriptions or classified advertising or sponsorship?

Find out the business priorities and make sure you keep abreast with changes in the industry.

If you have your sights set on a particular publication or company do lots of research. Read their company reports, the trade press and importantly view their media pack to see what packages they are offering their customers. This matters, because from the day you step through their doors, whether on placement or for a job interview, it will put you at an advantage to be informed. Being informed will help you come up with suggestions of how you can help that business grow.

More opportunities are being created

It is an exciting time for a journalist who has ideas for new projects, community campaigns or social media projects that might reach a new audience or just communicate with the existing audience in a new way. You might bring insights into a certain demographic or age group or specialism that the company has lacked previously. If so, use that to your advantage. Just as journalists are now required to report the story in different ways, they also can't afford to lose track of the company's focus.

Media groups are all competing for online readership, so you would be wise to familiarise yourself with analytics. It is one way you can help keep on top of your company's competitors, their contacts and campaigns. There are various analytical programmes which track every detail of an online story from web visits, how long someone reads the story, where the reader stumbled across the story, at which point they left and why this might be. Journalists are also ranked against each other for their online stories so you can see how your story is performing every second of the day.

Although this can bring another dimension of pressure for journalists, especially those writing content that might not go viral such as investigative reporting, it also plays right to the competitive drive of many journalists.

At a recent Facebook conference in London, I saw in action how the programme Crowdtangle is working with worldwide media corporations to give new insight into analytics. The application shows content from more than one million social media and newsfeeds. From the real-time dashboard you can not only source and research social content but benchmark your content against competitors. It is also helping journalists source content from communities, locally or online, by monitoring key words across social media platforms. Leading newspapers, broadcasters and magazines are all using this or another analytical tool and it pays a journalist to be on top of this technology.

Work placements

Getting work experience is absolutely vital to gaining an insight into the industry. The National Council for the Training of Journalists (NCTJ) recognises the importance of practical experience that complements the study of journalism.

Their research shows that work experience is an excellent way to put skills learned on a journalism course into practice and it may become the first step towards a successful career in the media.

The industry view

Emma Robinson, accreditation manager at the NCTJ, has worked as a journalist and a newspaper editor and has both untaken lots of work experience herself as well as training lots of placement students. "Practical work experience can be invaluable to a future journalist." Here she shares her advice on getting started.

> It is an excellent way to put the skills learned on a journalism course into practice and it may become the first step towards a successful career in the media. It is, therefore, essential that students make the most of their work experience placement.
>
> The key to a successful placement is preparation. Come prepared with your own ideas for stories and research the key issues in the area beforehand. Employers value creativity and initiative.
>
> Volunteer for any tasks that are suggested – whether it be phoning a press officer or going out to get vox pops – it shows enthusiasm and dedication. No task is too small. Being in the newsroom will help you refine your skills and learn new ones, giving you a taste of real-life decision-making and time management.
>
> Use this opportunity wisely – ask questions about the industry, build up your contacts and impress your new colleagues. Who knows what doors this placement could open?

Advice on work experience

Budding journalists studying on short journalism courses, distance learning and degrees across the UK are advised to study for the NCTJ Diploma in Journalism, which includes 60wpm shorthand or 100wpm for the gold standard. A very important part of this training is a work placement. Here's a list of useful tips from the NCTJ to help finding work experience:

- Start by contacting your local media outlets: newspapers, magazines, news websites, radio stations or broadcasters. Try to find out who deals with work experience so that you can call or email them directly.
- Editors are busy people, especially when their deadline is approaching. Find out what time of day is best to contact them.
- If sending an email, introduce yourself, explain that you are looking for work experience and suggest some dates. Attach an updated copy of your CV.
- Always give the media organisation enough notice to process any requests for work experience. Some companies have a waiting list of a couple of months

for placements. Do not expect to get work experience the week after sending a request.
- Tutors can be good sources of information about possible work experience placements – use your contacts.
- Don't take rejection personally: learn to be thick-skinned and, if at first you don't succeed, keep trying.

When on placement

It can be slightly daunting working in any new office or newsroom so here's a list of tips from the NCTJ to help you on your placement.

- Be prepared with your own ideas for stories. Employers value creativity and initiative.
- Be punctual – if you can't get to work on time, how can your editor be sure you'll be able to meet your deadlines?
- Volunteer for any tasks that are suggested, whether it be phoning a press officer or going out to get vox pops – it shows enthusiasm and dedication.
- Always have a notebook and pen at hand – you never know when you'll hear something that could make a good story.
- Talk to your colleagues – they are a mine of information and advice on the industry.
- Ask for feedback and/or a reference. Try and get a couple of minutes to sit down with your editor and ask for some constructive criticism – what did you do well and what could you have done differently? If you have completed an extended placement, getting a reference from an editor will be invaluable for any future job applications.

A graduate's perspective

Journalism student Liam Grace, who graduated in 2018 from Bournemouth University, describes his work experience at different media outlets as absolutely fundamental. He says:

> Getting the work experience I did at ESPN was the most significant thing that has happened to me in my career. It was the thing that changed everything for me and being thrown in at the deep end was exactly the right thing for me. It gave me the freedom to write feature articles, pitch ideas to editors and just really cement that this is the job for me.

Liam went on to win a prestigious university prize for the best placement feedback after his paid sandwich internship at sports TV channel and website ESPN UK.

In his appraisal by the lead editor he stated that the student's diligence, attitude, commitment and hard work as ESPN UK's editorial intern resulted in his stories being carried around the world on ESPN sites, including in Australia, Africa, India and the United States. In just a few months Liam went from work experience intern to editorial assistant. Following his graduation Liam went on to work for Sky Sports.

Here's Liam's top tips for getting the most from placements.

- Take every opportunity to get work experience, whether it is university or college magazines, radio stations or spending your holiday time at papers or magazines.
- Start your own blog and publish as often as possible, use this to showcase all your work.
- While on placement be bold, have ideas and work out how to pitch them. If you get the right balance people will really respect you and you'll find it easier the second time.

When applying for work experience take time to update your CV. Put your most important attributes in the header of the CV in a summary. If you are at the start of your journalistic career make sure you list every article you've published, perhaps while studying and list any other placements you have done. There are lots of free ways to get advice on your CV, from local library workshops to university and college careers advice and lots of great websites. Make sure you consult widely and above all make sure there are no mistakes.

It is also good practice to use a professional website such as LinkedIn and make sure this is updated to reflect your CV. Once you've been on a placement, connect with your colleagues and editors and ask for references on LinkedIn too. This permanent appraisal might just help you get a job in the future.

Build up a portfolio

Producing a portfolio or body of work is a key part to getting a job in journalism. Where portfolios used to be big folders full of cuttings and magazine pages, they are now often a portfolio website. These can be made quickly and cheaply using a range of online companies and are a great way to showcase all work, including video, opinion pieces, PDF articles or direct links. Take time to save every word published and make sure this portfolio site is prominent on your CV or LinkedIn page.

Jason Alner, Recruitment Business Partner for Haymarket Media Group, has expert advice on how a portfolio can help to get your foot in the door for work experience.

> Employers can be inundated with requests for work experience, so try to stand out amongst your peers. Examples of any previous work (links to published articles or blogs) are a great way of showing employers why they should give you a chance to work with them.

Cover letters or introduction emails are important when making first impressions. Flattery can work, but only goes so far. Talk about their industry or their company and tell them why you're interested and passionate to work with them.

If you can be knowledgeable about their subject or audience, you'll stand a much greater chance of working with them.

Mapping your future

In a changing industry such as journalism it pays to have a plan, but importantly be adaptable and react with change. Traditionally trainee journalists would get a job as a trainee or editorial assistant, work to complete their probation period or senior exams and then get experience working as a journalist, before perhaps gaining experience on a newsdesk or editing sections of a magazine. Those showing promise could work their way up to editor or deputy editor or perhaps move into sub-editing or a journalism specialism. Many followed this path and had a media ladder strategy to move from a small weekly, to a daily and then national publication. However, the changing nature of the industry means that the more senior roles are now available to journalists showing promise early on, or striving to take their own part of the market.

Some journalists prefer to stay as freelance and write for several publications. When you finish your course it is important to have a plan. What kind of publication do you want to work for? Can you do more work experience to gain more contacts and clippings for your portfolio? Focus your efforts on pitching ideas for articles to the commissioning editors, be persistent and show how passionate you are.

In today's job market journalists need to stay current by building their own brand. It is essential that aspiring journalists have a regularly updated blog and professional social media channels that can be used to promote your stories. A big attribute of hiring a young journalist is that they understand social media networks so use this to your advantage and broadcast live on channels such as Facebook, Instagram and Twitter. Use websites such as Reddit and Medium to build your own brand and keep working on it.

If successful you can use your online platform to network with peers, editors and the public and build on these connections. Editors will be impressed by this and it will help you to get a job in their organisation.

A word from the experts

If the last decade has taught us anything, it's that the industry has changed immeasurably. But having valuable work experience and making the right first impression is still fundamental. I asked four industry experts in both the newspaper and magazine industries and asked what their tips would be for, first, obtaining work experience and, second, how this would help a future career in the industry.

Toby Granville at Newsquest

Editorial Director for Newsquest Media Group, Toby Granville, emphasises how important work placements are to see if you are cut out to be a journalist.

Work experience is a crucial part of any trainee journalist's training in order for them to fully understand the industry away from the classroom. There is no better experience that can be taught than to actually be in a newsroom environment – to watch and be part of an exciting "news day" as it unfolds.

Getting work experience can help a prospective journalist know for sure whether they're cut out for the job. It's not 9–5 and you won't be uncovering "Watergate" scandals every day – but it's still the most exciting job in the world if you're the right type of person for the industry.

When applying for work experience there are two things you need to get absolutely right: GRAMMAR and SPELLING. Editors and news editors will simply press 'delete' straightaway if you have any errors like that – so make sure you check and then double check it again before pressing send.

What we look for in a work experience student is a confident, enthusiastic "can do" attitude – and brimming with story ideas. Certainly, nowadays they also need a good grasp of digital technology such as being able to make a compelling video on their smartphone – and know their way around social media like Facebook, Twitter and Instagram. They will also be shadowing our staff journalists going out on the "big" breaking news stories and should expect to get a few by-lines themselves during their placement. In fact, many reporters are hired after being remembered for a work experience stint – so there's nothing more important than making a strong lasting impression.

Editors at Newsquest consider trainees with the right qualifications first – but certainly those with impressive cuttings or links to great online stories gained through work experience will stand out ahead of the rest of the pack.

Rebecca Constable and Jason Alner at Haymarket

Head of Talent and Learning at Haymarket Media Group, Rebecca Constable and her colleague Jason Alner, Recruitment Business Partner, both say work experience is crucial to getting a job in the industry. Haymarket Media Group has more than 70 brands across the world including lots of top magazines. Rebecca and Jason underline the fact that a good placement can lead to a paid position and that being proactive is key.

In such a competitive market, I believe it's crucial for trainee journalists to show how they stand out from other candidates. Taking ownership of their careers and proactively seeking out work experience opportunities to demonstrate their passion for a brand as well as their technical journalistic skills is key to this.

Work experience can be the small differentiating factor between 1st and 2nd place at an interview. Work experience is a brilliant opportunity to stand out to employers, but also crucial in understanding if there is a preferred area of focus for the trainee journalists. Experiencing different organisations, industries and medias (video, online, newspapers/news, features, opinion etc.) and finding what you love (or hate!) can be a huge help when planning the first steps in your career.

Employers will expect that trainee journalists will not be a master of the industry, but will expect them to have done some research. A good prior understanding of a particular industry and a genuine interest is crucial in landing that work experience job. After showing an initial interest, employers will be more willing to take the time to train and share their crucial experience. Often work experience placements will be spending time with different members of a team, allowing trainees to draw from different individuals with their own unique experiences.

At Haymarket we look for a trainee journalist who is proactive, can articulate what they can offer and what they are hoping to learn. Someone who demonstrates their passion for the brand and industry and other related experience or activities they have completed in that field.

Someone who is willing to learn from the ground up and will maximise the opportunity presented to them.

While in the business, how do they present themselves? What they wear, how punctual they are, are all important. What else can they learn while they are here – what other conversations can they have to explore what sort of experience they should be building in the early stages of their career? Building breadth of experience and skills is more important than being an expert in one.

When roles do become available our hiring managers always reflect on the quality of students they have had and who we should be proactively contacting for our shortlist. Being on the shortlist puts them at the front of the queue.

Jonathan Telfer at Warners Group Publications PLC

Editor of Writing Magazine, *Jonathan Telfer, gave this sound advice about taking on new staff writers.*

Most of all, I look for enthusiasm and interest. Almost everything else can be learnt or acquired … but doing so takes commitment, which would be wasted if the applicant's enthusiasm or interest waned and they left six months later.

I would be turned off by poor use of language or grammar though. If you have reached employment age without picking up fluency in your native tongue, this might not be the right job.

16 Law and ethics
A rough guide

David Mascord

It's easy to get caught up with polishing an article's structure or thinking up a great intro, but ignorance of the law can be costly. The law affects all forms of journalism – and all journalists, including staff writers, freelancers, bloggers and tweeters. In-depth articles and reviews are open to the same potential legal dangers as news stories or news features. And these days writers can't always rely on sub-editors to spot their legal problems for them – some brands don't have them anymore.

This rough guide gives an overview of some of the main areas of law affecting feature articles, including libel law, restrictions on reporting legal cases, and the right of individuals to protect their work and their privacy. For more detail it's worth investing in the latest editions of *McNae's Essential Law for Journalists* (Hanna and Dodd, 2018) or Frances Quinn's *Law for Journalists* (2018). The law in Scotland is broadly similar in relation to journalism but there are some differences, so a text such as *Scots Law for Journalists* (McInness, 2010) is a useful guide for Scottish writers.

To keep up to date with changes in media law and current debates and cases, follow the media law coverage on www.pressgazette.co.uk and the NUJ's *The Journalist* magazine. Also, be aware of the content of the NUJ Code of Practice and the Independent Press Standards Organisation (IPSO) Editors' Code of Practice (see Appendices 4 and 5) which offer best practice guidelines on journalism ethics and standards that are not necessarily specified in law.

Copyright

In 2011, writer and columnist Johann Hari was suspended by *The Independent* for plagiarism. He admitted to using other writers' material in his articles without making reference to it. In particular, in profile features he had written, he used quotes which had been given by his interviewees to other journalists without attributing the original source. Hari said he genuinely believed he was doing nothing wrong. Clearly, ignorance is no defence so don't make assumptions about what you can and can't use when it comes to work produced by other people.

According to the 1988 Copyright, Designs and Patents Act (CDPA), the creator of a piece of work is the first owner of copyright in that work until either they assign (i.e. sell or grant permission to use) the copyright in the work; or they license the use of the material for a particular length of time or format. The owner of a work has the right to sue anyone who infringes their copyright.

This includes work – especially images – on websites and social media. There is a common misconception that all material, whether words, images or video, posted online is "in the public domain" and therefore free from copyright protection. This is not the case. The creator owns it – even if they share it online – unless the site's terms and conditions state otherwise. Photographers and their agents are particularly vigilant when it comes to protecting their work and will use the law to enforce their rights. Remember this simple mantra: just because material is easy to access doesn't make it free to use.

This is not to say that you cannot quote or reuse some elements of another copyright work. The defence of "fair dealing" allows writers to quote sections from other texts e.g. for reviews as long as the source text is acknowledged, the work has already been made available to the public, and as long as the extract quoted is not "substantial". Frustratingly, the CDPA doesn't clearly define what a substantial extract looks like: it doesn't state how much of a text can be quoted, for example. However, over time case law has come to interpret substantial material as referring not only to the amount published, but also to the importance of the extract used.

So, quoting a couple of lines from a book because it's in the news or for a review should be fine – as long as it doesn't give away the plot twist. But, for anyone wanting to quote a lengthy extract of a key piece of material from a text, the best advice is to check with the copyright holder.

Note, though, that fair dealing does not apply to pictures. All elements of pictures are thought to be equally substantial. It is a copyright infringement to reproduce them as whole or to publish extracts of them without permission or payment of a fee.

Libel

Copyright may be the most common legal issue to bear in mind for a journalist, but libel is perhaps the area of law that can be the most costly in money and time for media defendants. Libel is material in permanent form (including words, pictures and images that are in printed, online, or broadcast) that lowers a person's or company's reputation in the eyes of a "reasonable person".

The Defamation Act places the burden of proof on those who published the material in question, i.e. the publisher and/or journalist. They must show that they had a defence to publication (see Defences to libel below), which may have to be argued in a lengthy and expensive court case.

A libel claimant who wishes to sue a writer or publication has to show:

- that the material was **published**;
- that it **identified** them (not necessarily by name);
- it could be thought to be **defamatory** (see criteria above);
- and that it **caused, or is likely to cause, serious harm** to reputation.

But what is serious harm? An individual claimant has to show that the material in question caused, or was likely to cause, serious harm to their reputation. Meanwhile, a company ("an organisation trading for profit") must show that the material caused, or was likely to cause, serious financial loss. These relatively new legal criteria were designed to make claimants think twice before bringing "trivial" libel cases or using the law as a threat to strike fear into the hearts of journalists. However, the question of what a claimant needs to demonstrate to prove serious harm has been the subject of much legal argument in recent libel cases. A ruling in the *Lachaux v Independent and others* case in 2017 suggests that evidence of likely or actual serious harm to an individual's reputation is not necessarily required in order to bring a case, it may be implied. So be sure you have your story straight, your facts right and you've considered your defences before you publish.

Defences to libel

The main defences in the 2013 Defamation Act are listed in detail below in Table 16.1. The most commonly-used defences are: Truth, Privilege and Honest Opinion as outlined in the table.

The defence of truth sounds straightforward, but remember a media defendant will need evidence that stands up in court. Simply reading back notes from an interview is not enough – a writer who is a defendant will need to produce documents, recordings and, possibly, witnesses if they have to go to court.

Reviewers and opinion writers will largely rely on the defence of honest opinion but they must ensure that they do not make any assertions of fact that

Table 16.1 Main defences in the 2013 Defamation Act

Truth	Honest opinion (formerly Fair Comment)	Privilege
The defendant has to show the material was substantially true "on the balance of probabilities".	A defence for opinion and reviews. The material in question must be recognisable as comment and be based on true facts, or on privileged matter. It must indicate, in general terms, the facts on which it is based.	Applies to fair and accurate reports of matters of public interest being discussed in specific privileged (i.e. protected) meeting places. This includes reporting on evidence and statements given in court cases; parliamentary debates and committees; company meetings; public meetings; and reports on articles in peer-reviewed academic journals.

cannot be backed up. For example, if a food critic eats a meal they don't enjoy they are within their rights to tell readers why. They can describe what they ate, and explain what they felt was good or bad about their experience of the food, the service and the restaurant ambience. But, for example, they cannot draw the conclusion that the person who cooked the food is the worst chef in the world. Sticking to the foodie theme, in 2006 TV chef Gordon Ramsay successfully sued the *Evening Standard* for libel over a review of his *Kitchen Nightmares* TV show that wrongly claimed some scenes in a particular episode were faked. The reviewer may not have enjoyed the programme, and they were within their rights to say why, but they would need proof to back up their allegation that scenes were supposedly faked.

The defence of privilege, meanwhile, is a powerful tool for journalists reporting matters from court, council meetings, public meetings and other events of public interest. It offers protection as long as the reporting is done fairly and accurately – and without adding any "spin" or colour.

Other defences include:

- **Publication in the public interest.** This is a new defence in the 2013 Defamation Act that for the first time gives journalists a defence of public interest if they published material in a responsible manner.
- **Innocent dissemination.** A defence that can be applied by a publisher where material is transmitted by a person over whom they have no effective control: e.g. in a live broadcast, or in an unmoderated online comment space.
- **Operators of websites defence.** A new defence for publishers and web hosts who actively moderate user comments. It imposes a formal process on hosts for handling comments that individuals or organisations claim are defamatory of them.
- **Consent.** The claimant agreed to publication. (This is often more difficult to prove that it may seem.)
- **Proceedings were not started within the limitation period.** This period is one year from first publication.
- **The complainant has died.** A dead person cannot be libelled. Any ongoing action dies with the complainant.
- **Offer of amends.** A defendant must give a written offer to make a suitable correction and apology; publish the correction in a reasonable manner; and pay suitable damages and costs.
- **Accord and satisfaction.** When an apology has been accepted as full and final settlement.

Good practices for avoiding libel

Of course, the best form of defence is to avoid getting into a position in which there's a risk of being sued. There are a few common-sense steps to take to help ensure articles, and even social media updates, are as legally safe as possible:

- Check all facts before you publish.
- Don't repeat someone else's claim without checking. Just because another title says it, it doesn't mean it's true.
- Keep evidence: notes, documents, recordings, etc.
- Offer a right to reply.
- Apply defamation criteria and consider potential defences before you publish. Do the quotes, observations and facts you have included stand up to legal scrutiny?
- Take care with potential danger words such as "sacked". The term carries specific implications. Was the person sacked, which implies incompetence or wrongdoing? Or were they made redundant or laid off, which means they lost their job through no fault of their own?
- Think before you tweet. Individuals on social media are the authors and publishers of work. If they make libellous statements they may be sued.
- Get advice from someone with more experience.
- Check again.

Contempt

The law allows a fair degree of freedom of expression but protecting the right to a fair trial is paramount. The media cannot debate whether someone arrested for, or charged with, a crime is guilty when the accused person has not yet been the through legal process. A criminal case becomes "active" when any of the following take place: a warrant for arrest is issued; an arrest has been made; or a suspect is charged; or a summons is issued. Any report can be in contempt of court – risking a fine for the publication and editor under the "strict liability" rule – if it creates a substantial risk of prejudice to active legal proceedings.

The rule is strict because your intention is irrelevant. As in other areas of media law, a lack of knowledge is not an excuse. In contempt law, neither is a simple mistake. "Sorry, your honour, I didn't mean it" is no defence.

GQ magazine's coverage of the trial of senior *News of the World* staff on charges related to phone-hacking included an "observational piece" by US journalist Michael Wolff in its April 2014 UK issue. Published several months into the lengthy trial at London's Central Criminal Court, the Old Bailey, the feature looked at the issues involved and speculated on how much the defendants really knew and whether others not on trial were also to blame. It may have been an engagingly-written piece, but unfortunately it was in breach of the Contempt of Court Act. Hearing the case against GQ, the Lord Chief Justice, Lord Thomas said the material on defendant Rebecca Brookes, the chief executive at the newspaper group, "was an improper attack on a defendant in the course of her trial" (*Attorney-General v Conde Nast Publications*, [2015] EWHC 3322). He also said the article was seriously prejudicial to the trials of both Brookes, who was later acquitted, and her co-defendant former *News of the World* editor, Andy Coulson.

The principle of "open justice" states that a public trial in progress can be reported, but it's vital to stick to accurate reporting of what is said in court without embellishing it. Publishing Wolff's article during legal proceedings was a poor editorial decision. That said, contempt law does recognise that issues raised by court cases and trends in crime are a subject of public interest, so it does not limit the publication of a feature article that contributes towards public debate. The defence of "a general discussion of public affairs" (section 5 of the Contempt of Court Act) recognises that a general feature on, for example, the incidence of knife crime in the UK can be published as long as it does not make any direct, prejudicial reference to a current court case on that subject.

Much of contempt law is about common sense: ask yourself, "If I report this, will it affect the defendant's right to a fair trial?"

Anonymity for vulnerable people

The law has very few powers to restrict reporting of the identity of adult defendants in court trials. However, there are a number of restrictions on the identification of vulnerable people involved in court cases as defendants, or those making accusations as alleged victims.

Judges have the power to ban the identification of juveniles (i.e. under-18s) who are defendants, victims or witnesses involved in serious court proceedings involving a jury if they wish. And they often do. Journalists reporting from the press bench in court have some rights to challenge these orders in line with the open justice principle. Get advice from an editor or legal advisor on how to go about this.

Another anonymity restriction can affect journalists even if they are not covering court cases. Under the Sexual Offences Act, alleged victims of sexual offences automatically receive lifelong anonymity from the moment the allegation is made. The anonymity rule applies even if the accused is eventually found not guilty, and even if the alleged victim never reports the matter to the authorities. This can often affect writers of real-life human-interest pieces and sometime those who write celebrity profiles. If an interview subject chooses to "open up" to a journalist for the first time about a past sexual assault on them, their right to anonymity must be respected unless they consent in writing to waive that right. If they are under 16 their anonymity must remain intact regardless.

Breaching any alleged victim's anonymity, even unwittingly or accidentally, will result in a breach of the Act as happened in 2005 when Marie O'Riordan, editor of *Marie Claire* magazine, was fined for publishing the name and photograph of a teenage girl who was the victim of sexual offences. Also, take care with identifying an alleged attacker. If the person being accused of committing a sexual offence by your interviewee has not been to court and found guilty, you are defaming them.

Rights and restrictions when reporting court cases

Newcomers to reporting on trials should be aware of a few general restrictions:

- Making audio recordings in court is not permitted.
- Taking photos or filming in "court precincts" is banned.

- You can't approach jurors and interview them – their deliberations are confidential.

However, also be aware of journalists' rights:

- Trials held in public can be reported as long as no reporting restrictions are breached.
- Live-tweeting a trial contemporaneously from the court press bench is permitted as long as reports comply with the requirements of relevant laws.
- Reporters can ask court staff to confirm details relevant to a case such as charges, and names and addresses of defendants.

The HM Courts & Tribunals Service has issued a series of documents under the heading *Guidance to Staff on Supporting Media Access to Courts and Tribunals* (HMCTS, 2018). If court staff claim you do not have the right to report on a trial be prepared to politely argue your position, and refer them to the guidelines.

Privacy and data protection

The law relating to privacy is a developing area. There is no single statute on privacy, but case law on what the courts have termed the "misuse of private information" has developed via the extension of the law of breach of confidence and the application of the Human Rights Act (HRA).

The HRA recognises two competing principles: the right to a private and family life and the right to freedom of expression. These were put to the test when Naomi Campbell sued *The Mirror* in 2004 over the publication of stories about her being in recovery after a drug addiction and the publication of secretly-taken photographs of her leaving a meeting of Narcotics Anonymous. Campbell won on some of her claims. The case established the principle that even people in the public eye have a reasonable expectation of privacy in certain situations, unless the public interest outweighs this right. More recently, a 2016 privacy case involving the publication of pictures of the children of rock star Paul Weller established that children have a reasonable expectation of privacy that is arguably greater than that of adults.

Data Protection law and General Data Protection Regulation

Data Protection law covers a very specific area of private information in the form of sensitive personal data such as addresses and medical records. The 2018 Data Protection Act (DPA) recognises the principles of the EU's General Data Protection Regulation (GDPR) which, among other things, requires that personal data must be processed lawfully, collected for legitimate specified purposes only, and kept securely.

This affects publishers and journalists: because they store and process personal information, they are data processors or controllers and have a duty to handle data responsibly as required under the law and get necessary permissions, if relevant. For example, if an interview subject gives a journalist their personal email address the interviewee's expectation will be that the journalist will use it to contact them. But the journalist cannot pass the information to the media brand's marketing team for them to use, unless the interview subject has consented. In order to avoid confusion, writers may find that they have to be increasingly clear about how and where any personal data may be used when talking to interviewees.

Journalists and writers should also be aware that "data protection" and "GDPR" can often be cited incorrectly by contacts as reasons why information cannot be made available to them. You may need to remind them that the DPA covers personal data only, not data in general. In addition, the Act does offer journalistic exemptions for personal data that is being obtained or published in the public interest. It's recommended that writers keep an eye on the application of this potentially complex area of law and get advice where appropriate. The website www.journalism.co.uk offers useful brief guides to current topics such as what GDPR means for journalists.

Ethical concerns

The law may be necessarily strict at times, but it does its best not to be overly prescriptive. Courts balance the right to report against the right to protect reputation or private information, and in a free society there is an emphasis on "light touch" media legislation. As a result, newcomers to writing are sometimes surprised to find out how often the law does NOT specifically state what writers can and can't do. These "gaps" in the law are often covered by media regulation in the form of editorial Codes of Conduct and Practice.

Importantly, the editorial codes also list criteria for what is deemed as being in "the public interest". This term is used often by journalists, but not always correctly, so writers are advised to familiarise themselves with the codes' definitions. A formal public interest defence is also applicable in some areas of media law such as libel and privacy, but not in the law of copyright or the Contempt of Court Act.

The codes also offer some guidelines of tricky issues such as recording, secret filming and the ethics of interviewing minors:

- **Children:** there is no law against interviewing children, but get permission from parents or guardians, especially when children are at school or their welfare is involved. See IPSO Editors' Code clause 6.
- **Recording phone calls:** it is not a legal offence to record calls you are involved in, without informing the other participant. The general ethical approach is to explain that the call is being recorded, unless it makes sense not to reveal it.

- **Use of clandestine devices and subterfuge:** the ISPO Code says the press must not use hidden cameras and recorders, or engage in misrepresentation or subterfuge, unless it can be justified in the public interest. It says these methods should be considered and employed only when the material cannot be obtained by other means.
- **Privacy:** the codes echo the law, stating that everyone is entitled to respect for his or her private and family life. IPSO says editors are expected to justify intrusions into any individual's private life. Its code says it is unacceptable to photograph individuals in private places without their consent.

The paragraphs in this chapter may suggest that journalists are often restricted in what they can freely report. However, editors and writers should not allow an awareness of law and ethics to cause them to censor their reporting unnecessarily. Many of the requirements above can be met by practising good journalism. When writing and interviewing, always be aware of how far you can go while staying within the law and without breaching codes.

17 Last word

An editor's perspective, with Jonathan Telfer

Jonathan Telfer, editor of Writing Magazine *(Figure 17.1) reveals how he got his first break in journalism, sharing those experiences that have shaped him as a journalist. He also offers his perspective on what makes a good writer and has some sage advice for those starting out.*

When starting out in journalism I was fortunate enough to get my first break at a time when backdoors and sideways steps were still possible. I joined the *Yorkshire Evening Post* and *Yorkshire Post* as a copytaker, a role, though nobody knew at the time, that would become obsolete within a few years. The copytaker's main job was to sit on the end of a phone and input news copy from reporters who wouldn't have a chance to get back to the newsroom for deadline, or any other material provided on typed or handwritten sheets. I wanted to work in journalism but hadn't expected, as an entry-level job, to be handling front page news copy to meet three deadlines a day.

I wasn't a writer but got the job because of my solid grammar and awareness of style. Unlike the other, somewhat older, copytakers, who'd just type what they were told, I was proud to serve as a first filter and would pull up the reporters for repetition, suggest alternative phrasing or serve as an on-the-fly thesaurus. It gave me a great grounding in writing well, quickly, and exposed me to all the newsroom wisdom a cub journalist needed.

That opened two doors for me.

As one of the youngest people in the newsroom, who would return every lunch break laden with record bags, I always happy to help with anything, whether it fitted my job description or not. My "can-do" attitude led to contributing to freelance work – initially club and event listings, then album and film reviews, then pop culture features too. I did for over a decade, until the demands of my day job increased, and freelance budgets at the papers decreased.

At that time, *Writing Magazine* (*WM*) and *Writers' News* were owned by the newspapers' parent company, and shared some resources ... such as copytakers. When an opening came up for an editorial assistant on the mags, I jumped at the chance. Especially as the topic area so closely matched my own interests and experience.

My proper first by-line was for album reviews in the newly launched *Yorkshire Post* culture supplement. Having spent most of the previous decade longing to be

Figure 17.1 Cover of Writing Magazine. Credit: Writing Magazine

a music journalist, and devouring every bit of music coverage from broadsheets to fanzines, I knew how to write. Despite this, the practical side was a complete learning curve – how to get pre-releases especially. This became much easier once I had a few weeks' worth in print, to demonstrate I wasn't just some kid trying his luck.

I went on to interview people I genuinely admired (which is harder than for those whom you have no strong feelings about) and contribute op-eds and features. The one article I still cringe about was an almost entirely misguided rant about how I felt justified in pirating music because the industry was such a rip-off. Sadly, that's one of the few pieces of mine that still exists online.

It's always the mistakes or the missteps that you remember. A lot of the time I felt blessed to be largely unsubbed, but looking back I think I could have benefitted from firmer editing.

The person who perhaps made the biggest impact on my career was Derek Hudson, former chief reporter at the *Yorkshire Post*, and editor of WM when I joined. He wasn't one to preach or wax lyrical but applied a newshound's nose to everything we ever worked on, which I think is an essential lesson. There really is a story in anything, if you find the right angle, and ask the right questions. He was also big on writing everything as tightly as possible, which I still try to do, and using the inverted pyramid to ensure nothing gets missed in the subbing.

Like I said, he wasn't one to hold court on the virtues of this or that but one thing he said stands out: "You don't always have to agree with them."

This wisdom came from his news background. Derek would often have to interview people whose opinions he didn't share. It arose after I interviewed a lexicographer who happened to believe that the rapper Eminem was a brilliant poet, with a natural ear for metre, ingenious word use, and so on. In my interpretation, Derek was surprised that this belief went unchallenged in my resultant article.

As it happens, I perhaps don't believe it as strongly as that lexicographer, but I don't disagree either. But he was right. I hadn't considered the credibility of the statement or the bias of the speaker… In my naivety, I was trying to befriend everyone I interviewed, therefore avoided taking an opposing position.

Challenging your interviewee makes for a more vibrant conversation, which in turn brings – and this is the crux of it all – better copy.

This was one of many lessons learned while working my way up the later at WM, after joining as an editorial assistant. Having a literary education – my degree was in literature with a lot of my time spent on analysis, structure and form – I was well versed in the magazine's speciality. Promotion to staff writer soon followed before being appointed editor of our sister title, *Writers' News* (now absorbed into WM), then WM editor, which I've been for just under a decade now.

Throughout my journalism career I've learned while on the job. My skillset is now rather narrowly focused on the way we do things but since I pretty much get to decide the way we do things, that's not too much of a problem.

However, there are two things that I've found difficult to embrace, both are linked: the growth of the Internet, and the shift in editorial and commercial balance.

Despite not joining the industry until near the end of the golden age of print journalism (and perhaps shaped by my early exposure to all those cynical old hacks), my stance was always the same – editorial is king.

And then there's the Internet …

On a textual level, writing for the Internet is something I had to learn. And as the readers and advertisers shift online, we now spend more time doing just that. While there are transferable elements and skills such as writing tight or using the inverted pyramid, deliberately repeating key phrases (even though that's not as important as it used to be) or writing to grab attention in a crowded news feed don't come naturally.

Early in the digital era once we'd started taking Internet copy seriously, the feeling was that features written for the web needed to be far shorter than print. Although that may have been true at that time, there is more mileage now for longer articles online.

To me, that looks to be about users: 15 years ago, the Internet was for people who'd spent their entire lives reading at print pace, who perhaps felt uncomfortable reading on screen, or who were looking solely for a "quick dip" answer to a question. As the technology, and base audience matures, we're all far more attuned to reading on tablets, phones, Kindles, whatever, and our websites are also more refined to accommodate longer articles. And I, for one, welcome following a link to an interesting article and realising it's an in-depth read, not another list of soundbites.

As far as changes to print go, the influence has perhaps been biggest in terms of the tone. We now see more articles aiming for a clickbait-y style, which of course should be avoided as nobody likes feeling misled. But other changes are not unwelcome. For example, list or chunk-based articles, or step-by-step tutorials, give welcome texture in a publication otherwise full of prose articles. Being easy to read and attention-grabbing should be our aim in any medium.

While our reading habits are changing, that doesn't necessarily negatively impact feature writing. If anything, it's making the print experience more of a luxury – relishing a curated read of a journal with a particular style or interest – and, as I said, online outlets are coming back round to the full-length article approach.

As a feature writer, your overriding needs are still the same: be readable, be entertaining, be informative. When commissioning articles, it's perhaps alarming how quickly an editor can establish whether a pitch has potential. Writers have seconds, perhaps not much longer than it takes your email to open, to justify why an editor should spend longer reading your proposal.

In any pitch I look for the following:

- A clear idea. All too often I get suggestions for "an article about freelancing" or "writer holidays". If you can't pull the article into focus for the length of a

short sentence or (at most) paragraph, why would an editor trust you can stay on topic and structure an article?
- A solid grasp of spelling and punctuation.
- An awareness of the magazine, its style, readership and tone. Most editors also get a bit sniffy, and probably justifiably, if you don't know who they are. Do your research. The best magazine for you to submit to is the one you read by choice but to survive as a freelance, you need to spread the net a bit wider. You can't cut corners though – read the magazine, study the length of articles and tone of voice. Does it address readers at arm's length, or like a long-standing friend? Only by reading a few issues can you be sure to address these questions and get your pitch right. And ensure they haven't just run an article identical to the one you're about to propose.
- Something new. What makes your proposal special? What makes you the right person to write it? To use a specific example from *Writing Magazine*: every one of our readers is a writer of some level or another. Virtually daily, I receive suggestions for diary columns of writers striving for publication or "How I wrote my novel" pieces. Why would I choose today's over tomorrow's, or last week's? The only ones that receive more than cursory consideration are the ones that can highlight why their story is unique, and what readers can learn from the one specific article being suggested.

If this sounds harsh, I'm sorry, but that is the industry we're in. Editors are busy, and, to an extent, we're in a privileged position. Give us the slightest reason to reject your idea and we can, because there will always be another along soon enough. To look at it from the other side, we're all looking for a writer we can trust to deliver copy, on time, to length, while fitting the brief. That copy must also be clear in thought and expression, informative and fresh. Don't give us a reason to doubt you.

I'd pick a well-formulated pitch from a writer with no publication history over an ill-conceived, loose idea from one with a packed CV. Similarly, a writer with whom I had an existing relationship, however scant, would be more trusted than an unknown. This might not work everywhere but being a name I recognise from informed opinions on social networks or even submissions to the letters page could help persuade me that you know our readership and style. There is a snowball effect, and it's just a case of getting that initial momentum so that you have the CV that instils editors with confidence resulting in further commissions.

Opinions are divided over the virtue of doing free articles to build your CV, but let's assume you want to start on a professional footing (being paid) and don't have any samples from student magazines, websites, your own blog...

There are a couple of ways to help you over that first hurdle if you think an editor could be interested in your article. One would be to write the whole article before you pitch, offering to send it for consideration. But don't just send it – many editors don't like being sent a finished article first thing. The other, requiring less of a time commitment without some interest at least, would be to offer to write it on spec, so the editor could refine your proposal and suggest a direction, and still see a finished article, without obligation if it doesn't work out.

Another issue is securing an interview with a potential source when not having a commission, which is tricky. That said, I've known interviewees back out after a definite commission, turn us down after we were originally approached by their own press officer, and try to remove approval even after an interview has happened.

To overcome this I would approach a potential interviewee with a concrete idea of where I would like the resultant article to appear, the area of interest (if not just a general profile) and length of the piece. You should be able to work out those details from your research of the target publication.

At this stage, it's all hypothetical though, so your approach might be something like: "Would you be open to an interview if I were to secure …?" Then when they say yes, you've got an easy pitch to the editor for your article, assuming you haven't misjudged the publication's interest levels.

Lastly, my advice to anyone wanting to forge a career in journalism (features) either as a staffer or freelance is to stick with it. The industry is constantly shifting, and job roles are changing all the time, as are freelance opportunities, but if you're flexible, enthusiastic and committed, you'll always find work.

It's the best job in the world – who wouldn't be enthusiastic about playing with words all day?

Appendix 1: Example of a freelance workflow income spreadsheet

ARTICLE	MAGAZINE/NEWSPAPER	DEADLINE	TIME SPENT	AGREED FEE	EXPENSES	TOTAL INVOICED	DATE PAID
Interview	*Writing Magazine*	10th April	5 hours	£150	£80	£230	6/3/2018

Appendix 2: NUJ Code of Conduct

The National Union of Journalist's (NUJ) code of conduct has set out the main principles of UK and Irish journalism since 1936. The code is part of the rules of our union. All journalists joining the NUJ have to sign up and agree they will strive to adhere to its professional principles.

A journalist:

1. At all times upholds and defends the principle of media freedom, the right of freedom of expression and the right of the public to be informed.
2. Strives to ensure that information disseminated is honestly conveyed, accurate and fair.
3. Does her/his utmost to correct harmful inaccuracies.
4. Differentiates between fact and opinion.
5. Obtains material by honest, straightforward and open means, with the exception of investigations that are both overwhelmingly in the public interest and which involve evidence that cannot be obtained by straightforward means.
6. Does nothing to intrude into anybody's private life, grief or distress unless justified by overriding consideration of the public interest.
7. Protects the identity of sources who supply information in confidence and material gathered in the course of her/his work.
8. Resists threats or any other inducements to influence, distort or suppress information and takes no unfair personal advantage of information gained in the course of her/his duties before the information is public knowledge.
9. Produces no material likely to lead to hatred or discrimination on the grounds of a person's age, gender, race, colour, creed, legal status, disability, marital status or sexual orientation.
10. Does not by way of statement, voice or appearance endorse by advertisement any commercial product or service save for the promotion of her/his own work or of the medium by which she/he is employed.
11. A journalist shall normally seek the consent of an appropriate adult when interviewing or photographing a child for a story about her/his welfare.
12. Avoids plagiarism.

The Code of Conduct has been reproduced with the permission of the NUJ. For more details visit www.nuj.org.uk.

Appendix 3: IPSO – Editors' Code of Practice

The Code

The Code – including this preamble and the public interest exceptions below – sets the framework for the highest professional standards that members of the press subscribing to the Independent Press Standards Organisation have undertaken to maintain. It is the cornerstone of the system of voluntary self-regulation to which they have made a binding contractual commitment. It balances both the rights of the individual and the public's right to know.

To achieve that balance, it is essential that an agreed Code be honoured not only to the letter, but in the full spirit. It should be interpreted neither so narrowly as to compromise its commitment to respect the rights of the individual, nor so broadly that it infringes the fundamental right to freedom of expression – such as to inform, to be partisan, to challenge, shock, be satirical and to entertain – or prevents publication in the public interest.

It is the responsibility of editors and publishers to apply the Code to editorial material in both printed and online versions of their publications. They should take care to ensure it is observed rigorously by all editorial staff and external contributors, including non-journalists.

Editors must maintain in-house procedures to resolve complaints swiftly and, where required to do so, co-operate with IPSO. A publication subject to an adverse adjudication must publish it in full and with due prominence, as required by IPSO.

1. Accuracy

i) The Press must take care not to publish inaccurate, misleading or distorted information or images, including headlines not supported by the text.

ii) A significant inaccuracy, misleading statement or distortion must be corrected, promptly and with due prominence, and – where appropriate – an apology published. In cases involving IPSO, due prominence should be as required by the regulator.

iii) A fair opportunity to reply to significant inaccuracies should be given, when reasonably called for.

iv) The Press, while free to editorialise and campaign, must distinguish clearly between comment, conjecture and fact.
v) A publication must report fairly and accurately the outcome of an action for defamation to which it has been a party, unless an agreed settlement states otherwise, or an agreed statement is published.

2. *Privacy

i) Everyone is entitled to respect for his or her private and family life, home, health and correspondence, including digital communications.
ii) Editors will be expected to justify intrusions into any individual's private life without consent. In considering an individual's reasonable expectation of privacy, account will be taken of the complainant's own public disclosures of information and the extent to which the material complained about is already in the public domain or will become so.
iii) It is unacceptable to photograph individuals, without their consent, in public or private places where there is a reasonable expectation of privacy.

3. *Harassment

i) Journalists must not engage in intimidation, harassment or persistent pursuit.
ii) They must not persist in questioning, telephoning, pursuing or photographing individuals once asked to desist; nor remain on property when asked to leave and must not follow them. If requested, they must identify themselves and whom they represent.
iii) Editors must ensure these principles are observed by those working for them and take care not to use non-compliant material from other sources.

4. Intrusion into grief or shock

In cases involving personal grief or shock, enquiries and approaches must be made with sympathy and discretion and publication handled sensitively. These provisions should not restrict the right to report legal proceedings.

5. *Reporting suicide

When reporting suicide, to prevent simulative acts care should be taken to avoid excessive detail of the method used, while taking into account the media's right to report legal proceedings.

6. *Children

i) All pupils should be free to complete their time at school without unnecessary intrusion.

ii) They must not be approached or photographed at school without permission of the school authorities.
iii) Children under 16 must not be interviewed or photographed on issues involving their own or another child's welfare unless a custodial parent or similarly responsible adult consents.
iv) Children under 16 must not be paid for material involving their welfare, nor parents or guardians for material about their children or wards, unless it is clearly in the child's interest.
v) Editors must not use the fame, notoriety or position of a parent or guardian as sole justification for publishing details of a child's private life.

7. *Children in sex cases

The press must not, even if legally free to do so, identify children under 16 who are victims or witnesses in cases involving sex offences.

In any press report of a case involving a sexual offence against a child –

i) The child must not be identified.
ii) The adult may be identified.
iii) The word "incest" must not be used where a child victim might be identified.
iv) Care must be taken that nothing in the report implies the relationship between the accused and the child.

8. *Hospitals

i) Journalists must identify themselves and obtain permission from a responsible executive before entering non-public areas of hospitals or similar institutions to pursue enquiries.
ii) The restrictions on intruding into privacy are particularly relevant to enquiries about individuals in hospitals or similar institutions.

9. *Reporting of crime

i) Relatives or friends of persons convicted or accused of crime should not generally be identified without their consent, unless they are genuinely relevant to the story.
ii) Particular regard should be paid to the potentially vulnerable position of children under the age of 18 who witness, or are victims of, crime. This should not restrict the right to report legal proceedings.
iii) Editors should generally avoid naming children under the age of 18 after arrest for a criminal offence but before they appear in a youth court unless they can show that the individual's name is already in the public domain, or that the individual (or, if they are under 16, a custodial parent or similarly responsible adult) has given their consent. This does not restrict the right

to name juveniles who appear in a crown court, or whose anonymity is lifted.

10. *Clandestine devices and subterfuge

i) The press must not seek to obtain or publish material acquired by using hidden cameras or clandestine listening devices; or by intercepting private or mobile telephone calls, messages or emails; or by the unauthorised removal of documents or photographs; or by accessing digitally-held information without consent.

ii) Engaging in misrepresentation or subterfuge, including by agents or intermediaries, can generally be justified only in the public interest and then only when the material cannot be obtained by other means.

11. Victims of sexual assault

The press must not identify or publish material likely to lead to the identification of a victim of sexual assault unless there is adequate justification and they are legally free to do so.

12. Discrimination

i) The press must avoid prejudicial or pejorative reference to an individual's, race, colour, religion, sex, gender identity, sexual orientation or to any physical or mental illness or disability.

ii) Details of an individual's race, colour, religion, gender identity, sexual orientation, physical or mental illness or disability must be avoided unless genuinely relevant to the story.

13. Financial journalism

i) Even where the law does not prohibit it, journalists must not use for their own profit financial information they receive in advance of its general publication, nor should they pass such information to others.

ii) They must not write about shares or securities in whose performance they know that they or their close families have a significant financial interest without disclosing the interest to the editor or financial editor.

iii) They must not buy or sell, either directly or through nominees or agents, shares or securities about which they have written recently or about which they intend to write in the near future.

14. Confidential sources

Journalists have a moral obligation to protect confidential sources of information.

15. *Witness payments in criminal trials*

i) No payment or offer of payment to a witness – or any person who may reasonably be expected to be called as a witness – should be made in any case once proceedings are active as defined by the Contempt of Court Act 1981. This prohibition lasts until the suspect has been freed unconditionally by police without charge or bail or the proceedings are otherwise discontinued; or has entered a guilty plea to the court; or, in the event of a not guilty plea, the court has announced its verdict.

*ii) Where proceedings are not yet active but are likely and foreseeable, editors must not make or offer payment to any person who may reasonably be expected to be called as a witness, unless the information concerned ought demonstrably to be published in the public interest and there is an overriding need to make or promise payment for this to be done; and all reasonable steps have been taken to ensure no financial dealings influence the evidence those witnesses give. In no circumstances should such payment be conditional on the outcome of a trial.

*iii) Any payment or offer of payment made to a person later cited to give evidence in proceedings must be disclosed to the prosecution and defence. The witness must be advised of this requirement.

16. *Payment to criminals*

i) Payment or offers of payment for stories, pictures or information, which seek to exploit a particular crime or to glorify or glamorise crime in general, must not be made directly or via agents to convicted or confessed criminals or to their associates – who may include family, friends and colleagues.

ii) Editors invoking the public interest to justify payment or offers would need to demonstrate that there was good reason to believe the public interest would be served. If, despite payment, no public interest emerged, then the material should not be published.

The public interest

There may be exceptions to the clauses marked * where they can be demonstrated to be in the public interest.

1. The public interest includes, but is not confined to:
   - Detecting or exposing crime, or the threat of crime, or serious impropriety.
   - Protecting public health or safety.
   - Protecting the public from being misled by an action or statement of an individual or organisation.
   - Disclosing a person's or organisation's failure or likely failure to comply with any obligation to which they are subject.
   - Disclosing a miscarriage of justice.

- Raising or contributing to a matter of public debate, including serious cases of impropriety, unethical conduct or incompetence concerning the public.
- Disclosing concealment, or likely concealment, of any of the above.
2. There is a public interest in freedom of expression itself.
3. The regulator will consider the extent to which material is already in the public domain or will become so.
4. Editors invoking the public interest will need to demonstrate that they reasonably believed publication – or journalistic activity taken with a view to publication – would both serve, and be proportionate to, the public interest and explain how they reached that decision at the time.
5. An exceptional public interest would need to be demonstrated to override the normally paramount interests of children under 16.

The Independent Press Standards Organisation (IPSO) is happy to give pre-publication advice and welcomes approaches from editors and journalists for non-binding advice relating to the Editors' Code or the public interest – or any other concerns prior to publication. For more details visit www.ipso.co.uk/press-standards/guidance-for-journalists-and-editors/

Editors' Code of Practice © 2017 Regulatory Funding Company has been reproduced with the permission of IPSO.

Appendix 4: The Society of Authors' Guide to Copyright and Permissions

This guide offers basic advice on when permission is needed to use extracts from the works of others. It does not explore how far indirect copying, paraphrasing or the use of copyright works in other ways may amount to infringement. Members are welcome to contact the office for more detailed guidance.

Every reasonable effort has been made to ensure that the information provided in this Guide is reasonably comprehensive, accurate and clear and up-to-date as at the date stated in the Guide. However, the information provided is necessarily general and should not be relied on as specific legal or professional advice. If you have any specific queries, contact our advisers or a suitably qualified lawyer or professional. If you think you may have noticed any error or omission, please let us know.

1. Is the work in copyright?

a) General rule

Copyright in the United Kingdom for most works lasts until 70 years after the end of the year of the author's death ("life plus 70"). The same applied most places in the world.

For a work of joint authorship, such as a work by two or more authors in which the contributions of the authors are not discrete, the period of protection runs from the death of the author who dies last.

b) Variations in how long copyright lasts

There are a number of exceptions to the "general rule" given above.

(i) (a) Works not made available to the public during the author's lifetime

This exception particularly affects those wishing to quote from old letters and diaries. Works not made available to the public during the author's lifetime, where the author died after 1 August 1989, are protected for life plus 70 years – as with published material. However, where the author died before 1 August 1989, written works, photographs and engravings (note: this does not apply to other artistic works) still unpublished at the time of the author's death remain in copyright until 50 years from the end of the year in which they were first posthumously made available to the public, or until 31 December 2039, whichever is sooner. If life plus 70 is longer than the shorter of those two periods, life plus 70 will prevail.

(i) (b) "2039"

From 31 December 2039, works will go out of copyright 70 years after the end of the year of the author's death, whether or not they have ever been published. However, from that date, the person who publishes for the first time a previously unpublished work for which copyright has expired is entitled to a 25-year "publication right". How restrictive that right will be is not yet clear but, in the meantime, we understand that the public exhibition – before 31.12.39 – of an unpublished work (e.g. the public display of a letter) may disqualify that work from an entitlement to the publication right.

(ii) Works by non-European authors

If the author's country provides for a shorter period of copyright protection, that shorter period will also apply to works from that country when they are exploited in the UK (this equal-treatment exception does not apply to any foreign period of protection which is longer than life plus 70). For the duration of copyright in other countries, go to portal.unesco.org and enter "collection of national copyright laws" in the search box.

(iii) US copyright

In the US the period of copyright, particularly for older works, is different from the UK, and complex. As a general rule, for works created after 1 January 1978, US copyright protection lasts for life plus 70. For anonymous and pseudonymous works, and work made for hire, US copyright lasts until 95 years from the year of first publication or 120 years from the year of the work's creation, whichever is the shorter. For works created before 1978, it is unsafe to generalise as the term will vary depending on a range of factors and advice should be sought on a case by case basis.

(iv) Anonymous and pseudonymous works

This would include, for example, newspaper articles whose author is not identified. The period of protection is 70 years from the end of the calendar year in which the work is first made available to the public unless during that period the identity of the author comes to light, in which case the period is life plus 70.

(v) Crown and Parliamentary copyright

Different provisions apply to works "made by an officer or servant of the Crown in the course of his/her duties". For details go to www.nationalarchives.gov.uk and search for "crown copyright FAQs". For work made under the direction or control of either of the Houses of Parliament go to www.parliament.uk/site-information/copyright.

(vi) The publisher's copyright

The publisher automatically owns the copyright in the "typographical arrangement of a published work", which is to say the layout and general appearance of the published version. This means that the work cannot, for example, be photocopied or reproduced in facsimile form without the publisher's consent. This copyright lasts until 25 years from the end of the year in which the edition containing that arrangement was first published.

(vii) Translations

Remember that the original work and the translation are each entitled to copyright – copyright in the translation belongs to the translator and exists in addition to, rather than instead of, the copyright in the underlying work.

(viii) Letters

The copyright in letters is as at point 1.b)(i). Remember that while the letter itself in most cases belongs to the recipient, the copyright in its contents remains with the writer.

2. Need for permissions

a) How much may be quoted from a copyright work without permission?

You need permission to quote from works that are in copyright. For quotations other than those in the limited circumstances described below, you should ask permission to use any "substantial" extract from a copyright work.

The difficulty is that the meaning of "substantial" is not defined in the Copyright Act, but is a matter of fact and degree. A short extract may be a vital part of a work and it has often been said that the test is much more about quality than quantity. A few sentences taken from a long novel or biography are unlikely to constitute a "substantial part", but a few lines of poetry may be. It can be helpful to imagine you are the rights holder – how would you feel about the proposed use? The only safe course, if in doubt, is to ask permission if the quotation is not covered by the exceptions described at points 2.a) and b).

Bear in mind also: song lyrics are protected by copyright. Some record companies are notoriously rigorous about charging even for very short extracts, and the charges can be substantial. Permission should be obtained for any quotation of copyright material to be included in an anthology. The fact that a work has been reproduced on the internet (whether that use was authorised or not) does not alter its copyright status.

b) Exceptions

(i) Quotations

You can quote without needing copyright permission if all of the following apply

- the work you are quoting from has been previously published;
- the use is fair dealing;
- you quote "no more than is required by the specific purpose for which it is used";
- the use is genuinely for the purpose of quotation; and
- you include proper acknowledgement.

(Before 1 October 2014, this exception was restricted to quotations for the purpose of criticism or review of that or another work, or for reporting current events.)

(ii) Caricature, parody and pastiche

You can use extracts of a copyright work for purposes of parody, caricature or pastiche, provided that:

- the use is fair dealing;
- you rely on no more than a limited, moderate amount of the underlying work;
- you include proper acknowledgement (generally the title and the author's name).

"Parody, caricature and pastiche" are not defined, leaving their interpretation to the Courts. In addition, you still need to be careful that:

- your work is not defamatory;
- it does not infringe any trademark rights (particularly beware if you are making use of existing characters);
- it could not be deemed "passing off" (which would arise if the public is confused into thinking it had been created or licensed by the copyright owner of the underlying work and that copyright owner has suffered financial loss as a consequence);
- it does not breach any rights of confidentiality or privacy and that it does not give the impression that it has been created by or has the approval of the original copyright owner, which could be an infringement of that author's

moral rights not to have their work subject to "derogatory treatment" and not to have work falsely attributed to them.

(Before 1 October 2014, there was no exception for purposes of caricature, parody and pastiche.)

(iii) Educational purposes

You can copy extracts of works in any medium for the purposes of teaching as long as:

- the work is used solely to illustrate a point;
- the use of the work is not for commercial purposes;
- the use is fair dealing; and
- it is accompanied by a sufficient acknowledgement.

This means minor uses, such as displaying a few lines of poetry on an interactive whiteboard, are permitted, but uses which would undermine sales of teaching materials (for instance, photocopying material to distribute to students) would need a licence. Schools, colleges and universities still have to pay for third party teaching materials which are available under licence.

c) What is "fair dealing"?

Fair dealing only applies to work which has, with the authorisation of the copyright holder, been made available to the public. The leading reference book *Copinger & Skone James on Copyright* says that "If a work is unpublished, no dealing is likely to be fair." The law does not give specific guidelines on what constitutes fair dealing; but it may be relevant to take into account:

- does using the new work affect the market for the original work? If use of the new work acts as a substitute for the original, causing the owner to lose revenue, it is unlikely to be fair;
- is the amount of the original which is being used reasonable and appropriate? Was it necessary to use the amount that was taken? Usually, only part of a work may be used.

d) *Contract override*

If you want to make use of a copyright work and have been refused permission in accordance with the less liberal copyright provisions applying before the 2014 changes were introduced, but what you intend to do is permitted under the current provisions, you can go ahead. Members should consult the SoA on a case by case basis if this question arises.

3. Obtaining permissions

a) Who is entitled to grant, and whose job is it to obtain, copyright permissions?

If you have been asked to grant permission for use of your work, the first step is to check that it is indeed you rather than your publisher who controls anthology and quotation rights.

If you are quoting from other works, it is likely that under your publishing contract it will be your responsibility to obtain permission for the use in your book of any copyright material not original to you.

Who pays any fee charged by the rights holder is a subject for negotiation. It is often the author's responsibility, but sometimes the publishers may be persuaded to pay at least some part of such fees, or to pay in the first instance then deduct a corresponding amount from your royalties. Where quotations are an essential element of the work (e.g. an anthology or textbook) it may be more appropriate for the publisher to pay all the fees.

When it comes to clearing rights in illustrations, photos, maps or diagrams, bear in mind that the owners of the image (e.g. a museum or picture library) may well charge fees for loan and reproduction (separately from and in addition to any copyright permission fee which may be required). If you are responsible for such costs, you should ideally get quotes from the owners at the outset, so you have a realistic idea of what the outlay will be before you finalise the contract with your publisher.

b) Who and what to ask

With published material, it is best to write first to the publishers of the original edition of the book, who are most likely to hold the rights for anthology use or quotations. Address your letter to the Permissions Department. If the original publishers do not control the rights, they should forward your letter to whoever does. This could be the author, his/her agent or heir or, possibly, a subsequent publisher of the book

It is very much in your interest to clear permissions as early as possible. Some publishers can be very slow to respond and you may be put in a difficult position if your book is about to go to press and permission is refused or the requested fees are very high. As a first step, go to www.plsclear.com which offers a fast-track service linking to publishers' permission departments.

When contacting the rights holder for permission, you should be sure to include the following information:

- Your name and address (and your publisher's name and address if they are paying the fee – be clear about who should be invoiced).
- The title of your publication.
- The name of your publisher and the date of publication, if known.

- Details of the extract you want to quote. Give the name of the author, the title, the number of words if prose, number of lines if poetry and language (if not English).
- What editions you need to clear rights for (e.g. hardback, paperback, electronic).
- What territories you need to clear rights for (e.g. the World, the UK and Commonwealth).
- The size of the print-run(s) and the retail price(s).
- A lower fee may be charged if your work is scholarly or an anthology, so include relevant extra details.
- When sending a permission fee to a rights holder state what it is for, giving the permission reference number (if relevant) or the source (title and author) of the extract and not just the name of the book in which the quotation is to be used.

c) How much will the fee be?

Copyright owners (and those controlling anthology and quotation rights) should bear in mind that they may well on occasion be on the other side of the fence, wishing to quote from others' works. "Do as you would be done by" is a useful maxim when dealing with permissions.

Because there are so many variables, and to comply with competition legislation, the SoA cannot recommend rates. However, the rates which the SoA applies when licensing rights for the literary estates which it represents can be found at www.societyofauthors.org/estates/permissions. They do not constitute recommended or guideline rates; and it should also be noted that they apply to the licensing of, in many cases, classic works by major authors. The SoA will be happy to advise members on specific instances.

Rights holders often ask to be sent a free copy of the book containing their material on publication. Your publisher can generally be persuaded to foot the bill for such copies, on request.

4. What if the rights holder will not answer my request?

If you know who owns the copyright, but they do not answer your letters, a possible course is to send a recorded delivery letter explaining the situation and saying that if you hear nothing more within four weeks, you will assume that there is no objection to the extract being used. Note, however, that this course is not supported by law and should only be used as a last resort.

5. What if I cannot trace whoever is entitled to give permission?

If you have done a diligent, thorough and search in good faith but the copyright owner of an old work is unidentifiable or untraceable, the work will be considered "orphan". You can make certain limited uses of orphan works.

a) What constitutes "diligent search"?

Here are some suggestions of resources you may wish to use in tracing a rights holder:

- WATCH (Writers, Artists and their Copyright Holders) www.watch-file.com
- ALCS (Authors' Licensing and Collecting Society) www.alcs.co.uk if the book you want to quote from was published by a firm no longer in existence (you can check with Companies House at www.companieshouse.gov.uk) write to the publishers of another book by the same author; they may be able to tell you who owns the author's copyrights
- the Association of Authors' Agents www.agentsassoc.co.uk
- the British Library www.bl.uk
- the National Library of Scotland www.nls.uk
- the National Library of Ireland www.nli.ie
- the Location Register of Literary Manuscripts www.reading.ac.uk/library/about-us/projects/lib-location-register.aspx
- the US Library of Congress Copyright Office www.loc.gov/copyright
- for TV, film and theatre writers: the Personal Managers Association www.pma.org.uk, the BBC TV and radio rights departments, and the Writers' Guild of Great Britain www.writersguild.org.uk
- unpublished works held in a library: the librarian may be able to put you in touch with the right person
- the Will of the author. Where copyrights are not separately mentioned in a Will, they simply form part of the testator's residuary Estate. For more information on tracing UK Wills, see the National Archives website nationalarchives.gov.uk/records/looking-for-person/willafter1858.htm
- publish a letter seeking information in an appropriate publication (e.g. the *Times Literary Supplement* for literary biographies, or a specialist journal in the copyright owner's field of expertise).

The Intellectual Property Office also has guidance on how to do a diligent search: gov.uk/government/publications/orphan-works-diligent-search-guidance-for-applicants

If a diligent search has drawn a blank, your next step would be to follow the Intellectual Property Office's procedure for obtaining a licence to exploit what will now be deemed an orphan work (be aware that such licences extend only to limited use and only within the UK). Information about the orphan works scheme can be found at gov.uk/guidance/copyright-orphan-works

6. Permission licence model letter

From [name and address of the person granting the licence]

To [name and address of the person seeking the licence]

Licence No:............................

Date:...............................

Title [of the work in which the quote will appear]

To be published by: [publisher and imprint] Territory: [e.g. UK and EEA or world]

Extent of use: [e.g. English language/all languages volume form publication as print/ebook/password-protected website, in one/all editions]

Name [of the work/description of the extract to be quoted]

I can give you permission to use the work mentioned above on the following terms:

- Fee: £:........................
- Payment is due on publication, or within 12 months of the date of this licence, whichever is earlier, failing which this permission automatically terminates.
- Permission is limited to the territories and rights specified above. It does not include the right to issue new or revised editions in a different format or under another publisher's imprint.
- When sending the fee, and in future correspondence, please quote the number and date of this licence and the author and title of the work(s) used.
- On publication a copy of your book/periodical should be sent to: ....
- Wording of the acknowledgement:...........................

If we do not hear from you to the contrary within four weeks from the date of this licence we shall assume that the terms have been accepted. Inclusion of the work in your publication also indicates your acceptance of these terms.

Signed:..

© Society of Authors, 2016. This guide has been reproduced with the permission of The Society of Authors. For more details visit www.societyofauthors.org

Appendix 5: Syndicates, news and press cuttings agencies

Syndicates

If you hold copyright for your work, you can sell it to a syndication agency. In most cases, syndication agencies will pay you around 50 per cent of the fee that they sell the article for, although percentages usually range between 40 and 60 per cent.

- **Andrews McMeel Syndication:** accepts comic strips, cartoons, features, columns and games. Full submission guidelines for writers and artists can be found on the agency's website.
  Contact details: via website only visit http://syndication.andrewsmcmeel.com/contact
- **Famous:** a celebrity picture and feature agency, supplying showbiz content for over 20 years to newspapers, magazines, websites, TV stations, mobile phone companies, books and advertisers worldwide.
  Contact details: T: 0207 284 1074 | E: info@famous.uk.com | W: www.famous.uk.com
- **Hayters Teamwork:** a specialist sports reporting agency providing news and interviews with some of the world's leading sports stars for newspapers, TV and digital. It also has a growing sports TV production team, working with clubs, brands and sponsors to produce high-quality video content for global distribution.
  Contact details: T: 07836 280 244 | E: sport@hayters.com | W: www.hayters.com
- **Lifestyle Features:** a South African agency, which resells decorating, travel and food features around the globe.
  Contact details: E: info@lifestylefeatures.com | W: http://lifestylefeatures.com

News agencies

These provide newspapers and magazines with a range of news stories and features.

- **National Association of Press Agencies (NAPA):** founded in 1982, the Association draws most of its membership from the premier agencies providing news, pictures and features from every town and city in the UK. Its membership also includes agencies operating from the EU and the USA.

NAPA is a self-help body, administered on a largely voluntary basis by members of the Association. Its main objectives are to further the interests of its members and maintain professional standards of conduct.
Contact details: E: enquiries@napa.org.uk | W: www.napa.org.uk
- **Press Association (PA):** the UK's leading provider of multimedia content and services was established in 1868. PA remains the national news agency for the UK and Ireland, serving a broad range of customers including major media and digital brands around the world, businesses and public sector organisations. In addition to its newswire, PA's products and services span pictures, video, data APIs, hosted live blogs, graphics, listings pages, social media curation and page production.
  Contact details: T: 020 7963 7000 | E: info@pressassociation.com | W: www.pressassociation.com
- **Reuters:** the news and media division of Thomson Reuters is the world's largest international multimedia news provider. It provides trusted business, financial, national and international news to professionals. May accept some freelance work.
  Contact details: via website visit https://agency.reuters.com
- **Solent News and Photo Agency:** an independent press agency based in the UK, which sends news around the world. Accepts freelance work.
  Contact details: T: 023 8045 8800 | E: info@solentnews.co.uk | W: http://solentnews.co.uk
- **South West News Stories (SWNS):** produces a newswire service comprising over 100 original pieces of copy and 1,000 photographs and videos daily. It is one of the single largest sources of content for the major news publishers in the UK, US and beyond.
  Contact details: T: various regional numbers see website | E: news@swns.com | W: https://swns.com

Press cuttings

- **Gorkana (previously Durrants):** monitors the most comprehensive list of global media across all channels: press, online, broadcast and social. Its huge team of in house editors filter the white noise, so clients receive just the coverage that's relevant to them.
  Contact details: T: 020 7674 0200 | E: marketing@gorkana.com | W: www.durrants.co.uk/pr-products/media-monitoring
- **International Press-Cutting Bureau (IPCB):** the last national family run print media monitoring agency in the UK which was started in 1920 and has undergone major changes to reflect the developments in information technology over the past few decades. IPCB offers a full range of services including the traditional hard copy press cuttings as well as digital services with accompanying monthly reports and media analysis. Its media list covers the UK and Ireland. Major overseas national titles can also be included.
  Contact details: T: 020 7708 2113 | E: ipcb2000@aol.com | W: www.ipcb.co.uk

References

Anon. *Brexit: The Pros and Cons of Leaving the EU.* The Week, 22 May 2018. www.theweek.co.uk/brexit-0. Accessed 3/7/2018.

Anon. *Business Breakfast Held at Kingston Maurward College.* Southern Daily Echo. www.dailyecho.co.uk/news/16372630.It_was_all_about_education_at_this_business_breakfast/. Accessed 10/9/2018.

Anon. Guidance to staff on supporting media access to Courts and Tribunals. GOV.UK. www.gov.uk/government/publications/guidance-to-staff-on-supporting-media-access-to-courts-and-tribunals. Accessed 28/8/2018.

Anon. *Livingetc Launches Website.* InPublishing, February 2018. www.inpublishing.co.uk/news/articles/livingetc_launches_website_11650.aspx. Accessed 2/2/2018.

Anon. *We're Living the Mamma Mia Dream.* Woman & Home Magazine, August 2018, pp42–46.

Attorney-General v Conde Nast Publications QBD [2015] EWHC 3322 (Admin). www.judiciary.uk/wp-content/uploads/2015/11/hm_-attorney_general_v_conde_nast_publications_limited_final.pdf. Accessed 14/7/2018.

Barber, L. 2002. *Caution: Big Name Ahead.* The Observer, Life and Style, 27 January 2002. www.theguardian.com/theobserver/2002/jan/27/features.magazine47. Accessed 12/10/2018.

Barker, S. 2018. *Should you Downsize to a Retirement Development?* Money, The Daily Telegraph, 28 July 2018, p5.

Barnett, C. 2018. *Tributes to Cyclist Killed in Van Crash.* Worcester News, 11 January 2018 edition, p1.

Belsey, A. and Chadwick, R. 1992. *Ethical Issues in Journalism and the Media.* Chapter 8, Objectivity, bias and truth (Edgar, A). London: Routledge, p112.

Bennett, R. 27 March 2018. *Depression Risk for Pupils who Fall Behind Aged 11.* The Times. www.thetimes.co.uk/article/depression-risk-for-pupils-who-fall-behind-aged-11-dv8h76zvd. Accessed 29/3/2018.

Blamires, D. 1998. *Mink Meet Grisly End.* Independent, 11 August 1998 edition. www.independent.co.uk/news/mink-meet-grisly-end-1171089.html. Accessed 8/1/2018.

Boyd, W. 2008. *Anton Chekhov (1).* Bamboo. London: Bloomsbury, p246.

BRAD. OK ABC print circulation figures July–December 2017. https://brad.mediatel.co.uk/profile/press/6467#circulation. Accessed 28/3/2018.

BRAD. Regional Newspapers. https://brad.mediatel.co.uk/browse/p. Accessed 4/01/2017.

Brown, M. 2018. *Acting is Now a Job for the Well-off, says Head of Equity.* The Guardian, 13 August 2018, p7.

Callan, J. 2018. *There's Something About Mary.* Good Housekeeping, January 2018, pp20–25.

Clark, N. 2018. *Year of Three Popes*. Daily Express, 13 August 2018, p13.

Clayton, J. 1994. *Interviewing for Journalists: How to Research and Conduct Interviews you Can Sell*. London: Piatkus, pxiii.

Cole, P. 2008. *News Writing*. Guardian, 25 September 2008. www.theguardian.com/books/2008/sep/25/writing.journalism.news. Accessed 12/7/2018.

Colley, J. and Gordon, C. 20 June 2006. *Damages for Ramsay Over 'Faked Scenes' Claims*. Independent. www.independent.co.uk/news/uk/crime/damages-for-ramsay-over-faked-scenes-claims-404791.html. Accessed 24/7/2018.

Connolly, K. 22 November 2009. *Friedrich von Schiller: The Romantic love*. The Guardian. www.theguardian.com/stage/2009/nov/22/friedrich-schiller-anniversary-film-biography. Accessed 28/11/2017.

Crowdtangle. www.crowdtangle.com/customers. Accessed 30/10/2018.

Davis, E., Michener, J., Cerf, B. and Russell, B. 1953. *Saturday Review Reader No. 2*. New York: Bantam Books.

Davis, H.W. 1927. *The Column*. The Rotarian, February 1927, p28. https://books.google.co.uk/books?id=d0MEAAAAMBAJ&pg=PA28&lpg=PA28&dq=The+good+reporter+and+the+good+feature+writer+do+not+encourage+us+to+inquire+into+things.+Even+the+editorial+writer+does+not+often+ask+us+to+look+on+both+sides.+But+the+columnist+is+ever+flipping+things+upside+down+and+wrong+side+out+and+inviting+us+to+loo&source=bl&ots=_kSc3kbup5&sig=nIQYNL2_PgzjXXshZnGWeSF04b4&hl=en&sa=X&ved=2ahUKEwimzaXuqcfdAhXJIcAKHcf7BA0Q6AEwAXoECAYQAQ#v=onepage&q&f=false. Accessed 19/9/2018.

Definitions of Advertising. 2018. Institution of Advertising Practitioners. www.ipa.co.uk/Page/What-is-advertising#.W5EZrn4nZTY. Accessed 6/9/2018.

Definition of Public Relations. Chartered Institute of Public Relations. www.cipr.co.uk/content/policy/careers-advice/what-pr. Accessed 6/9/2018.

Develin, K. and Tominey, C. 17 June 2018. *£600M A Week Brexit Bonus for NHS*. Sunday Express, p1.

Dobson, L. 2017. *The Key to Surviving Prostate Cancer*. Saga, July 2017 edition, pp95–97.

Dool, G. 17 October 2017. *National Magazines Take On the Harvey Weinstein Scandal*. Folio www.foliomag.com/national-magazines-take-on-the-harvey-weinstein-scandal-industry-notes/. Accessed 23/11/2017.

Empire, K. 2017. *Coldplay Review – Charge of the Bright Brigade*. The Observer, 16 July 2017. www.theguardian.com/music/2017/jul/16/coldplay-live-review-principality-stadium-cardiff-a-head-full-of-dreams-tour. Accessed 1/10/2018.

Everton, G. 2018. *Saigon, Saigon*. Traveller. Volume 48, No. 1, p50.

Fearn, H. 21st February 2017. *Teachers are Leaving the Profession in their Droves – and Little Wonder. Who Would Want to be One in Modern Britain?* Independent. www.independent.co.uk/voices/teachers-crisis-education-leaving-profession-jobs-market-droves-who-would-be-one-a7591821.html. Accessed 29/3/2018.

Fixter, A. 14 July 2005. *O'Riordan Fined for Naming 12-year-old*. Press Gazette. www.pressgazette.co.uk/oriordan-fined-for-naming-12-year-old/. Accessed 28/8/2018.

Foges, C. 2018. *Workplace Equality Targets Undermine Women*. The Times, 13 August 2018, p21.

Food and Travel. Media Information – magazine fact sheet. https://foodandtravel.com/assets/img/content/general/Media_information_2016.pdf. Accessed 22/1/2018.

Ford, J. and Plimmer, G. 12 February 2018. *Momentum Stalls on UK's Private Prisons*. The Financial Times. www.ft.com/content/3c356914-0d9c-11e8-839d-41ca06376bf2. Accessed 29/3/2018.

Fuentes, A. 2018. *Are We as Awful as We Act Online?* National Geographic, August 2018, pp17–20.

Glover, S. (ed.) 2000. *The Penguin Book of Journalism: Secrets of the Press.* 'Editors and Egomaniacs, p46. Henry Porter. London: Penguin.

Goldhill, O. 6 March 2015. *Homework Around the World: How Much is Too Much?* The Telegraph. www.telegraph.co.uk/education/educationnews/11453912/Homework-around-the-world-how-much-is-too-much.html. Accessed 29/3/2018.

Hanna, M. and Dodd, M. 2018. *McNae's Essential Law for Journalists.* 24th edition. Oxford: OUP.

Hartley, A. 2002. *Me Frodo, You Jane.* The Spectator Magazine, 22 June 2002, p22. http://archive.spectator.co.uk/article/29th-june-2002/22/me-frodo-you-jane. Accessed 10/8/2018.

heat. Issue 978, 17–23 March 2018.

Hemingway, E. 1964. *A Moveable Feast.* Palimpsest. www.thepalimpsest.co.uk/2009/12/ernest-hemingway-writing-in-pencil.html. Accessed 28/11/2017.

Hogarth, M. 1997a. *An Ancient Craft in Modern Times.* Hampshire The County Magazine, August 1997, pp38–39.

Hogarth, M. 1997b. *Is Mark's Woodland Craft Doomed?* Andover Midweek Advertiser, 26 August 1997, p7.

Hogarth, M. 2002. *First-timer Lands Major Film Deal with Latest of the Grown-up Chic-lit Sagas.* Writers' Forum. September 2002, pp29–30.

Hogarth, M. 2009. *A Writer Never Stops.* Writer's Forum, October 2009, pp7–8.

Hogarth, M. 2015. *Opening the Door to an Agent.* Self Publishing Magazine. Issue 37, Winter 2015, pp5–9.

Hogarth, M. 2016a. *Alexandra Shulman Interview.* In Publishing, September/October 2016, pp18–20.

Hogarth, M. 29 March 2016b. *Five Minutes with Freya North.* Lovereading.co.uk, www.lovereading.co.uk/blog/author-talk/five-minutes-freya-north-5792. Accessed 16/7/2018.

Hogarth, M. 2016c. *Five Minutes with Tony Parsons.* Lovereading.co.uk, 26 May 2016. www.lovereading.co.uk/blog/author-talk/five-minutes-with-tony-parsons-6445. Accessed 15/10/2018.

Hogarth, M. 2016d. *Life Lessons.* Writing Magazine, March 2016, pp28–29.

Hogarth, M. 13 March 2018. *When Should a Publisher Adopt a Membership Model?* What's New In Publishing. https://whatsnewinpublishing.com/2018/03/13/when-should-a-publisher-adopt-a-membership-model/. Accessed 27/6/2018.

Hogarth, M. (ed.) and Jenkins, J. 2014. *How To Launch A Magazine In This Digital Age.* A Gap in the Market, p5. London: Bloomsbury.

Hough, G. (ed.) 1983. *Chambers Dictionary of Dates.* Chambers.

Hoyle, F. and Wickramsingh, C. 1986. *Astronomer Believes Aids Has Far-out Origin.* Chicago Tribune, 18 December 1986.

Hughes, D. 2018. *The Wife Review.* Empire, 24 September 2018. www.empireonline.com/movies/wife/review/. Accessed 1/10/2018.

Hulonce, L. 2017. *Paupers' Brave New World.* BBC History Magazine, March 2017, pp23–27.

Jackson, I. 1986. *The Provincial Press and the Community.* Manchester: Manchester University Press.

Johnson, I. 9 January 2017. *Fake Beggars 'Have Homes and Pocket More Than £2,000 a Month in Benefits' While Pretending to Sleep Rough.* Mirror. www.mirror.co.uk/news/uk-news/fake-beggars-have-homes-pocket-9588720. Accessed 5/4/2018.

Koppelman, A. 3 December 2017. *What I Know Now as a Teen with Dyslexia*. HuffPost. www.huffingtonpost.com/anna-koppelman/the-gigantic-parts-of-my-dyslexia-have-shrunk----except-the-shame_b_6855402.html. Accessed 29/3/2018.

Kunova, M. 15 May 2018. *What Does GDPR Mean for Journalists?* Journalism.co.uk www.journalism.co.uk/news/what-does-gdpr-mean-for-journalists-/s2/a721821/. Accessed 29/8/2018.

Lachaux v Independent Print Ltd, Court of Appeal – Civil Division, September 12, 2017 [2017], EWCA Civ 1334.

Landesman, C. 2001. *Harmless Fun*. Prospect. www.prospectmagazine.co.uk/magazine/harmlessfun. Accessed 28/3/2018.

Lawson, M. 2018. *Trial by Laughter Review – Private Eye Team's Tribute to Embattled Satirist*. The Guardian, 27 September 2018. www.theguardian.com/stage/2018/sep/27/trial-laughter-review-watermill-newbury-william-hone-ian-hislop-private-eye-nick-newman. Accessed 1/10/2018.

Lazarsfeld et al. 2017. *Two-Step Flow Theory*. Communication Theory. http://communicationtheory.org/two-step-flow-theory-2/. Accessed 22/11/2017.

Lovereading UK www.lovereading.co.uk.

Marshall, S. 2011. *How To: Syndicate Freelance Articles Abroad*. Journalism.co.uk. 1 September 2011. www.journalism.co.uk/skills/how-to-syndicate-freelance-articles-abroad/s7/a545852/. Accessed 22/10/2018.

Martin, M. 1999. Art Buchwald: He'll Always Have Paris. *The New York Times*. 22 January 1999. www.nytimes.com/1999/01/22/style/IHT-art-buchwaldhell-always-have-paris.html. Accessed 21/10/2018.

May, G. 2018. *Hard Luck: Why Male Impotence is on the Rise*. Marie Claire. April edition, pp89–90.

McInnes, R. 2010. *Scots Law for Journalists*. 8th edition. Edinburgh: W Greens.

McKay, J. 2013. Chapter 4, Freelance Journalism. *The Magazines Handbook*. 3rd Edition. Abingdon: Routledge, pp44–45.

Milford, H. 1917. *The Table Talk and Omniana of Samuel Talyor Coleridge*. Oxford University Press, p73. PDF of works: https://ia802705.us.archive.org/23/items/tabletalkomniana00coleuoft/tabletalkomniana00coleuoft.pdf. Accessed 21/6/2018.

Mitford, N. 2010. Main Ed. *Poison Penmanship: The Gentle Art of Muckraking*. New York: New York Review Books Classics. Now Let Us Now Appraise Famous Writers, p156.

Morrish, J. and Bradshaw, P. 2012a. *Magazine Editing In Print and Online*, 3rd edition. London: Routlege. Chapter 5, The Right Words, p119.

Morrish, J. and Bradshaw, P. 2012b. Magazine Editing In Print and Online, 3rd edition. London: Routledge. Chapter 6, Pictures and Design, p162.

Muir, R. 2018. *The Power of the Muse*. Vogue, May 2018, p108.

Mumby, D. 2018a. *It's a Great Quality of Life Here, Why Wouldn't You Want to Stay if the Work was Available?* Western Gazette, edition Thursday 9 August 2018, p12.

Mumby, D. 2018b. *Successful Online Gift Business to Quit Town*. Western Gazette. 4 January 2018 edition, p3.

NCTJ. www.nctj.com/downloadlibrary/work_experience.pdf. Accessed 22/10/2018.

Ogilvy, D. 2011. *Confessions of an Advertising Man*. Harpenden: Southbank Publishing, p125.

Osnos, E. 2018. *Can Mark Zuckerberg Fix Facebook Before It Breaks Democracy?* The New Yorker. 17 September 2018. www.newyorker.com/magazine/2018/09/17/can-mark-zuckerberg-fix-facebook-before-it-breaks-democracy. Accessed 15/10/2018.

Overview of the UK population. Office of National Statistics. www.ons.gov.uk/people populationandcommunity/populationandmigration/populationestimates/articles/overviewoftheukpopulation/july2017. Accessed 30/3/2018.

Ponsford, D. 2018. *Mail on Sunday Columnist Liz Jones Reveals she has been Declared Bankrupt.* Press Gazette, 2 January 2018. www.pressgazette.co.uk/mail-on-sunday-columnist-liz-jones-reveals-she-has-been-declared-bankrupt/. Accessed 21/9/2018.

Quinn, F. 2018. *Law for Journalists.* 6th edition. London: Pearson.

Regional labour market statistics in the UK: January 2018. Office for National Statistics. www.ons.gov.uk/employmentandlabourmarket/peopleinwork/employmentand employeetypes/bulletins/regionallabourmarket/january2018. Accessed 10/9/2018.

Reynolds, D. 2017. *Junk Mood or Junk Food?* Running. September/October 2017, pp68–71.

Reynolds, N. 15 October 2002. *The Poet Laureate Relies on Metre and Malady.* The Telegraph. www.telegraph.co.uk/news/uknews/1410230/The-Poet-Laureate-relies-on-metre-and-malady.html. Accessed 28/11/2017.

Runciman, D. 2018. *Democracy's Aging Problem.* TIME, 20 August 2018, p17.

Scanlan, C. 2002. *Making Friends with a Clock: Time Management for Writers.* Poynter.org. 19 November 2002. www.poynter.org/news/making-friends-clock-time-management-writers. Accessed 29/09/2017.

Sofroniou, A. 2012. *Good and Bad Forms of Government.* Aristotle's Aetiology. Lulu.com, p43.

Spratt, V. 17 May 2017. *Why Scrapping Tuition Fees isn't Necessarily the Answer to Young People's Problems.* The Debrief. https://thedebrief.co.uk/news/opinion/scrapping-tuition-fees-isnt-necessarily-answer-young-peoples-problems/. Accessed 29/3/2018.

Stone, J. 18 October 2017. *Brexit: What Happens if Talks Collapse and There's No Deal?* Independent. www.independent.co.uk/news/uk/politics/brexit-talks-collapse-negotiations-eu-uk-theresa-may-david-davis-no-deal-wto-a7955471.html. Accessed 12/7/2018.

Stretton, R. 2018. *School Children go to the Polls to Elect MYPs to Serve County.* Dorset ECHO. 8 January 2018 edition, p15.

Stuart, A. 2017. *Crisis Reporting and Citizen Journalism: 7/7 Changed the Way we Experience News.* http://theconversation.com/crisis-reporting-and-citizen-journalism-7-7-changed-the-way-we-experience-news-44369. Accessed 15/10/2018.

UK Activists Warn of More Mink Releases. BBC News, 18 August 1998. http://news.bbc.co.uk/1/hi/uk/153504.stm. Accessed 5/1/2018.

Urquhart, C. 20 July 2012. *Johann Hari Leaves the Independent after Plagiarism Storm.* Guardian. www.theguardian.com/media/2012/jan/20/johann-hari-quits-the-independent. Accessed 31/7/2018.

Vaughan, R. 14 September 2017. *'Tens of Thousands' of Students to Protest Against Tuition Fees.* iNews. https://inews.co.uk/news/education/tens-thousands-students-protest-tuition-fees/. Accessed 29/3/2018.

Wansell, G. 2013. *A Nasty Little Thug to the End.* Daily Mail, 18 December 2013. www.geoffreywansell.com/RonnieBiggs.html. Accessed 2/7/2018.

Waterhouse, K. 1993. *Waterhouse on Newspaper Style.* London: Penguin Books. What is Style? p244 and p246.

Webb, J. 2017. *The Spy who Hates Trump.* Radio Times, 1–7 April 2017, p19.

Wheen, F. 2002. *Why Facts Must Figure.* The Guardian, 25 February 2002. www.theguardian.com/media/2002/feb/25/mondaymediasection.bookextracts. Accessed 24/9/2018.

Bibliography

Books

Get to know the best local library, with a good reference section, in your area. If you get into writing research features, you can buy second-hand books online and it may be worthwhile to join the British Library. The great majority of the books in these lists have been published a year or two before the date of the edition of this book. Older books are included if they have the status of classics or near-classics. As far as possible obtain the latest editions. Check online for dates of these and availability.

Reference

Basic reference library

The following is a rough guide to a writer's basic reference library. Although you can look up words online it's a good idea to have a hard copy of the following books. You will add to this according to how your interests develop.

1. English dictionary (Oxford or Chambers).
2. Thesaurus.
3. *The Oxford Writers' Dictionary*, compiled by R.E. Allen.
4. *The Oxford Manual of Style*, edited and compiled by R.M. Ritter.
5. *Hart's Rules for Compositors and Readers*, Oxford University Press.
6. *The Oxford Dictionary for Writers and Editors*, Oxford University Press.
7. Hanna, M. and Dodd, M. 2016. *McNae's Essential Law for Journalists*, 23rd edition, Oxford University Press.
8. *The Economist Style Guide* or *The Times Style Guide*.
9. A selection of Penguin dictionaries: politics, economics, religions, etc.
10. A dictionary of quotations.
11. *Writers' and Artists' Yearbook*, A&C Black.
12. *The Writer's Handbook*, Macmillan.
13. *Writer's Market*, Writer's Digest Books.
14. *Photographer's Market*, Writer's Digest Books. Annual.
15. World atlas and gazetteer.

16 A concise world history.
17 *Dod's Parliamentary Companion.* Annual. Gives names and backgrounds of MPs.

Other reference resources

Guinness Book of Records. Annual.
Hollis Press and Public Relations. Annual.
International Who's Who.
The Statesman's Year Book, Palgrave Macmillan. Annual.
Who's Who. Annual.

Publications

Amis, M. 2006. *The Moronic Inferno and Other Visits to America.* Vintage.
Barber, L. 1999. *Demon Barber: Interviews by Lynn Barber.* Penguin.
Blaine, M. 2014. *The Digital Reporter's Notebook.* Routledge.
Bonnett, A. 2011. *How to Argue.* 3rd edition. Prentice Hall.
Burchill, J. 2001. *The Guardian Columns 1998–2000.* Gollancz.
Burgess, M. 2015. *Freedom of Information: A Practical Guide for Journalists.* Routledge.
Butcher, J., Drake, C. and Leach, M. 2006. *Copy-Editing. The Cambridge Handbook.* 7th edition. Cambridge University Press.
Caunt, J. 2016. *How to Organize Yourself.* 5th edition. Kogan Page.
Cheney, T.A. Rees. 2005. *Getting the Words Right: 39 Ways to Improve Your Writing.* 2nd edition. Writer's Digest Books.
Christians, C.G., Fackler, M., Brittain-Richardson, K., Kreshel, P.J. and Woods, R.H. Jnr. 2011. *Media Ethics: Cases and Moral Reasoning.* 9th edition. Routledge.
Clayton, J. 1994. *Interviewing for Journalists.* Piatkus.
Coleridge, N. 2000. *Streetsmart.* Orion.
Crofts, A. 2007. *The Freelance Writer's Handbook.* 3rd edition. Piatkus.
Cutts, M. 2013. *Oxford Guide to Plain English Guide.* 4th edition. OUP.
Davies, H. 1994. *Hunting People: Thirty Years of Interviewing the Famous.* Mainstream Publishing.
De Burgh, H. 2008. *Investigative Journalism.* Routledge.
Foster, J. 2008. *Effective Writing Skills for PR.* 4th edition. Kogan Page.
The Granta Book of Reportage. 2006. Granta Books.
The Guardian Bedside Books. 2015. Guardian Books.
Hamilton, J.T. 2016. *Democracy's Detectives: The Economics of Investigative Journalism.* Harvard University Press.
Harmon-Butler, J. and Purwin-Zobel, L. 2012. *The Travel Writer's Handbook: How to Write and Sell Your Own Travel Experiences.* 7th edition. Surrey Books.
Hastings, M. 2003. *An Inside Story of Newspapers.* Pan.
Hennessy, B. and Hodgson, F.W. 1995. *Journalism Workbook.* Routledge.
Hicks, W. with Adams, S., Gilbert, H., Holmes, T. and Bentley, J. 2016. *Writing for Journalists.* 3rd edition. Routledge.
Hill, S. and Lashmar, P. 2014. *Online Journalism: The Essential Guide.* Sage.
Hogarth, M. (ed.) and Jenkins, J. 2013. *How to Launch A Magazine in This Digital Age.* Bloomsbury.

Hogarth, M. 2018. *Business Strategies for Magazine Publishing*. Routledge.
Huff, D. 1991. *How to Lie with Statistics*. Penguin Books.
Jones, L. and Mallon, J. 2012. *Freelance Writing*. Greatest Guides Ltd.
Keeble, R. 2014. *The Newspapers Handbook and Ethics for Journalists*. 5th edition. Routledge.
Keene, M. 2015. *Practical Photojournalism: A Professional Guide*. Ammonite Press.
Lamer, W. 2018. *Press Freedom as an International Human Right*. Palgrave Pivot.
Larkin, P. 2002. *Required Writing: Miscellaneous Pieces, 1955–82*. Faber & Faber.
Lee-Potter, E. 2017. *Interviewing for Journalists*. Routledge.
Leigh, R. 2017. *Myths of PR: All Publicity is Good Publicity and Other Popular Misconceptions*. Kogan Page.
Marr, A. 2004. *My Trade*. Pan Macmillan.
Martinez Standring, S. 2013. *The Art of Column Writing: Insider Secrets from Art Buchwald, Dave Barry, Arianna Huffington, Pete Hamill and Other Great Columnists*. 2nd edition. RRP International LLC.
Martinez Standring, S. 2013. *The Art of Opinion Writing: Insider Secrets from Top Op-Ed Columnists*. RRP International LLC.
McKay, J. 2013. *The Magazines Handbook*. 3rd edition. Routledge.
Morrish, J. and Bradshaw, P. 2011. *Magazine Editing: In Print and Online*. 3rd edition. Routledge.
O'Farrell, J. 2002. *Global Village Idiot*. Black Swan.
Parris, M. 2013. *Chance Witness: An Outsider's Life in Politics*. Penguin.
Silvester, C. 1994. *The Penguin Book of Interviews*. Penguin.
Pilger, J. 1993. *Hidden Agendas*. Vintage.
Meyer, K.E. 2001. *Pundits, Poets and Wits. An Omnibus of American Newspaper Columns*. Replica Books.
Quinn, C. 2010. *No Contacts? No Problem! How to Pitch and Sell Your Freelance Feature Writing*. Methuen Drama.
Randall, D. 2016. *The Universal Journalist*. 5th Edition. Pluto Press.
Rudin, R. and Ibbotson, T. 2015. *An Introduction to Journalism. Essential Techniques and Background Knowledge*. Focal Press.
Shrimsley, B. 2008. *The Silly Season*. JR Books Ltd.
Stewart, P. and Alexander, R. 2016. *Broadcast Journalism: Techniques of Radio and Television News*. 7th edition. Routledge.
Strunk, W. 2013. *The Elements of Style*. Denton & White.
Turabian, K. 2018. *A Manual for Writers of Research Papers, Theses and Dissertations*. 9th edition. University of Chicago Press.
Wardle, I. 2013. *Theatre Criticism*. Faber & Faber.
Waterhouse, K. 2010. *Waterhouse on Newspaper Style*. 3rd revised edition. Revel Barker.
Wimbs, D. 2007. *Freelance Copywriting*. A&C Black.
Writer's Digest Editors. 2017. *Writing Voice: The Complete Guide to Creating a Presence on the Page and Engaging Readers. 2017*. Writer's Digest Books.
Young, H. 2004. *Supping with the Devils: Political Journalism*. Atlantic Books.
Young, T. 2002. *How to Lose Friends and Alienate People*. Abacus.

Online

British Rate and Data (BRAD Insight) https://bradinsight.com/ Mediatel Ltd. Gives circulation and readership figures, etc. for newspapers and magazines in the UK. (This is online and can be often accessed for free via a university library.)

Campaign www.campaignlive.co.uk the B2B for the advertising industry, Haymarket Media Group Ltd.
Freelance Market News www.freelancemarketnews.com published by The Writer's Bureau.
Media www.theguardian.com/uk/media published by *The Guardian*.
Office for National Statistics www.ons.gov.uk/.
PPA (Professional Publisher's Association) www.ppa.co.uk represents and supports around 250 companies, ranging from consumer magazine publishers to business-to-business data and information providers, customer magazine publishers and smaller independents.
Press Gazette www.pressgazette.co.uk.
The Spotlight Casting Directory and Contacts www.spotlight.com. Covers the world of entertainment.

Indexes to articles

Many publications produce indexes. Some, like *The Times*, put them into volumes annually. Other annual volumes select from various publications. The following is a sample.
Applied Science and Technology Index.
Avery Index to Architectural Periodicals.
British Humanities Index: by ProQuest selects from quality newspapers, weekly reviews, selected magazines and professional journals.
The Clover Index: general and specialised interest magazines.
The Clover Newspaper Index: quality newspapers and selected magazines.
Research Index: indexes articles and news items of financial interest in the national press and business periodicals.

Magazines

The Author, Society of Authors. Quarterly, available to non-members on subscription.
British Journalism Review, quarterly, BJR Publishing Ltd.
Index on Censorship, quarterly.
PR Week, bi-monthly, Haymarket Media Group Ltd.
Writer's Digest, bi-monthly, F&W Media, USA.
Writing Magazine, monthly, Warners Group Publications.

Index

Note: page numbers in *italic* refer to figures and in **bold** refer to tables.

advertising: analysing 40; copywriting 170–171; definition 169; as distinct from PR 168–169
Allen, Stuart 243
Alner, Jason 248–249, 250–251
analytic tools 245
angle: developing more than one story 64, **64**, 89, 111, 131; finding an 20, 26, 32, 48, 80, 86
anonymity for vulnerable people 257
arguments: convincing 140–142; structuring 123–124
art exhibition reviews 206
articles, turning ideas into 72–90; case study 87–90; celebrity stories 74–76; children 76–77; crime 77–79; education stories 79–80; feature opportunities 73; health and medicine 80–81; old age or retirement stories 82–83; travel 83–87

Barber, Lyn 216
Barber, Richard 74
Barker, Paul 78
Barker, Sam 139
Barrie, Jackie 177–179
BBC History Magazine 136–137
Biggs, Ronnie 120
blogs 4, 38, 60, 71, 192, 201, 248; travel writing 89–90
book reviews 204–205
books as a source of ideas 31
BRAD Insight 53, 74
Bradshaw, Paul 75, 151
Brexit article 123–124
Buchwald, Art 238–239
BureauLocal 113
business: records 14–15; writing as a 11–13

business-to-business (B2B) magazines 40; ideas from 30–31; press releases 175; working at 190
business perspective: images from 159–160; publishing from 243–244

calendars 11
cameras 156–157
Campbell, Naomi 258
Canter, Lily 145–149
captions 73, 159
career paths, future 249
careers, getting started and advice 13; Alan Geere 52–53; Chris Wheal 187–190; Jackie Barrie 177–179; James Davies 6–7; Jill McCaffrey 69–71; Jill Starley-Grainger 87–90; Jonathan Telfer 251, 261–266; Liisa Rohumaa 209–210; Lily Canter 145–149; Suzette Martinez Standring 196–198; *see also* first break, getting
Castle, David 21–22
The Celebrity Bulletin 216
celebrity stories 74–76
Chambers Dictionary of Dates 31
Chartered Institute of Public Relations (CIPR) 169
charts 161
children: interviewing 259; stories about 76–77
Clayton, Joan 220
Codes of Conduct and Practice 259; IPSO Editors' Code of Practice 269–274; National Union of Journalists (NUJ) 268
Coldplay concert review 205
Cole, Peter 124–125

Index

columns 190–198; case study 196–198; fact-checking 194; key themes **195–196**; learning from the best 191–192; pitching 193; securing 192–193; selling worldwide 238–239; types of 193–194; working methods 194
commissioning editors: choosing right person for job 56–57; dealing with 68–69; engaging and building relationships with 4–5, 37, 57, 65
commissions, getting *see* first break, getting
Constable, Rebecca 250–251
consumer magazines 30, 40
contacts: apps/programmes to organise 11, 14–15, 93–94; building up your 49, 65, 93–94; establishing bonds with 107–108
contempt law 256
content analysis, magazine 41–43
contracts 16; copyright and 17–18; for regular work 16, 177
copyright: case study 17–18; law 252–253; negotiating 16; short extracts and quotes 107; Society of Authors Guide to, and Permissions 275–283; tracing holders of 281
Copyright, Designs and Patents Act (CDPA) 1988 252–253
copywriters 167–180; advertising 170–171; case study 177–179; fees and payment 178; from journalism to PR 168; obtaining work 175–177; from PR to journalism 171–175; press releases 172–175; research 169–170; resources 179; techniques 179; trade releases 175
courses 2
court reporting, rights and restrictions 257–258
creative: development of ideas 32–33; questions 101–103
crime stories 77–79
Crowdtangle 245
curriculum vitae (CVs) 248
customer publishing 40

Daily Mail 120
The Daily Telegraph 139, 192
data journalism 112
data organising, tools for 11
data protection law 258–259
Davies, James 6–7
Davis, Hallam Walker 190
The Debrief 79
Defamation Act 2013 253, 254, **254**
description: to add colour 103; avoiding too much 84, 85, 137; in detailed, in-depth articles 121; getting it right 136, 146, 148; and narration 122–123, 137; in publicity writing 179
Dool, Greg 23
Dropbox 99, 157

editorial teams: engaging 4–5; shrinking 57, *57*
editors *see* commissioning editors
education stories 79–80
email 37, 52; interviews 107, 219; organising commissions via 65; pitching via 60, 62, 70
empathy 111
Empire 208, 212
Empire, Kitty 205
endings 115, *126*, 130, 134
equipment 10
essays 142
ethical concerns 259–260
Evening Standard 78, 255
Everton, Guy 122–123
expenses 15, 72, 84, 237
experience, gathering 3–4
experts, assessing 96
explanation, thorough 138–140, 148

Facebook 4, 5, 13, 95; conference 245; Zuckerberg interview 228–229
face-to-face interviews 217–218
fact-checking 187, 189, 194
"fair dealing" 253, 279
Fearn, Hannah 79
feature packages 2, 10, 26–27, *126*, 130–132, 134, *130–132*, **131**
feature plans 115–117, **116**
features 46–52; in local papers 47–48; local stories 48–49; local stories becoming national stories 51–52; in national papers 49–50; opportunities 73; organising commissioned 65–67; problem 67, 68; reporting experience 49; topical 50–51; writing engaging 117–124; *see also* specialist features
fees 12, 15–16, 45, 66, 70, 160, 177, 178
figures, verifying 109
film reviews 207–209
first break, getting 4, 6, 13, 62, 87, 145, 197, 201, 209, 210, 261; *see also* careers, getting started and advice
first drafts 124–127; key components 127–130; three-stage map *125*
five Ws 171, *171*

food critics 255
Food and Travel 41, 43, *44*, 63; magazine facts 41, *42*; pitching to 62
formula ideas 33–34
free pictures 159
Freedom of Information Act (FOI) requests 93, 112
freelance, life as a 9–19; books, equipment and resources 9–11, 17; business of writing 11–13; case study 17–18; fees and rights negotiations 15–17; workflow and business records 14–15
freesheets 49

Geere, Alan 52–53
General Data Protection Regulation (GDPR) 258–259
Givhan, Robin 198
Good Housekeeping 24, 74
GQ 256–257
Grace, Liam 247–248
Granville, Toby 250–251
The Guardian 28, 29, 74, 124–125, **143**, 145, 183, 194, 206–207, 212

Hari, Johann 252
Hartley, Aiden 137
Haymarket Media Group 250–251
headlines 33–34, 88–89, 127–128
health and medicine stories 80–81
heat magazine 74–75
Hello! 76
Hollis Find a Client 94
how-to approach 120–121, 139
Hudson, Chris 163–165
Hudson, Derek 263
Hughes, David 208–209
Hulonce, Lesley 136–137
Human Rights Act 1998 258

iCloud 99, 157
ideas 20–38; advertising copywriting 171; case study 36–38; checklist 35–36; developing specialisms 34–35; as a freelance 25–31; mind mapping 26, *26*; as a staff writer 20–25; techniques to grow 31–34; where to look for 28–30; *see also* articles, turning ideas into
images 151–166; adding impact 152–153; from a business perspective 159–160; cameras, tips and resources 156–159; captions 73, 159; case study 163–165; charts 161; copyright 253; for features 154–156; free pictures 159; infographics 160; mapping a publication's feature 153, *153*; maps 161–162; negotiating fees 160; online resources to create a range of 162; relevance of 154, 155; sending/uploading/storing 157–158; stock 159; submission requirements 73; timelines 162; *see also* photographs
The Independent 51, 79, 252
Independent Press Standards Organisation (IPSO) Editors' Code of Practice 269–274
infographics 160
Instagram 13, 52, 249
Institute of Practitioners in Advertising (IPA) 169
Intellectual Property Office 282
interactive engagement 24–25
internships *see* work placements
Interviewing for Journalists 220
interviews 212–232; "approval" requests 107, 216, 230; background research 92, 96–97, 98, 214, 219–220; case study 230–231; challenging your interviewees 263; choosing interviewees 213–214; contact methods 215, *215*; difficult interviewees 223; editing transcripts 224–225; email 107, 219; encouraging revelations 223–224; face-to-face 217–218; five essential steps 97, *97*; follow ups 224, 229–230; formats for writing up 226–229; interviewing techniques 221–224; narrative 228–229; notes 99–108, **102**; "off the record" 105, 224; options 106–107, 217–219; phone 218–219; pitching 214; preparing questions 148, 213, 219–221; profiles 212, 229; Q&A 226–228; recording 10, 98, 99, 218; setting up 66–67, 148, 215–217, 265–266; strategies 96–99; target markets 213; tough questions, techniques for 222–223
introductions, feature 115, *126*; good 128–130, 134
inverted feature pyramid model 126–127, *126*
investigative journalism 44, 93, 115–117; case study 110–113

Jackson, Ian 47–48
jargon 186–187
Jenkins, John 230
Jones, Liz 191
Judd, Alan 140

KISS theory 128, 148

Lashmar, Paul 110–113
law 252–260; anonymity for vulnerable people 257; contempt 256; copyright 252–253; court reporting, rights and restrictions 257–258; data protection 258–259; ethical concerns 259–260; libel 253–256; privacy 258; resources 252
Lawson, Mark 206–207
learning your trade 2
legal advice 100, 105, 111–112
legwork research 92–93, 136, 187
letters' page 24
libel 253–256; avoiding 255–256; defences to 254–255
linear-logical thinking 34
LinkedIn 13, 110, 182, *215*, 248
local magazines 40
local papers 47–49; local stories 48–49; local stories with national implications 51–52
London 7/7 bombings 243–244
Lovereading.co.uk 43–45, 129, 227

magazine: facts 41, *42*; hierarchy model 57, *57*; markets, researching 40–43
maps 161–162
Marie Claire 80, 257
market research 39–54; case study 52–53; emphasis on features 46–52; magazine markets 40–43; newspaper markets 45–46; online opportunities 43–45; overseas markets 236–237; resources 45, 53
Martin, Mitchell 238–239
Martinez Standring, Suzette 196–198
Mascord, David 17–18
May, Gareth 80
McCaffrey, Julie 69–71
media kits 40–41, 53, 169–170, 234, 240
Men's Running 21–22, *21*
mind maps 26, *26*
minders, getting past 216–217
The Mirror 258
Mitford, Nancy 223–224
Morrish, John 75, 151
Moss, Tyler 132–134
multimedia perspective 27, 126, 130–132, **131**, 134
multiple pitches 62–65, **64**; case study 239–242
music reviews 205–206

narrative: compelling 137–138; descriptive 122–123, 137; interviews 228–229
National Geographic Traveller (UK) 163–165, *164*, *165*
national newspapers 49–50; categories **50**; local stories in 51–52; supplements 183
National Union of Journalists (NUJ) 16–17, 66; Code of Conduct 268; *Freelance Guide* 15; *The Journalist* 17, 252
networking 3–4, 177–178
The New York Times 93, 238–239
The New Yorker 228–229
news agencies 284–285
news stories 22–23
News of the World 256–257
newspapers: case study 52–53; emphasis on features 46–52; local 47–49; markets 45–46; national 49–50; supplements 183; topical features 50–51
Newsquest 244, 250

The Observer 205, 216
"off the record" 105, 224
Ogilvy, David 169
OK! magazine 74
old age or retirement stories 82–83
online: articles, length of 264; magazines, researching 43–45; readership, competition for 245; sources 93, 95–96, 109–110
opinion pieces 142
organising commissioned articles 65–67
Osnos, Evan 228–229
outlines, writing 66, 117, 124, 134
overseas markets *see* worldwide markets

Panama papers 112
paraphrasing 100
Parsons, Tony 227
payment: late and non- 16, 70; terms 16
Pearson, Alison 192
permissions: Society of Authors Guide to Copyright and Permissions 275–283; tracing whoever entitled to give 281–282
persuasion techniques 104–105
phone: calls, recording 219, 259; cameras 157; interviews 218–219; pitches via 58–59
photo libraries, digital 160
photographer, working with a 158
photographs: basic techniques for taking 157; creating digital libraries

160; getting permission to take 155; relevance 154, 155; specialist 155–156; submission requirements 73; travel stories 73, 85, 154, 156; *see also* images
picture agencies 159
picture editors 152
pictures *see* images; photographs
pitches 4, 55–71; case study 69–71, 145; column 193; demonstrating value 60–61, 60; developing a network of contacts 65; an editor's advice on 37, 264–265; from an editor's point of view 56–57, 132; email 60, 62, 70; an example 61–62; interview 214; keeping records of 14, **14**; multiple 62–65, **64**, 239–242; overseas markets 235–236, 236–237, 239–242; phone examples 58–59; preparing 57–58; specialist publication 184
plagiarism 100, 252
polemics 142
Popbitch 75
Porter, Henry 55
portfolios 3–4, 176
press cuttings 92, 285
press releases 23–24, 172–175
press trips 72–73, 85–86, 89
privacy 258, 260
problem features 67, 68
productivity 12
profiles 212, 229
public relations: definition 169; as distinct from advertising 168–169; from, to journalism 171–175; from journalism to 168; obtaining work 175–177; press releases 172–175; research 169–170; trade releases 175
publicists 104, 216

Q&A 226–228
qualifications 2
questions: awkward 105; creative 101–103; not to ask 104; preparing interview 213, 219–221; techniques for asking tough 222–223
quotes 100; eliciting good 105–106; guide to how many 127; from other works 253, 278; summarising **225**

Radio Times 138
Rankin, George 43, 62
rate cards 41
Reader's Digest 140

readers' interests, focus on 119–120
recording: apps 10, 85; face-to-face interviews 217, 218, 222; hidden 260; interviews 98, 99; phone calls 219, 259
records, business 14–15
reference books 10, 31, 53, 291–292
regular contributor, becoming a 29–30
rejections 39, 58, 64–65, 68–69
research: advertising and PR 169–170; background 92, 96–97, 98, 214, 219–220; case study 110–113; finding reliable sources 91–96; legwork 92–93, 136, 187; specialist features 187, 189; summary of key 101, **102**; target market 27–28, 36–37, 43; verification skills 108–110
resources: pooling of 112; skills and 2–6
retirement or old age stories 82–83
reviews 198–210; art exhibition 206; book 204–205; case study 209–210; core components 201–202, **203**; getting started 199–200; music 205–206; potential markets 200–201; reviewer's map 199, 200; television and film 207–209; theatre 206–207; writing-up 202
Reynolds, Deborah 121
Riddell, Pat 163–165
rights: serial 16, 18, 240–241; in worldwide markets 234–235, 240–241; *see also* copyright
Robinson, Emma 246
Rohumaa, Liisa 209–210

Scanlan, Chip 12
Sedge, Michael 234, 235, 239–242
serial rights 16, 18, 240–241
single-use licences 18
skills and resources 2–6
slogans 170–171
social media: building your brand on 13, 249; getting an editor's attention on 52; interactive engagement 24–25; letters' pages and 24, 25; personal and professional life on 17; posts to signpost features 27, 131; as a resource 95–96, 112
Society of Authors Guide to Copyright and Permissions 275–283
software 11, 132
sources: acknowledge your 107; assessment of 94–95; finding reliable 91–96; mapping to note headings 117, *118*; online 93, 95–96, 109–110

spec, sending articles on 67–68, 265; dealing with rejection 68–69
specialisms 47, 176–177; developing 34–35, 181, 182
specialist features 181–190; case study 187–190; content 184–185; fact-checking 187, 189; finding opportunities 182; jargon 186–187; keeping-up-to-date 183, 188–189; pitching 184; publishing strategy 183; research 187, 189; structure 185; using right language 185–186
The Spectator 137
Spratt, Vicky 79
Starley-Grainger, Jill 87–90
start-ups, targeting new online 45
stock images 159
structure 114–135; case study 132–134; components 114–117, **116**; engaging features 117–124; feature packages 126, 130–132, **131**, 134; first draft 124–127; first draft, key components 127–130; in interviews 220; inverted feature pyramid model 126–127, *126*; organising notes 117, *118*
style 136–150; analysis of different publications' writing 142, **143–144**; capturing a publication's 125–126; case study 145–149; convincing arguments 140–142; description 136; explanation 138–140; finding your own 142, 144; narration 137–138; newspaper 119
syndication agencies 238–239, 284

target markets: developing ideas and researching 27–28, 36–37, 43; for interviews 213
tax returns 15
television reviews 207–209
Telfer, Jonathan 251, 261–266
theatre reviews 206–207
three Cs 185–186
three whys 35–36, 61
time management 12–13
timelines 162
titles 33–34, 88–89, 127–128
touch typing 12–13
tough questions, techniques for 222–223
trade releases 175
translation of articles 235
travel expenses 72, 89, 237
travel freebies 72–73, 85–86, 89
travel writing 83–87; case study 87–90; descriptive narrative 122–123, 137; funding trips 237; images 73, 85, 154, 156; income 89
Traveller Magazine 122–123
Twitter 4, 13, 95

user-generated content 243–244

value, demonstrating 60–61, *60*
Vegan Living 146, *147*, 148
verification skills 108–110
voice, finding your own 142, 144
voice-recording apps 10, 85
voice typing tools 224–225

Wansell, Geoffrey 120
Warners Group Publications PLC 251
Waterhouse, Keith 119
Webb, Justin 138
website, create your own 13
The Week 123–124, 183, 205–206
Weinstein, Harvey 23
What's New in Publishing? 115; article for 115–117, **116**
Wheal, Chris 187–190
Wheen, Francis 194
Wolff, Michael 256–257
word associations and ideas 33
work placements 2, 5–6, 8, 245–247; advice on 246–247, 250–251; a graduate's perspective 247–248; industry view 246; tips to help you when on 247, 248
workflow charts 14, 15, 65, **66**, 267
workspace 3, 9, 10–11
worldwide markets 233–242; case study 239–242; finding opportunities 234–236; market research 236–237; online resources 234; pitches 235–236, 236–237, 239–242; rights 234–235, 240–241; studying the culture 236–237; syndication agencies 238–239; translation of articles 235; writing for different countries 236–238
Writers' & Artists' Yearbook 53
writer's block 38
Writer's Digest 132–134, *133*, 235
Writer's Market 53
Writing Magazine 129, 235, 261–266, *262*

Yellow Pages 31
Yes Minister 49

Zuckerberg, Mark 228–229